D1194112

THE PHILOSOPHY OF PLOTINUS

THE PHILOSOPHY
OF PLOTINUS

THE GIFFORD LECTURES AT ST. ANDREWS, 1917–1918

BY

WILLIAM RALPH INGE, K.C.V.O., D.D.

Dean of St. Paul's, 1911–1934

IN TWO VOLUMES

VOL. I

THIRD EDITION

LONGMANS, GREEN AND CO.
LONDON • NEW YORK • TORONTO

LONGMANS, GREEN AND CO. LTD
6 & 7 CLIFFORD STREET, LONDON, W.1

LONGMANS, GREEN AND CO. INC.
55 FIFTH AVENUE, NEW YORK 3

LONGMANS, GREEN AND CO.
215 VICTORIA STREET, TORONTO 1

ALSO AT MELBOURNE AND CAPE TOWN

ORIENT LONGMANS LTD
BOMBAY, CALCUTTA, MADRAS

New Impression 1948

Printed in England
SPOTTISWOODE, BALLANTYNE & CO. LTD.
London & Colchester

TO

THE VISCOUNT HALDANE OF CLOAN, F.R.S., K.T., O.M.
ETC., GIFFORD LECTURER AT ST. ANDREWS, 1902–4

All Truth is a Shadow except the last. But every Truth is Substance in its own place, though it be but a Shadow in another place. And the **Shadow** is a true Shadow, as the Substance is a true Substance.

ISAAC PENNINGTON.

PREFACE TO THE THIRD EDITION

IN preparing this final edition of my Gifford Lectures for the press, I have read through the whole of the *Enneads* again. I have also revised my book throughout, and have made some hundreds of small corrections and alterations.

A good deal of work has been done upon Plotinus in the last ten years. Professors Dodds and Sleeman have published a large number of textual emendations, some of which are important as clearing up obscurities caused by errors in the manuscripts. In spite of all that has been done to remove such errors, the text of Plotinus is still faulty in many places.

Of recent books on the philosophy of Plotinus, the most important is that of Fritz Heinemann (*Plotin*, Leipzig, 1921). Heinemann claims not only to have restored the chronological order in which the different parts of the *Enneads* were written, but to have discovered considerable interpolations, which he ascribes to friends and disciples of the philosopher. He also asserts that the doctrine of Plotinus changed materially between the earliest and the latest parts of his book. In the earlier chapters he cannot find the characteristic Plotinian doctrine of ' the One.' I have tried to judge this theory on its merits, but I am not convinced. It is unlikely *a priori* that a thinker who wrote nothing before the age of fifty, and died sixteen years later, should have altered his views on fundamental questions as he went on. Nor do I find anything more than a slight change of emphasis. On the Problem of Evil it might be possible to find contradictions between earlier and later books ; but I do not think that Plotinus ever dealt confidently with this problem. On the whole, I agree with Arnou, that ' la doctrine est bien la même dans tous les livres.'

Another book which I have found valuable is René Arnou, *Le Désir de Dieu dans la Philosophie de Plotin* (Paris). N. O. Lossky, *The World as an Organic Whole* (Oxford, 1928), is interesting as a modern philosophic work avowedly based on the *Enneads*.

Mr. Whittaker has brought out an enlarged edition of his admirable book *The Neoplatonists*. Mr. Stephen Mackenna has now translated the whole of the *Enneads* except the Sixth Book. The later volumes confirm the high opinion which I formed of his work after reading the first. I earnestly hope that he will endure to the completion of his labour of love. I have profited by some of Professor Taylor's criticisms of the first edition in *Mind* (1919).

There has been, I rejoice to observe, a great change in the estimate of Plotinus as a philosopher. Some of the errors against which I protested ten years ago are seldom any longer repeated, and it is now more generally recognised that he is one of the greatest names in the history of philosophy. Professor Dodds' little book, *Select Passages Illustrating Neoplatonism* (S.P.C.K., 1923), is very sound, and will be helpful to students beginning the subject.

My method of treating my subject was necessarily determined by the conditions of the Gifford Lectureship; this has been forgotten by one or two critics. But I was glad to be obliged to treat Neoplatonism as a living, not as a dead, philosophy; for so I believe it to be. In choosing so to deal with it, some parts of the *Enneads* seemed to me more vital than others. I could not, for example, include a detailed discussion of the Categories in the Sixth Ennead. I wish the book to be regarded as a contribution to the philosophy of religion, rather than a treatise on general metaphysics. My last reading ot Plotinus has only confirmed me in my conviction that his value as a religious philosopher can hardly be overestimated. I know no more powerful defence of the *religious* view of life, which bids us pass through things temporal 'in the spirit of a worshipper,' to use a phrase of Bishop Gore's. Plotinus sets himself to prove dialectically, as a Platonist must attempt to do, the soundness of the upward track which he is treading in his inward experience. He names the rungs on Jacob's ladder, but, as I have said, his view of reality is much rather a picture of a continuous spectrum, in which the colours merge into each other, unseparated by any hard lines. Most of the waverings and apparent contradictions which schematists have found in the *Enneads* are thus to be accounted for.

For him, 'the good life' itself is its own reward, and we must look for no other. He disdains the threats and promises of ecclesiasticism. His profound indifference to worldly affairs and the problems of civilisation puts the modern spirit out of sympathy with him ; but is not this indifference also characteristic of the Gospels ? The riddle of the Sphinx for the twentieth century is how to preserve what is true and noble in the idea of evolutionary progress, without secularising our religion and losing our hold on the unchanging perfection of God. This problem was not so insistent either in the first century or in the third. Plotinus will teach us that there can be no evolution except in relation to a timeless background which does not itself evolve. This is, of course, the Christian view, and I believe it will vindicate itself against the rival view of a Deity who is vitally involved in the fortunes of His creatures.

W. R. INGE.

DEANERY, ST. PAUL'S.
June 1928.

PREFACE TO THE FIRST EDITION

THE Gifford Lectureships have given many English and some foreign scholars the pleasantest of introductions to the life of the Scottish Universities. The unique charm of St. Andrews is but half realised by those who only know it as the Mecca of the golfer. Those who have had the privilege of being admitted to the academic society of the ancient city will understand why Andrew Lang confessed that even Oxford had a successful rival in his affections. The present writer will always look back upon his two visits to St. Andrews as the brightest interlude in four sad years.

It is my agreeable duty to acknowledge the help which I have received from several friends. I have been encouraged and gratified by the interest in my lectures shown by those two distinguished Platonists, Professors Burnet and Taylor, of St. Andrews. For several years I have received the kindest sympathy in my philosophical studies from Lord Haldane. Three Oxford friends have been good enough to read my book in manuscript or in the proof-sheets : Captain Ross, Fellow of Oriel ; the Rev. H. H. Williams, D.D., Principal of St. Edmund Hall ; and Mr. C. C. J. Webb, Fellow of Magdalen and at present Gifford Lecturer at Aberdeen.

SYLLABUS OF LECTURES I–XI

LECTURE I

INTRODUCTORY

Plotinus is generally regarded as the great philosopher of mysticism. The word is loosely used, and in many different senses. The psychical experiences which are often supposed to distinguish it are really a subsidiary and not indispensable part of the mystical quest, which is the journey of the soul, by an inner ascent, to immediate knowledge of God and communion with Him. The close agreement which we find between mystics of all ages and countries indicates that the mystical experience is a genuine part of human nature, and that it assumes the same general forms wherever it is earnestly cultivated.

Mysticism is now studied chiefly as a branch of the psychology of religion. But, valuable as these recent studies are, they remain outside the position of the mystics themselves, whose aim is the attainment of ultimate, objective truth. The mystic is not interested in the states of his consciousness ; he desires to unite himself with reality, to have a vision of the eternal Ideas, and perchance of the supreme Unity that lies behind them.

This kind of philosophy may not be in fashion just now ; but when we see what havoc popular subjectivism has made of religious philosophy, and how it has encouraged a recrudescence of superstition, we may be glad to return to Plato and his successors. For them, mysticism involves and rests upon metaphysics.

Mysticism, thus understood, is a spiritual philosophy, which demands the concurrent activity of thought, will, and feeling, which in real life are never sundered from each other. By the proper discipline of these faculties a man becomes effectively what he is potentially, a partaker of the divine nature and a denizen of the spiritual world. We climb the pathway to reality by a power which all possess, though few use it. It is the *amor intellectualis Dei* which draws us upward, and not merely a susceptibility to passionate or rapturous emotion.

No other guide on this pathway equals Plotinus in power and insight and spiritual penetration. He leaves us, it is true, much to do ourselves ; but this is because the spiritual life cannot be described to those who are not living it. He demands of us a strict moral discipline as well as intellectual capacity for learning.

On the intellectual side, Neoplatonism sums up the results of 700 years of untrammelled thinking, the longest period of free speculation which the human race has enjoyed. The greater part of it passed over into Christian philosophy, which it shaped for all time. Neoplatonism is part of the vital structure of Christian theology, and it would be impossible to tear them apart.

The neglect of Plotinus, alike by students of Greek philosophy and of Christian dogma, is therefore much to be regretted. It makes a gap where no gap exists. Apart from prejudices, which have operated from the side of the theologians, the extreme difficulty of reading the Enneads in the original has contributed to this neglect. [An account follows of the literature of the subject, with a criticism of some of the chief modern books on Plotinus.]

The lecturer has found Plotinus a most inspiring and fortifying spiritual guide, as well as a great thinker. In times of trouble like the present he has much to teach us, lifting us up from the miseries of this world to the pure air and sunshine of eternal truth, beauty, and goodness.

LECTURES II, III

THE THIRD CENTURY

Plotinus is the one great genius in an age singularly barren of greatness. It was a dismal and pessimistic age, when civilisation seemed to be stricken with mortal sickness. And though Plotinus deliberately detaches himself from current affairs, the great man always gives voice to the deepest thought of his own time, and cannot be understood apart from his historical setting.

A blight had fallen upon the Greek and Roman stocks, and the Empire was full of Orientals and Germans. This change of population profoundly affected the social life, the morals, and the religion of the Empire. Except in law, religion, and religious philosophy there was stagnation or retrogression everywhere.

The revival of the religious sentiments was strongly marked. Toleration and fusion of cults were general; only atheism and impiety were frowned upon. The old Gods were again honoured; but the religions of the East were far more potent. These came chiefly from four countries—Egypt, Syria, Phrygia, and Palestine. Characteristics of the worship of Isis, Cybele and Attis, Mithra.

The new syncretism ($\theta\epsilon o\kappa\rho a\sigma ia$) differed widely from the old polytheism. It was now the fashion to worship one God with many names. The deity, says Themistius, takes pleasure in the diversity of homage. Paganism had no dogma and no church. It tolerated Lucian, who made few disciples, and persecuted the Christians, who made many. But the real rivals of Christianity were the Eastern cults, not the official paganism, the object of the rhetorical polemic of the Fathers. The real enemy was ignored, not attacked, by controversialists on both sides. The Christians hardly mention Mithra; Plotinus leaves the Christians severely alone.

There was a great revival of superstition, especially of magic, white and black, and of astrology, which was called the queen of the sciences. We probably underestimate greatly the pernicious influences of these pseudo-sciences in the last age of pagan antiquity. Christianity deserves credit for reducing a permanent nightmare of the spirit to a discredited and slowly dying superstition.

Eschatology is always vague and contradictory, and it is most difficult to discover what was really believed in a past age. But it is clear that belief in immortality was much stronger in the third century than in the first. The Orphic and Neopythagorean faith in the essential imperishableness of the soul was quite independent of spiritualistic superstitions, and the Oriental cults owed much of their attractiveness to their definite promises of a future life. The revival of the ' mysteries ' was not unconnected with the same tendency.

Judaism could not offer this particular attraction ; and in our period it was returning to its former exclusiveness, and was relapsing into an Oriental religion.

Meanwhile, Christianity was developing rapidly into a syncretistic European religion, which challenged the other religions of the Empire on their own ground. A great change came over the Christian Church between Marcus Aurelius and Decius. In the second century the Christians appeared to their neighbours a *tenebrosa et lucifugax natio* ; they were heartily despised, but hated only by the mob. But in the third century they attracted many nobles and able professional men ; in Origen they could boast of the most learned man of his generation. The silence of Plotinus is not due to ignorance. He attacks at length the half-Christian Gnostics, who seemed to travesty his own doctrines ; with the school of Origen he could not have much to quarrel about ; and Roman churchmanship, already practical and political, would not claim his attention as a philosopher. He left it to Porphyry to assail Christian orthodoxy. The real quarrel between Neoplatonism and Christianity lay in their different attitudes towards the old culture, and towards the Roman Empire. Origen and Plotinus might exchange compliments ; but Minucius Felix calls Socrates *scurra Atticus*, and Cyprian speaks of the pagans as ' dogs and swine.' The pagans retorted by calling the Christians ' insolent barbarians.' The struggle was between two political traditions.

The moral reformation was not less conspicuous than the religious revival. Besides the growth of asceticism, we note the emergence of the clerical profession, the private chaplain, the sermon, and the pious tract. Civic virtue declined ; sexual purity and humanity increased. The Catholic type of piety was establishing itself.

LECTURES IV, V

THE FORERUNNERS OF PLOTINUS

The evolution of thought in Plato's mind was a foreshowing of what happened to his school. The history of Platonism is anticipated in Plato himself. But before the fusion of Greek philosophies in Neoplatonism could take place, there had to be a new development and transformation of the older schools. Heracleitus and the Cynics had a new life in Stoicism ; the Atomists and Cyrenaics joined to produce Epicureanism; the Eleatics and Megarians lived on, to some extent, in the Scepticism of the post-Aristotelian period. Plato influenced them all, except perhaps the Epicureans.

The best part of Plato—his spiritual vision—was not preserved by the Athenian professors who expounded his doctrines, and before long the Academy devoted itself to a rather arid and timorous moralising. But the school came back, through scepticism, to a position nearer Plato's own. Eclectic Platonism became a philosophy of revelation. The earliest philosophies had been cosmocentric ; the later anthropocentric ; the last phase was to be theocentric. By insisting on the supersensual as alone real, and on inspiration as alone blessed, it made a return to the true Plato.

But the cradle of Neoplatonism was not Athens but Alexandria, the meeting-place of East and West, hospitable to all ideas.

LECTURES VI, VII, VIII

THE PHILOSOPHY OF PLOTINUS—THE WORLD OF SENSE

There are two fundamental triads in Plotinus—that of the Divine Principles, the Absolute (τὸ ἀγαθόν, τὸ ἕν, τὸ πρῶτον) ; Spirit (νοῦς), and Soul (ψυχή) ; and the division of man into Spirit, Soul, and Body.

In their objective aspects, Body, Soul, and Spirit are respectively the world as perceived by the senses ; the world interpreted by the mind as a spiritual and temporal order ; and the spiritual world. The last alone is fully real. Reality is constituted by the unity in duality of the spiritual faculty and the spiritual world which it contemplates in exercising its self-consciousness. The reality of Soul and its world is derivative and dependent ; the phenomenal world does not possess reality (οὐσία).

Refutation of materialism. Plotinus sees the issue between materialism and the philosophy of spirit more clearly than any previous thinker. He argues against the Stoics that when we pass from Body to Soul, we have to deal with a different kind of existence, to which the quantitative categories do not apply. Justice and virtue cannot be stated in terms of extension. And the explanation of a thing must always be sought in what is above it in the scales of value and existence. The Stoics, while professing to be pantheists, slide into materialism.

Matter (ὕλη) is not material in our sense. It is the subject of energy, viewed by abstraction as separated from the energy which alone gives it reality.

In what sense does Plotinus regard Matter as evil ? The difficulty arises from the relation of the two standards, that of Value and that of Existence. In the scale of existence there are no *minus* signs ; but the value judgment has to register temperatures below zero. But we have to remember that there can be no world without Form working on Matter. Form and Matter together are ' one illuminated reality '; it is only when isolated by abstraction that Matter appears as that which resists the good. Matter can be perceived only ' by an illegitimate kind of reasoning.' The half-blinded spiritual faculty, the clouded perception, and the shapeless object, all belong together, and all ' desire ' to rise into a light where all will be transformed. But there is Matter in the spiritual world, since in every sphere the recipient of Form holds the position of Matter. This is enough to prove that Plotinus never dreams of making Matter the diabolical principle in his universe.

Matter was created, but not in time. It was created in order that the will-activities of Soul and Spirit might become actualities.

The world of appearance may be regarded either as the spiritual world seen through a distorting medium, or as an actual but imperfect copy of the archetype. The real-idealism of Plotinus holds these two views together. 'A feeble contemplation makes a feeble object of contemplation.' Our knowledge of this half-real world is a kind of half-knowledge.

Nature (φύσις) is the active faculty of the World-Soul, its outer life. On the other side, it is that which, added to Matter, gives it its substantiality. It is the lowest of the spiritual existences. 'All that is below Nature is but a copy of reality.'

The ground-form of all appearance is Extension. Mutual externality is the condition of things in the world of sense, as compenetration is the character of the spiritual world. 'Space is after everything else '— the lowest rung of the ladder. Spatial ideas are our clearest and our poorest ideas.

Time is the moving image of eternity. 'Things that are born are nothing without their future.' Perpetuity is the symbol and copy of the permanence of eternity. In eternity the whole is in each part ; in the world of Time the stages follow each other.

Time arose through the desire of the World-Soul to exert its active powers ; 'it desires always to translate what it sees in the eternal world into another form.' 'Time is the activity of an eternal soul, exercised in creation.'

Bergson's theory of Time is next discussed.

We cannot admit real causality without teleology. Things cannot be causes.

Time is the form of willed change.

The universe had no temporal beginning and will have no temporal end. But its history consists of an unending series of finite schemes, which have a beginning, middle, and end. This cosmology is alone consistent with modern science.

Categories of the world of appearance.

The dualism often ascribed to Plotinus—the two worlds theory—has no foundation in the Enneads.

The controversy with the Gnostics. 'Those who despise what is so nearly akin to the spiritual world show that they know nothing of the spiritual world except in name.' 'This world is worthy of its Author, complete, beautiful, and harmonious.' 'There is nothing Yonder which is not also Here.'

LECTURES IX, X, XI

THE SOUL

The Orphics were the first to teach that the Soul of man is ' fallen ' —' an exile from God and a wanderer.' Their doctrine of a multitude of immortal souls broke up the older doctrine that Soul generically is the active manifestation of one spiritual Being. The Orphic doctrine involved a theodicy. Plotinus thus inherited a double tradition—that which regarded Soul as analogous to the ' Wisdom ' of later Jewish literature, and that which thought not of Soul, but of souls on pilgrimage. He attempts to combine the best of both.

The Soul is in the centre, not at the summit, of being. 'It binds extremes together.' It is in vital connexion with both the spiritual and the phenomenal worlds. There is no limit to its possible expansion. It may rise into the realm of Spirit, where ' it will see God and itself and the all.' ' It will be unable to find a stopping-place, to fix its own limits and determine where it ceases to be itself ; it will give up the attempt to distinguish itself from the universal Being.' It is a stranger among the things of sense, which are only the shadow of Soul cast by the sun of Spirit. It is an energy thrown out by Spirit ; it is eternal and timeless. ' It is indivisible even when divided ; for it is all in all and all in every part.' From the desire of Soul to create after the pattern of Spirit, ' the whole world which we know arose and took its shapes.'

The World-Soul is not in the world ; rather the world is in it. ' There is nothing between Soul and Spirit except that Spirit imparts and Soul receives. But even the Matter of Spirit is beautiful and of spiritual form.' The World-Soul is the creator and the providence of the world. Its energy descends as low as vegetable life, and slumbers even in inorganic nature. *Omnia sunt diversis gradibus animata.* The World-Soul directs the world from above ; it is not involved in it. The creative Logoi of the World-Soul are ' an activity of contemplation.' Like Leibnitz and Fechner, Plotinus believes that the heavenly bodies have souls. The ancient opinion that ' There are in the universe many things more divine than man ' seems to me entirely reasonable, and far more respectable than the arrogant anthropocentrism of Hegel and others.

Individual Souls are not parts into which the *anima mundi* is divided : Soul cannot be divided quantitatively. Individual Souls are Logoi of Spirits. But their division from each other is an affection (πάθημα) of bodies, not of Soul itself. In the spiritual world there is distinction without separation. ' All Souls are one.' Individuality is a fact, but unity is also a fact. Plotinus is anxious to preserve individuality. Each Soul is an ' or'ginal cause.' Human sympathy proves our common life in the ' undivided Soul': ' we have a fellow-feeling with each other and with the All, so that when I suffer the All feels it too.' But on earth this sympathy is ' dull ' (ἀμυδρά).

The true being of each individual consists in its *raison d'être* (τὸ διὰ τί). Soul, as we know it, is a teleological category, though its home is in the realm of achieved purposes.

Faculties of the Soul. Sensation. This is not a passive impression, but an energy, a kind of force (ἰσχύς τις). Perception itself is largely the work of imagination. Berkeley's doctrine is very similar. The fact of sensation is due to a ' faint sympathy,' and is evidence of the living unity of nature. But there is no purely sensational experience : consciousness always involves perception.

Pleasure and pain belong neither to the Body nor to the Soul, but to the ' compound ' of them. They are not pure sensations, nor yet affections of the Soul. The soul can conquer them by living upon its own highest level.

Memory and *Imagination* are closely connected ; they belong to the Discursive Reason (διάνοια). Recollection (ἀνάμνησις) is the power of active search or recall ; it demands a higher kind of volitional and rational activity than Memory. Memory in a sense constitutes the empirical *ego*. It is of images only ; Spirit needs it not ; we do not remember νοητὰ—we possess them, or they us.

Imagination, Opinion, and *Reasoning* have their places in an ascending scale between Sensation and Spiritual Perception (νόησις). Plotinus, for whom φαντασία is rather *Vorstellung* than Imagination in the higher sense, does not give it such an exalted place as (*e.g.*) Wordsworth does. Wordsworth, Ruskin, J. C. Shairp on Imagination.

Reason (διάνοια) is the proper activity of the Soul, in which it discharges its characteristic function. Self-consciousness belongs to the reasoning faculty. But in the psychic life, 'we see ourselves as another'; Soul knows itself truly only when it knows itself as Spirit. Consciousness is aroused most sharply by what is alien and hostile; 'when we are well, we are not conscious of our organs.' We do things best when we are not thinking of ourselves as doing them. Thus what we usually call self-consciousness is consciousness of externality. R. L. Nettleship quoted. Strictly, there is no such thing as self-consciousness; every cognitive state has for its object something other than itself. There is a kind of unconsciousness in the highest states of the Soul, the 'waking state,' as Plotinus calls it. Discursive thought contains within itself neither the material nor the formal, nor the final causes of its own thinking. It is, in fact, never separated from νόησις at one end, and creativeness (ποίησις) at the other. Soul is the immediate experience of an organic individual; it is conscious and self-conscious in various degrees. Its ideal perfection is such an all-embracing experience as will break down the barriers between the individual Soul and universal Soul-life.

Plotinus' doctrine of consciousness illustrated from Leibnitz, Ferrier, Bain, Lewes. Drews attempts unsuccessfully to connect it with Hartmann's doctrine of the Unconscious.

Bergson's doctrine, in spite of superficial likeness, is incompatible with that of Plotinus, since Bergson makes the spontaneity of life reveal itself in motiveless diversity, while regularity is for him a proof of thraldom to blind mechanism. This is far removed from the Plotinian doctrine, which does not triumph in introducing the unpredictable into the predetermined, but rather rejoices in the harmonious working of what has been called cosmic consciousness.

'Each man's Self is determined by the principle of his activity'; we choose our own rank in the scale of Being. The Self is not given to start with.

In what sense is finite selfhood an illusion? Lotze's doctrine of personality. Royce's doctrine. The self is a teleological category.

'*The Descent of the Soul.*' The universe is a living chain of Being, a 'harmony' in the Greek sense of the word. The divine life overflows in an incessant stream of creative activity, so that every possible manifestation of divine energy, in degree as well as in kind, is somewhere represented. There is a corresponding centripetal movement of all created things back to the divine: such is the systole and diastole of universal life. There should then be no blame attaching to the Soul which has been 'sent down' to earth. But too often the Soul does not try to return, and the question arises, 'Would it not have been better if it had not come down?' Was it pride or curiosity, or wilfulness that brought it down? Plotinus is manifestly perplexed, and unable to find clear guidance in Plato. There is a want of firmness and consistency in his discussion of this subject. The Christian doctrine of the Incarnation—of the Divine voluntarily 'coming down,' impelled by love, might have helped him greatly. The human soul also, though it did not choose its lot, may have its share in redemptive work.

The question whether the Soul 'comes down' entire, or only the lower part of it, is discussed at length by Plotinus. We shall understand it better if we ask instead, ' Can the soul itself sin ? ' Is there, as the medieval mystics taught, a Soul-centre which can never consent to evil ? Plotinus says there is : most of his followers in the school differ from him. Proclus asks, ' If the will sins, how can we call the Soul impeccable ? ' Proclus also says definitely, that the Soul comes down ' to imitate the divine providence.' The inmost life and being of the Soul are safe, because the Soul is the child of God, but the Soul cannot remain always on the mount of vision, and it may miss its way back thither.

THE PHILOSOPHY OF PLOTINUS

LECTURE I

INTRODUCTORY

THE honour which the University of St. Andrews has conferred upon me has given me the opportunity of delivering in the form of lectures the substance of a book on which I have worked, with many interruptions, for about seventeen years. My interest in Plotinus began while I was writing my Bampton Lectures on Christian Mysticism, which I gave at Oxford in 1899.[1] Mysticism is a very wide subject, and the name has been used more loosely even than ' Socialism.' We are unable in English to mark that distinction between the higher and the lower kinds of mysticism which the Germans indicate when they call the one *Mystik* and the other *Mystizismus*. To many persons a mystic is a dreamer who takes a detached and unpractical view of life. Others suppose the essence of mysticism to be the search for ' loose types of things through all degrees,' as if nature were a divine cryptogram, the key to which is furnished through some kind of occultism. The Roman Catholic Church associates the word closely with what are called mystical phenomena, those strange experiences of the cloistered ascetic which

---

[1] My judgments of Plotinus in this early work are crude, and do not represent my mature opinions. Arnou's criticisms are quite justified, but I regret that he has not read the present volumes, which he mentions in his bibliography.

I.—B

that Church ascribes to the direct agency of supernatural powers, benign or maleficent, and which modern psychology believes to be purely subjective and for the most part pathological.   There are few stranger things in literature than the semi-official Roman Catholic books on 'mystical theology,' compiled with great learning and a show of scientific method, but consisting largely of cases of levitation, incandescence, transverberation, visions and auditions of every kind, which the mystics of the cloister, many of whom have been canonised as saints, have recorded as their own experiences.   The main task for the theologians and spiritual directors who collect these cases is not to establish the objective reality of these phenomena, which is taken for granted, but to show how 'divine mysticism' may be distinguished from diabolical imitations of it.   It is, however, only fair to say that the wisest of the Catholic writers on mysticism discourage the tendency to attach great importance to miraculous favours and temptations.   These experiences are a subsidiary and not indispensable part of the great mystic quest, which is the journey of the Soul, by an inner ascent, to the presence of God and to immediate union with Him.   The stages of this ascent are mapped out with the same precision as the supernatural visitations above mentioned, and these records of the Soul's progress have a recognised value for psychologists as well as for divines.   Although much importance must be allowed to the effects of suggestion in all matters of religious experience, the books of the medieval mystics have great value as first-hand evidence of the normal progress of the inner life when the mind and will are wholly concentrated upon the vision and knowledge of God.   The close agreement which we find in these records, written in different countries, in different ages, and even by adherents of different creeds (for Asia has here its own important contribution to make) can only be accounted for if we hold that the mystical experience is a genuine part of human nature, which may be developed, like the arts, by concentrated attention and assiduous labour, and which assumes the same general forms whenever and wherever it is earnestly sought.

There are some students of mysticism who are content to investigate the subject as a branch of psychology. They examine and tabulate the states of mind described in mystical writings, without raising the question what degree of intrinsic value or truth they possess. This is the right attitude for a scientific psychologist to take. But it is not the right attitude for one who wishes to understand the mystics. We cannot understand them as long as we confine ourselves within the limits which psychology, which is an abstract science, is obliged to accept. Mysticism is the pursuit of ultimate, objective truth, or it is nothing. ' What the world calls mysticism,' says Coventry Patmore,[1] ' is the science of ultimates, the science of self-evident reality.' Not for one moment can it rest content with that neutrality or agnosticism with regard to the source and validity of its intuitions, which the psychologist, as such, is pledged to maintain. For psychology is a branch of natural science. It may be defined as the science of behaviour, or as that part of physiology from which the physiologist is self-excluded by his assumption that all vital functions can be explained mechanically.[2] The mystic is not interested in the states of his consciousness. He cares very little whether he is conscious or unconscious, in the body or out of the body. But he is supremely interested in knowing God, and, if possible, in seeing Him face to face. His inner life is not an intensive cultivation of the emotions. It develops by means of what the later Greek philosophy calls ' the dialectic,' which Plotinus[3] defines as ' the method and discipline which brings with it the power of pronouncing with final truth upon the nature and relation of things, also the knowledge of the Good and of its opposite, of

[1] *The Rod, the Root, and the Flower*, p. 39.
[2] My own belief is that ' mechanism ' and ' purposive action,' when contrasted with each other, are both false abstractions.
[3] I. 3. 4.

the eternal and of the temporal.' This knowledge gained, the dialectic, now freed from all deceit and falsehood, ' pastures the Soul in the meadows of truth' ; it has a clear vision of the eternal Ideas, and points the way to the supreme Unity that lies behind them. Then at last, and not before, it rests, leaving behind the operation of the discursive reason and contemplating the One who is also the Good.

I am well aware that this philosophy runs counter to a very strong current in contemporary thought. It is possible to write a book on the philosophy of religion, as Höffding has done, in which the three parts are epistemology, psychology, and ethics, that is to say, the science of knowledge, the science of mental states, and the science of conduct, without touching on the question which to the Platonist seemed the necessary starting-point and the necessary goal of the whole inquiry—the question, ' What is ultimate reality ? ' But when I observe what this popular relativism has made of religion and philosophy ; when I see that it has helped to break down the barriers which divide fact from fancy, knowledge from superstition, I am confirmed in my conviction that when the philosophy of religion forsakes ' its old loving nurse the Platonic philosophy ' (to quote one of the Cambridge Platonists of the seventeenth century), it is in danger of falling from its high estate, and playing into the hands of those who are willing to exploit the superstitions of the vulgar. Pragmatism is defenceless against obscurantism ; the ' Gospel for human needs ' rehabilitates those half-suppressed thought-habits which are older and more tenacious than civilisation.

Thus it soon became clear to me that mysticism involves a philosophy and at bottom is a philosophy. Although it never leaves the pathway of individual and concrete experience, it values that experience precisely as being not merely subjective, not merely individual, but a revelation of universal and eternal truth. And while the intelligence itself is continually enriched and strengthened by the experiences which come to it, so that it changes progressively in correspondence with the growth of its knowledge, it is never a passive spectator of the energies of the will and the raptures of the emotions, but on the contrary is ever active, co-ordinating, sifting, and testing the whole content of experience, and maintaining a mental discipline not less arduous and not less fruitful than the moral discipline which accompanies it.

Mysticism is a spiritual philosophy which demands the concurrent activity of thought, will, and feeling. It assumes from the outset that these three elements of our personality, which in real life are never sundered from each other, point towards the same goal, and if rightly used will conduct us thither. Further, it holds that only by the consecration of these three faculties in the service of the same quest can a man become effectively what he is potentially, a partaker of the Divine nature and a denizen of the spiritual world. There is no special organ for the reception of Divine or spiritual truth, which is simply the knowledge of the world as it really is. Some are better endowed with spiritual gifts than others, and are called to ascend greater heights ; but the power which leads us up the pathway to reality and blessedness is, as Plotinus says, one which all possess, though few use it.

This power is emphatically not a mere susceptibility to passionate or rapturous emotion. Mysticism has indeed been defined as 'an extension of the mind to God by means of the longing of love ' ; and there is nothing to quarrel with in this definition. But it is 'the *Spirit* in love ' of Plotinus, the *amor intellectualis Dei* of Spinoza, which draws us upward. It is the whole personality, unified and harmonised under the leadership of what the Stoics called the ruling faculty, that enters the holy of holies. There are some admirers of the mystics who speak as if the intellect were an intruder and almost an obstacle in the life of holiness. Against such I will be content to quote the words of one of our foremost theologians, the Roman Catholic layman, Baron Friedrich von Hügel. ' It is impossible to see why, simply because of their superior intellectual gifts and development, men like Clement of Alexandria and Origen, Cassian and Duns Scotus, Nicholas of Coes and Pascal, Rosmini and Newman, should count as necessarily less near to God and Christ, than others with fewer of these gifts and opportunities. For it is not as though such gifts were considered as ever of themselves constituting any moral or spiritual worth. Nothing can be more certain than that great mental powers can be accompanied by emptiness or depravity of heart. The identical standard is to be applied to these as to all other gifts : they are not to be considered as substitutes, but only as additional material and means for the moral and spiritual life ; and it is only inasmuch as they are actually so used, that they can effectively help on sanctity itself. It is only contended here that such gifts do furnish additional means and materials for the devoted will- and grace-moved soul, towards the richest and deepest spiritual life. For the intellectual virtues are no mere empty name : candour, moral courage, intellectual honesty, scrupulous accuracy, chivalrous fairness, endless docility to facts, disinterested collaboration, unconquerable hopefulness and perseverance, manly renunciation of popularity and easy honours, love of bracing labour and strengthening solitude ; these and many other cognate qualities bear upon them the impress of God and His Christ. And yet they all find but a scanty field of development outside the intellectual life.'[1] The same writer makes, as it seems to me, a most acute comment on the influence which Realism and Nominalism have respectively exercised upon the intellectual factor in religion. ' Whereas,' he says, ' during the prevalence of Realism, affective, mystical religion is the concomitant and double of intellectual religion, during the later prevalence of Nominalism, Mysticism becomes the ever-increasing supplement, and at last ever

[1] F. von Hügel, *The Mystical Element of Religion*, Vol. I. p. 79.

more largely the substitute, for the methods of reasoning.'[1] In other words, it is the alliance of mysticism with that great school of thought which can be traced back to Plato, which saves it from *Schwärmerei* and the vagaries of unchecked emotionalism. The 'contemplation' of the Platonic mystic is only what St. Paul means when he says, 'I will pray with the Spirit and I will pray with the understanding also.'

Such being the truth about the mystical element in religion, as I was led by my studies to believe, I was naturally brought to pay special attention to the great thinker who must be, for all time, the classical representative of mystical philosophy. No other mystical thinker even approaches Plotinus in power and insight and profound spiritual penetration. I have steeped myself in his writings ever since, and I have tried not only to understand them, as one might try to understand any other intellectual system, but to take them, as he assuredly wished his readers to take them, as a guide to right living and right thinking. There is no Greek philosopher who did not intend to be an ethical teacher ; and in Plotinus the fusion of religion, ethics, and metaphysics is almost complete. He must be studied as a spiritual director, a prophet and not only a thinker. His is one of the most ambitious of all philosophical systems, for he not only attempts to unite and reconcile what was best in all Greek philosophy, but he claims to have found the way of deliverance and salvation for the soul of man, in whatever circumstances he may be placed. And, as he is never tired of telling us, we can only understand him by following him, and making his experience our own. The quest is for him who will undergo the discipline and follow the gleam. Spiritual things, as St. Paul says, are spiritually discerned ; the carnal mind, however quick in apprehending the appearances of the world of sense, cannot know the things of the Spirit. We can only judge of what is akin to ourselves. He says : 'As it is not for

[1] *Id.* Vol. I. p. 62.

those to speak of the beauties of the material world who
have never seen them or known them—men born blind,
for instance, so must those be silent about the beauty of
noble conduct and knowledge, who have never cared for
such things ; nor may those tell of the splendour of virtue
who have never known the face of justice and temperance, beautiful beyond the beauty of the morning and
evening star.'[1]   There is much in philosophy (so Plato
himself felt) that cannot be explained in words.   In his
Seventh Epistle, which I think, with Professor Burnet,[2]
we may accept as genuine, he declares his intention of
publishing nothing on what he must have regarded as
the crown of his philosophy, the Idea of the Good.   ' There
is no writing of mine on this subject, nor ever shall be.   It
is not capable of expression like other branches of study ;
but as the result of long intercourse and a common life
spent upon the thing, a light is suddenly kindled as from
a leaping spark, and when it has reached the Soul, it
thenceforward finds nutriment for itself.   I know this
at any rate, that if these things were to be written
down or stated at all, they would be better stated
by myself than by others, and I know too that I
should be the person to suffer most by their being badly
set down in writing.   If I thought that they could be
adequately written down and stated to the world, what
finer occupation could I have had in life than to write
what would be of great service to mankind, and to reveal
Nature in the light of day to all men ?   But I do not
even think the effort to attain this a good thing for man,
except for the very few who can be enabled to discover
these things themselves by means of a brief indication.
The rest it would either fill with contempt in a manner
by no means pleasing, or with a lofty and vain presump-
tion as though they had learnt something grand.'   So
in the *Timaeus* he says, ' To find the Father and Maker
of this universe is a hard task ; and when you have found
him, it is impossible to speak of him before all people.'

---

[1] I. 6. 4.   [2] Burnet, *Greek Philosophers*, pp. 221, 337.

We find exactly the same feeling in Clement, who is important as illustrating the methods of teaching philosophy at Alexandria in the generation before Plotinus. 'To write down everything in a book,' he says in the *Stromateis*, ' is as bad as putting a sword into the hand of a child.' ' The safest thing is not to write at all, but to learn and teach orally ; for what is written remains.' The *disciplina arcani* of the Christian Platonists probably consisted in an allegorical and philosophical interpretation of certain historical dogmas ; but there was also the perfectly legitimate feeling that spiritual teaching is for the spiritually minded ; and this is the motive of such reticence as we find in Plotinus. Plotinus himself learnt the duty of reticence from Ammonius ; and we must remember this principle in dealing with any mystical philosopher. Even St. Paul had seen in a vision things ' unlawful to utter ' ; and Samuel Johnson blames Jacob Böhme for not following the apostle's example in refraining from attempts to utter the unutterable. Nevertheless I do not think that Plotinus has suppressed anything except the indescribable. The Enneads are notes of conferences held with the inner circle of his disciples.

My study of Plotinus has therefore been, by necessity, a moral as well as an intellectual discipline. And I have not found that he fails his disciples in good fortune or in evil. Like Wordsworth, he is an author whom a man may take up in trouble and perplexity, with the certainty of finding strength and consolation. He dwells in a region where the provoking of all men and the strife of tongues cannot annoy us ; his citadel is impregnable even when the slings and arrows of fortune are discharged against ourselves or our country. For he insists that spiritual goods alone are real; he demonetises the world's currency as completely as the Gospels themselves. The good life is always within our power ; and ' if a man seeks from the good life anything beyond itself, it is not the good life that he is seeking.' It is a severe utterance ; but there is what Emerson calls a ' tart cathartic virtue ' in it, which is bracing when we are battling through a storm. I have found him, I say, a wise and inspiring spiritual guide ; and if I have also found his philosophy intellectually satisfying, it is partly because a religious philosophy must satisfy religious needs as well as speculative difficulties. The two cannot really be separated, unless we try to divide our minds into water-tight compartments, which is unnecessary, since we are in no danger of being torpedoed in this voyage.

It is a satisfaction to me to know that in thus confessing myself to be a disciple and not merely a student and critic of the philosopher whose system I have undertaken to expound, I am in harmony with the intentions of the founder of this lectureship, as expressed in the deed of foundation. He wished his lecturers to study the nature of the supreme Reality, within which we live and move and have our being. He wished them to consider the duty and destiny of man, determined by his relations with the powers above him. And he desired that the knowledge to which these studies may lead us shall be a knowledge that is our own, not depending on any external special revelation, nor enjoined by any sacrosanct authority. To such knowledge Plotinus promises to conduct us, and his last word to us is, ' Remember that there are parts of what it most concerns you to know which I cannot describe to you ; you must come with me and see for yourselves. The vision is for him who will see it.'

The great constructive effort of Neoplatonism, in which the speculations of seven hundred years are summed up, and after which the longest period of unimpeded thinking which the human race has yet been permitted to enjoy soon reached its end, is of very great importance in the history both of philosophy and of theology. Historically, this is what Platonism came to be ; this is the point at which it reached its full growth— its τέλος or φύσις, as Aristotle would say, and then stopped. The Neoplatonic philosophy underwent no further development of importance after Plotinus, but it absorbed into itself most of the rival theories which had flourished alongside of it, so that it seemed to later students to have unified Plato and Aristotle, and the Stoics to boot. But its later history, from an earlier date than the closing of the Athenian schools of philosophy by Justinian in 529, must be sought not among the crumbling ruins of Hellenism, but within the Christian Church. If it be true, as Eunapius said, that ' the fire still burns on the altars of Plotinus,' it is because Christian theology became Neoplatonic. This involved no violent changes. From the time when the new religion crossed over into Europe and broke the first mould into which it had flowed, that of apocalyptic Messianism, its affinity with Platonism was incontestable. St. Paul's doctrines of Christ as the Power and the Wisdom of God ; of the temporal things that are seen and the eternal things that are invisible ; his theory of the resurrection, from which flesh and blood are excluded, since gross matter ' cannot inherit the Kingdom of God ' ; and his psychology of body, soul, and spirit, in which, as in the Platonists, Soul holds the middle place, and Spirit is nearly identical with the Platonic *Noûs*—all show that Christianity no sooner became a European religion than it discovered its natural affinity with Platonism. The remarkable verse in 2 Corinthians, ' We all with unveiled face reflecting like mirrors the glory of the Lord, are transformed into the same image from glory to glory,' is pure Neoplatonism. The Fourth Gospel develops this Pauline Platonism, and the Prologue to the Gospel expounds it in outline. One of the Pagan Platonists said that this Prologue ought to be written in letters of gold. The Christian writers of the three generations after the Johannine books are, on the intellectual side, less interesting ; but from the beginning of the third century we have an avowed school of Christian Platonism at Alexandria, which lives for us in the writings of that charming man of letters, Clement, and in the voluminous works of Origen, the most learned

Biblical scholar of his time. After this, Greek Christianity remained predominantly Neoplatonic ; Gregory of Nyssa and Basil are full of echoes of Plotinus and his school. With Augustine Latin theology follows the same path. Plotinus, read in a Latin translation, was the schoolmaster who brought Augustine to Christ. There is therefore nothing startling in the considered opinion of Rudolf Eucken, that Plotinus has influenced Christian theology more than any other thinker (since St. Paul, he should no doubt have added). From the time of Augustine to the present day, Neoplatonism has always been at home in the Christian Church. The thoughts of Plotinus were revived and popularised in Boëthius, long a favourite author with medieval students ; his spirit lives again in Scotus Erigena and Eckhart ; and the philosophy of Proclus (or perhaps rather of Damascius, the contemporary of the writer) was invested with semi-apostolic authority when the treatises of the pseudo-Dionysius the Areopagite, which seem to have been written under his influence, were ascribed to St. Paul's Athenian convert. The Arabs included some Neoplatonic treatises in their Aristotelian collection, and through them another rivulet from the same source came back into European philosophy, and influenced the theology of the schoolmen.[1] It is impossible that a union thus early formed and so frequently cemented can ever be dissolved. Platonism is part of the vital Christian theology, with which no other philosophy, I venture to say, can work without friction. It is gratifying to me to find that Troeltsch, one of the deepest thinkers in Germany, has said that the future of Christian philosophy depends on the renewal of its alliance with Neoplatonism.

If this is so, the neglect with which the Enneads have been treated is not a little surprising. In most of our Universities where Greek philosophy is studied (I can

---

[1] In the controversy between Realism and Nominalism the adherents of the former were Christian Neoplatonists. Their opponents were not slow to accuse them of pantheism.

speak at any rate for Oxford and Cambridge), it has been almost assumed that nothing later than the Stoics and Epicureans is worthy of attention. Some histories of ancient philosophy end earlier still. The result is that a very serious gap seems to yawn between Hellenic and Christian philosophy, a gap which does not really exist. There were quarrels between Christian and Pagan philosophers, but they were based mainly on violent prejudices with which intellectual differences had not much to do ; for neither in philosophy nor in ethics were the differences very great. It is therefore regrettable that students of Greek philosophy should think it natural to ignore Christian thought, and that students of Christian dogma should often have no intimate knowledge of Greek philosophy. An example of this limitation is furnished by a very famous book, Harnack's *History of Dogma*. Professor Harnack is one of the most learned men in Europe, and his survey of the whole field of Christian speculation and dogmatic controversy is admitted to be masterly ; but he has little or no sympathy with Greek philosophy, and does not seem to be very well acquainted with it. Neither his article on Neoplatonism in the *Encyclopædia Britannica* nor his chapter on the subject in the first volume of the *History of Dogma* seems to me worthy of its author. He regards the Hellenic element in Christianity with unmistakable impatience and irritation ; it is for him, one may almost say, an unwelcome intruder. Other German theologians, who belong without qualification to the Ritschlian school (which cannot be said of Harnack himself) show this animus with no disguise ; and the Catholic Modernists, in spite of their quarrel with Liberal Protestantism, see in the Christian Platonists only the spiritual fathers of their *bête noire*, St. Thomas Aquinas. We have thus to face a revolt against Platonism both in Protestant and Catholic theology. Those who sympathise with this anti-Hellenic movement are not likely to welcome my exhortations to read Plotinus. But if they would do so, they would understand better the real continuity between the old culture and the new religion, and they might realise the utter impossibility of excising Platonism from Christianity without tearing Christianity to pieces. The Galilean Gospel, as it proceeded from the lips of Christ, was doubtless unaffected by Greek philosophy; it was essentially the consummation of the Jewish prophetic religion. But the Catholic Church from its very beginning was formed by a confluence of Jewish and Hellenic religious ideas, and it would not be wholly untrue to say that in religion as in other things *Græcia capta ferum victorem cepit*. Catholicism, as Troeltsch says, is the last creative achievement of classical culture. The civilisation of the Empire, on its moral and religious side, expired in giving birth to the Catholic Church, just as on the political side the Cæsars of the West handed over their sceptre, not so much to the Holy Roman Emperors as to the priestly Cæsar on the Vatican.

I regret that the scope of these lectures cannot be enlarged so as to include a survey of the development of Christian Platonism. Valuable books on the subject already exist; but none of them, so far as I know, treats this school of Christian thought as a continuation, under changed conditions, of the latest phase of Greek philosophy. The assumption is that the Christian religion may be traced from the Old Testament Scriptures, through the canonical books of the New Testament, and so to the Councils of the Catholic Church. This is like tracing a pedigree from one parent only, for the Hellenic element in the New Testament is usually almost ignored.

To the student of historical evolution, whether in the political sphere or in the growth of ideas, the great interest of this period is the reciprocal influence of East upon West, and of West upon East. The classical civilisation was driven in self-defence to import certain alien elements which properly belong to the East, and which are exotic to that type of culture which was developed on the shores of the Mediterranean. The

ancient system of self-governing city states, with their
vivid social and intellectual life, and their devotion
to art, science, and letters, was too weak to withstand
the menace of northern barbarism. The empire of
Augustus became inevitable from the time when the
Republic was driven to suspend constitutional forms and
empower Gaius Marius to raise a professional army.
The fate of liberty was sealed when, after a century of
military revolutions and pronunciamientos, the Empire
was centralised and turned into a Sultanate by Diocletian.
The establishment of a State Church, from which it was
penal to dissent, followed as a necessary part of this
Orientalising of Europe. The change was easier because
the free Mediterranean races had long been declining
in numbers and energy. But neither absolutism nor
Cæsaro-papism belongs to the natural evolution of
European civilisation. It was no accident that as soon
as political conditions permitted the rise of free cities
in Italy and elsewhere, the study of classical culture
began again where it had been dropped a thousand
years before. From that time to this our civilisation has
been inspired by Græco-Roman ideas, kept alive by the
fragments of the old literature which fortunately survived
through the Dark Ages. The continuity of thought has
been less broken than that of political and religious
institutions. Catholic theology has stood firmly by its
ancient philosophical tradition, and has kept it alive and
active. As long as St. Thomas Aquinas is the norm of
scientific orthodoxy, the philosophy of the Church must
remain predominantly Neoplatonic.[1]

The neglect of Plotinus himself, in spite of the immense
influence of his teaching, is partly accounted for by the
reluctance of ecclesiastics to acknowledge obligations to
a Pagan, who was the master of that formidable anti-
Christian apologist, Porphyry. But it is partly due to
the extreme difficulty of reading the Enneads in the

[1] To me at least it is clear that St. Thomas is nearer to Plotinus than
to the *real* Aristotle.

original. The obscurities of his style baffle at first even
a good Greek scholar, and the arrangement is chaotic.
We have in fact only isolated conferences in the *Seminär*
of Plotinus, in which some particular difficulty is discussed.
Hence endless repetition, and often the impression of
keen young students heckling their professor. In one
place (5. 5. 6) ' you have said ' is allowed to stand. When
after much labour the student has become familiar
with the mannerisms of the author, he has his reward.
The sustained elevation of thought ; the intense honesty
of the man, who never shirks a difficulty or writes an
insincere word ; the deep seriousness which makes him
disdain all ornament and fine writing, but frequently
moves him to real eloquence by the grandeur of his
intellectual visions ; the beauty of holiness which pervades even the abstruse parts of the dialectic, produce a
profound impression on those who have given themselves
time to surmount the initial difficulties of reading the
Enneads. But these difficulties are certainly formidable,
and they have in fact deterred many who would have
found the labour well repaid. It has not hitherto been
possible to read Plotinus in a really good translation.
There is a Latin version by Marsilio Ficino, the well-
known Renaissance Scholar (1492). The enthusiastic
English Platonist, Thomas Taylor, published partial
translations between 1787 and 1834. The volume, which
was first issued in 1817, has been edited by Mr. G. R. S
Mead in Bohn's Series. It is very useful to the English
reader, but is incomplete and not immaculate in scholarship. Bouillet's French translation (1857) has long been
out of print. It contains the whole of the Enneads, with
valuable notes, introductions, and appendices. As a
translation it has the merit of being always lucid and
readable, and the demerit of being often inaccurate.
Müller (1878) has translated the whole with great care
into very crabbed German. In 1905 another German,
Otto Kiefer, published a translation of selected portions,
which I have not seen, but which Drews praises for its

style. But in the near future it will be possible for any
English student to make the acquaintance of Plotinus in
an excellent English version. This we shall owe to the
devoted labour of Mr. Stephen Mackenna, who is translating the whole into admirably clear and vigorous
English.[1] The most convenient Greek text is that of
Volkmann, in the Teubner Series, 1883-4. He and other
editors have done something to clear the text of cor-
ruptions, but several passages are mutilated beyond
repair.[2]

The literature of Neoplatonism is extensive. Three
works in French—those of Matter (1817), Jules Simon
(1845), and Vacherot (1846)—are still worth studying,
though in some important points I have found them
unsatisfactory, especially in their disposition to find un-
Hellenic elements in Plotinus. They are all excellently
written. A more recent French work, Chaignet's *Histoire
de la Psychologie des Grecs* (1887), in five volumes, seems
to me very sound but not very brilliant. The fourth
volume is devoted to Plotinus. There is a large number
of German monographs. I have consulted, with varying
degrees of profit, those of Steinhart (1840), Kirchner
(1854), and Richter (1867), as well as the well-known
work of Zeller, whose citations I have found more valuable
than his interpretation of them. The pages of Ueberweg-
Heinze[3] and of the Real-Encyclopädie which deal with
the subject are useful. Hartmann's comments on Plotinus
are good ; and his disciple, Arthur Drews, has published
a book called *Plotin* (1907), which contains valuable
criticism, though he is too anxious to find Hartmann's
' Unconscious ' in Neoplatonism. Essays in German and
French on the influence of Plotinus upon Augustine and
Basil have also been consulted. Rudolf Eucken has a

---

[1] I have not seen Bréhier's translation in three volumes (1922–25).
It is well spoken of.

[2] The numerous and valuable emendations of Professors Dodds
and Sleeman are mentioned in the Preface.

[3] Especially the new edition of Ueberweg, edited by Karl Praechter
(1926).

I.—C

fairly long discussion of Plotinus in his *Lebensanschauungen Grosser Denker*, which marks an advance on earlier criticisms of the philosophy. Eucken fully recognises the great importance of Plotinus in the history of thought, and especially of Christian thought; but he has not escaped the common error of finding metaphysical dualism in Plotinus, and he has not understood the doctrines of the One and of Spirit in relation to each other. The account of Neoplatonism in Windelband's *History of Philosophy* is short but very acute, and he traces with great ability the influence of Plotinus upon Christian philosophy. Of English works, by far the best is Mr. Whittaker's volume, *The Neoplatonists* (1901), an admirable survey of the subject. An independent contribution to an understanding of our author is the chapter on ' The Spiritualism of Plotinus ' in Mr. Benn's *Greek Philosophers*. Mr. Benn is not afraid to claim that in some respects Plotinus shows a real advance upon the teachings of Plato and Aristotle. But this writer declares roundly that ' the speculations of Plotinus are worthless,' an *ex cathedra* pronouncement which no philosopher should have the hardihood to utter. Dr. Bigg's little volume on Neoplatonism (1895) is marked by the liberality, penetration, and humour which distinguish all his writings. Writing as a Christian theologian, he is a little inclined to treat the Pagan philosophers *de haut en bas*; but for all that, his account of the Neoplatonists is one of the best in English.[1]

Of other English books on the subject I am unable to speak with the same satisfaction. Max Müller notices Plotinus in his lectures on Psychological Religion; but he has been at so little pains to verify the information which he has gathered from other books, that he prints *in extenso*, with a few Greek words in brackets, a purely fictitious ' letter from Plotinus to his friend Flaccus,' remarking that a man's real opinions may sometimes be

[1] It is difficult to know what to say of *Plotinos, Complete Works*, by Kenneth Sylvan Guthrie, University of the South, U.S.A. The translation is readable and fairly accurate, but the notes and excursuses are very poor.

discovered more accurately from his correspondence than from his published works. The letter is a cento of Plotinian phrases, compiled, without any intent to deceive, by R. A. Vaughan, in his *Hours with the Mystics*. Vaughan has not made it quite clear that the document is his own composition, and I have found four later writers caught in the trap thus inadvertently laid for them. This incident throws some light on the careless-ness which critics have shown in dealing with the subject of these lectures. An American, Mr. Fuller, has published an essay on *The Problem of Evil in Plotinus*. The subject is not happily chosen, for Plotinus makes no attempt to hide his embarrassment in dealing with this insoluble problem, and throws out several suggestions which have no appearance of finality.

I wish that I could speak with a more whole-hearted appreciation of Dr. Edward Caird's chapters on our subject in the Gifford Lectures, entitled *Theology in the Greek Philosophers*, delivered at Glasgow in 1900–02. The book as a whole is as instructive as it is delightful, and it is no light matter to differ from one of the master-minds of his generation. But I must take my courage in both hands, and say that he seems to me to have attempted to stretch Plotinus on his Hegelian bed of Procrustes, and to have grievously distorted him in the process. When I read that the method of Plotinus ' involves a negation of the finite or determinate in all its forms ' ; that he makes unity the ' direct object of thought ' ; that for him ' religion ceases to be the consecration of life ' ; that ' the world of pure intelligence is opposed in the sharpest way to the world of spatial externality and temporal change ' ; that he ' develops to its extremest form the dualism of form and matter ' ; that he escorts us to a region in which ' all that concerns the individual life is left out ' ; that in the ascent ' spirit divests itself of one element of its life after another,' I cannot resist the con-clusion that Dr. Caird has in some important respects entirely misinterpreted the doctrine of the great Neo-platonist. I shall have to return to all the points raised

by his criticisms, in the course of my lectures. Here it
will suffice to say that Dr. Caird takes no notice of the
doctrine of ἐνέργεια, the creative activity of the higher
principles, which is an essential part of this philosophy ;
that in criticising Plotinus he assumes that because in
the material world no movement can take place without
loss of energy on the part of the mover, the same law must
hold in the spiritual world ; and finally, that he virtually
ignores the κόσμος νοητός, the world of Spirit, which for
Plotinus is the sphere of ultimate existence, and speaks
as if the universe of Plotinus consisted of the supra-real
One and the infra-real Matter, thus reducing to absurdity
a system which assuredly deserves a different treatment.
I do not mean to imply that Dr. Caird's treatment of
Plotinus is throughout hostile and unsympathetic ; that
is far from being the case. Many of his strong points are
generously acknowledged. But it is taken as proved that
the philosophy is vitiated by certain fundamental errors
which must prevent it from possessing much more than
a historical interest. The errors and inconsistencies
which Dr. Caird finds in him are of a kind which could not
have escaped the notice of Plotinus himself, who was
no lonely thinker, but lived in an atmosphere of free
criticism, which he always encouraged. And in fact
there is not one of the objections which cannot be either
answered out of the Enneads, or proved to rest on a
misunderstanding of their teaching.

I will conclude this introductory lecture by quoting
a few laudatory estimates of Plotinus as a philosopher,
by writers whose names carry weight. I will omit the
eulogies of later members of his own school, with whom
loyalty was a point of honour, and honorific epithets a
matter of custom. While other Platonic teachers were
deemed to have deserved the name of 'divine,' the
superlative 'most divine' (θειότατος) was reserved for
Plotinus. Augustine, who, as Grandgeorge has proved,
shows acquaintance with each of the six Enneads, and
quotes Plotinus by name five times, speaks of him

in the following terms. 'The utterance of Plato, the most pure and bright in all philosophy, scattering the clouds of error, has shone forth most of all in Plotinus, the Platonic philosopher who has been deemed so like his master that one might think them contemporaries, if the length of time between them did not compel us to say that in Plotinus Plato lived again.'[1] The precise form of laudation is not happy ; but the words leave no doubt that Augustine, at this early period of his career, was an enthusiastic admirer of Plotinus. In his later writings, Augustine speaks of the 'very acute and able men' who formed the school of Plotinus at Rome ; regrets that some of them were led astray by curious arts (the theosophy and theurgy into which the Pagan revival betrayed the Neoplatonists in the fourth century), and thinks that if Plotinus and his friends had lived a little later, they would have 'changed a few words and phrases and become Christians, as many of the Platonists in our generation have done.'[2] In the *De Civitate Dei* he explains how little they would have had to change, though he criticises one or two of their doctrines sharply enough.

Of modern critics, Réville considers Plotinus 'one of the most vigorous thinkers that humanity has produced.' Vacherot calls the Enneads ' *la synthèse la plus vaste, la plus riche, la plus forte peut-être qui ait paru l'histoire de la philosophie.*' Harnack thinks that his main influence was in the ' creation of an ethical and religious mood, the highest and purest ever attained in antiquity.' Whittaker calls him ' the greatest individual thinker between Aristotle and Descartes '; Drews, ' the greatest metaphysician of antiquity.' Benn, whose almost contemptuous estimate of the sytem has been quoted, admits that ' no other thinker has ever accomplished a revolution so immediate, so comprehensive, and of such prolonged duration.' Eucken speaks of the ' *Welt-*

---

[1] Augustine, *Contra Academicos*, 3, 18.
[2] *Epist.* 118 ; *De Vera Religione,* 12.

beherrschenden Geist des Plotin.' The words of Troeltsch, already referred to, are : ' In my opinion the sharper stress of the scientific and philosophical spirit in modern times has made the blend of Neoplatonism and New Testament Christianity the only possible solution of the problem at the present day, and I do not doubt that this synthesis of Neoplatonism and Christianity will once more be dominant in modern thought.'

Encouraged by these opinions, I shall endeavour to put before you the teaching of this great man, in the hope that you will find it, as I have done, full of intellectual light and practical guidance. Nor am I without hope that, as we study him together, we shall find in him a message of calm and confidence for the troublous time through which we are passing. It is not worse than the period in which Plotinus himself lived. And yet he was able to breathe freely in the timeless and changeless world which is the background of the stage on which each generation struts for its brief hour and then is gone. He lives among the eternal Ideas ; he never refers to the chaos which surrounded his peaceful lecture-room. It is not callousness or indifference that makes him avert his eyes from the misfortunes of the Empire ; he knows that the earth is full of darkness and cruel habitations ; but he is convinced that evil is not the truth of things ; he cannot regard it as having a substance of its own. ' Evil,' he says, ' is not alone. By virtue of the nature of Good, the power of Good, it is not Evil only. It appears necessarily, bound around with bonds of Beauty, like some captive bound in fetters of gold ; and beneath these it is hidden so that, while it must exist, it may not be seen by the gods, and that men need not always have evil before their eyes, but that when it comes before them they may still be not destitute of images of the Good and Beautiful for their remembrance.'[1] In another place he says, in words as true as they are consoling, ' Wickedness is always human, being mixed with something contrary

[1] I. 8. 12, Mackenna's translation.

to itself.' It is human, and therefore not wholly evil and not wholly incurable ; for the Soul of man comes from God, and cannot be utterly cut off from Him. And above the Soul of man is the great Soul, the Soul of the world. This, for Plotinus, as for Eastern thinkers down to Rabindranath Tagore, is no mere metaphor but a truth. The world has, or is, a Soul, which, as the Wisdom of Solomon says, sweetly ordereth all things. If our ears were attuned to the Divine voices we should, in the words of the great living poet and prophet of India, ' hear the music of the great I AM pealing from the grand organ of creation through its countless reeds in endless harmony.' The Soul of man is bidden to take its part in the great hymn of praise which the world sings to its Creator. The body and its organs are the lyre on which the Soul discourses its music. We must take care of our lyre while we can ; but when the lyre is broken or worn out, then, says Plotinus, ' we must sing without accompaniment.' No losses or misfortunes, whether public or private, can hurt the hidden man of the heart, our real self ; still less can they impair the welfare of the universal life in which our little lives are included. The real or spiritual world is a kingdom of values ; and all that has value in the sight of the Creator is safe for evermore. ' Nothing that has real existence can ever perish.' If Plotinus sometimes seems to speak a little heartlessly of such calamities as have lately befallen some unhappy communities of men and women, it is because his philosophy will not permit him to doubt for a moment that a noble life cannot possibly be extinguished by death, that the cause of justice and righteousness cannot possibly suffer final defeat, and that no earth-born cloud can long prevent the beams which stream from the eternal fount of light from illuminating the dark places of this lower world. He bids us, as his master Plato had done, to ' flee hence to our dear country.' But this flight is no shirking of our duties ; it is, as he puts it, ' a being made like to God'; and this we can achieve without any running away; for the spiritual world is all about and within us; 'there is not much between us and it.' And when we have, in heart and mind, reached our dear country, all earthly troubles fade into insignificance. So it may be that others besides myself will find in this prophet of a sad time a helper in public and private sorrows, and that they will say of Plotinus what he said of his master Ammonius, 'This is the man I was looking for.'

LECTURES II, III

THE THIRD CENTURY

PLOTINUS is the one great genius in an age singularly barren of greatness. The third century is a dull and dark period, which has been avoided by historians for its poverty of material and lack of interest.[1] It was a depressing age even to those who lived in it. When the death of Marcus Aurelius on the banks of the Save or Danube closed a long series of good emperors, even those who had ridiculed the imperial saint were saddened; all men had a misgiving that a troublous time was coming. Aurelius himself had been oppressed by the gathering gloom; he exhorts himself to courage and resignation, not to hopefulness. In the generations which followed, pessimism was prevalent. Cyprian, in rebutting the charge that the Christians are the cause why plague, famine, and drought ravage the world, says, ' You must know that the world has grown old, and does not remain in its former vigour. It bears witness to its own decline. The rainfall and the sun's warmth are both diminishing; the metals are nearly exhausted; the husbandman is failing in the fields, the sailor on the seas, the soldier in camp, honesty in the market, justice in the courts, concord in friendships, skill in the arts, discipline in morals. This is the sentence passed upon the world, that everything which had a beginning should perish, that things

---

[1] ' There is no period of the Roman Empire concerning which we are so little informed as the third century,' Cumont, *Oriental Religions in Roman Paganism*, p. 13. Renan, Friedländer, Boissier, Dill, and others have made the death of Marcus Aurelius their limit.

which have reached maturity should grow old, the strong weak, the great small, and that after weakness and shrinkage should come dissolution.'[1] Tertullian finds in the state of the world ample corroboration of the sombre apocalyptic dreams in which he loves to indulge. This is indeed, he exclaims, the *fin de siècle* (*ipsa clausula saeculi*), which threatens horrible misfortunes to the whole world.[2] Pagan literature is equally pessimistic. Dion, Lampridius, and Censorinus all lament the progressive decay of the world, which to Julian, in the fourth century, seemed to be 'at its last gasp.'[3] It would no doubt be possible to find parallels to those lugubrious vaticinations in the most flourishing periods of Greek and Roman culture. The idea that the world is deteriorating was very commonly held in antiquity, though the opposite belief in progress also finds frequent expression. But such a chorus of woe as rises from the literature of the third century had not been heard before.

It has been customary to blame both Christianity and Neoplatonism for encouraging and justifying this pessimistic temper. Pagan apologists were not slow to ascribe the decay of civilisation to the 'third race,' the adherents of the new faith.[4] Modern historians too, lamenting the wreck of the ancient culture and the destruction of its treasures in the stormy night of the Dark Ages, have felt a thrill of sympathy with the melancholy prophecy of a certain Antoninus, son of Eustathius, that soon 'a fabulous and formless darkness shall tyrannise over the fairest things on the earth.' And as for Neoplatonism, was not Plotinus a mystic, and does not the mystic's soul

---

[1] Cyprian, *Ad Demetr.* 3 (abridged). Just a thousand years later the same language is heard. The Abbé Rigord, of Saint Denis, writes, 'The world is sick; it relapses into infancy. Common report has it that Antichrist has been born at Babylon and that the day of judgment is at hand.' Luchaire, *Social France*, p. 1.

[2] Tertullian, *Apol.* 32.

[3] τὴν οἰκουμένην ὥσπερ λιποψυχοῦσαν. Further references in Rohde, *Psyche*, II. 397; and cf. Dion, 75, 4; Lampridius, *Diad.* 1; Censorinus, *De Die Nat.* 17.

[4] The Christians retaliated, attributing the anger of heaven to 'paganorum exacerbata perfidia,' Rohde, *Psyche*, II. 398.

dwell in a house with 'rich windows that exclude the light, and passages that lead to nothing'? Did he not notoriously regard this world only as a good place to escape from ?

As regards Christianity, subsequent history has shown the absurdity of attributing the world-weariness of any age or people to its influence. Christian idealism has taken many forms, but it would be difficult to name any period when it has quenched men's hopes or paralysed their energies. The true account of the matter is that the mysterious despondency which brooded over the Roman world at this epoch, attacked the new religion and infected it with a poison from which it was slow to recover. The Christian Church was no contributory cause of the disease. And if the *tædium vitæ* of the third century nearly swamped the buoyant ship of Christianity, it will be necessary for us to examine closely the other-worldliness of Plotinus, in order to disengage if possible the accidental from the essential in his obvious neglect of social life and its problems. Our object is to understand his philosophy, which, as I hope to show, has a permanent value far greater than is usually supposed. With this aim before us, we shall desire to give full weight to the conditions under which the Enneads were written, and in estimating the value of their moral teaching to consider rather the logical implications of the author's system than the want of emphasis on social and civic duties which we may observe in the work itself. This caution is the more necessary, because Plotinus follows what was really a literary convention of his age in avoiding any references to contemporary problems. There is nothing in the Enneads to indicate that their author was a subject of Decius and the Gordians ; he might be writing in and for a timeless world. We may excuse him, for the age was not favourable to the study of political philosophy. The time was not yet ripe for St. Augustine's *De Civitate Dei*, which was written when the death-throes of the first Latin Empire were heralding the yet wider sway of the second, the crowned and sceptred ghost of Cæsarism which Hobbes beheld sitting amid the ruins of its ancient power.

It would no doubt be possible to discuss the philosophy of Plotinus as a thing independent of the date and locality in which it appeared. Mysticism, above all other types of human thought, is nearly the same always and everywhere. Plotinus would perhaps have preferred that his work should be so dealt with. But there is much in Neoplatonism besides the mystical element, much that can only be understood when it is replaced in its historical setting. And if we are to treat Plotinus as the last of the great Greek philosophers, as indeed he was, we must try to picture to ourselves the strange and uncongenial influences with which Hellenism had to contend in the third century, and take account of the inevitable modifications which Platonism underwent in such an atmosphere. A thinker may be in advance of his contemporaries, but not of his age. The great man gives voice to the deepest thought of his own epoch.

The salient features of this period—the fusion of religious cults, the inroads of Orientalism, the growth of superstition, the reverential deference to antiquity, the profound but half unconscious modification of the older pagan ethics, and the intense individualism of the contemplative life are all phenomena which have their explanation in the uprooting of nationalities which resulted from the Roman state-policy, and still more from the Roman slave-system. The racial factor had a decisive influence in the religious movements under the empire, and helped largely to bring about the defeat of those traditions and aspirations with which Neoplatonism, after the death of Plotinus, more and more allied itself.

A very few words will suffice to indicate the nature of the imperial government. When Septimius Severus lay dying at York in 211, he flattered himself that he was leaving in profound tranquillity an empire which he had found torn with dissensions of every kind.[1] He was the last emperor for eighty years who died in his bed. His sons, whose 'concord' and 'brotherly love' were celebrated on coins and commemorated in an annual festival, agreed no better than Cain and Abel. Caracalla was assassinated after a reign of six years; Macrinus, his murderer and successor, fourteen months later. The next emperor was a young Syrian priest, who for four years exhibited in his own person the worst aberrations of unclean nature-worship. Next the army appointed a boy named Alexander, who called himself Severus and reigned for thirteen years, devoting his time to the practice of a vague eclectic religiosity, in which Apollonius and Jesus, Orpheus and Abraham, divided the honours of his chapel. When he too was murdered by the soldiers, a period of anarchy set in. There were seven emperors in fourteen years (235–249). It was during this chaos that Plotinus arrived at Rome (in 244). Then came Decius and a futile conservative reaction, which as usual took the form of a persecution of the Christians. His death in battle with the Goths—no emperor had before fallen under the enemy's sword in Roman territory—ushered in another period of wild confusion, during which an emperor died the captive of the Persian king. One able ruler, Aurelian, appeared, and was soon murdered. His reign witnessed a bloody pitched battle in Rome itself. The Illyrian emperors, of whom the last and greatest was Diocletian, restored order by bringing to an end the lawless rule of the army, and accepting in principle the Sultanate towards which all indications had been pointing since the time of the Antonines.

A vigorous nation can survive a long period of revolutions and bad government, conditions to which the ancient world was only too well accustomed. But the two great races of antiquity were no longer vigorous.

[1] Septimius Severus was a very able statesman, whose policy anticipated the centralised despotism of Diocletian. The weakness of his successors undid his work, and caused the misery and chaos of the third century.

The system of city-states is a forcing-house of genius, but terribly wasteful of the best elements in the population. From the fifth century B.C. onwards, war, massacre, and banishment steadily eliminated the most virile members of the Greek cities. Originally a very prolific race, as is proved by the extent of its colonisation, the Hellenic stock dwindled rapidly. The Spartiates became almost extinct. Polybius speaks of Greece generally as an empty country, and by the time of Plutarch large tracts of land were absolutely deserted. The decline was in quality as well as quantity ; by the time of Cicero the Greeks had already ceased to be a handsome people. Complete racial exhaustion had practically destroyed the Hellenes before the period which we are considering.

The same blight began to attack Italy in the second century before Christ. The ravages of the Social War and the proscriptions only aggravated a disease which would have run its course without them, and which even peace and good government could not cure. Marcus Aurelius settled large bands of Marcomanni in Italy, a proceeding which would be inconceivable if tracts of good land had not been lying fallow. In the fourth century not only the country but the towns were almost deserted. Bologna, Modena, Piacenza, and many other cities in Northern Italy were largely in ruins. Samnium remained the desert which Sulla had left it ; Apulia contained only sheep-walks and a few farm-slaves. Rome itself seems to have shrunk by more than one-half between Augustus and Septimius Severus. This decline, which was not caused by want, but mainly by a deficiency of births, received a sudden acceleration from the great plagues of the second and third centuries. In a healthy society the losses due to pestilence, like those due to war, are quickly made good by a spontaneous rise in the birth-rate ; but in the Roman empire the loss was probably permanent.

The exceptions to the universal depopulation are found, not in the Romanised provinces of Gaul and

Spain, which seem to have dwindled, though less rapidly than Greece and Italy, but in the Semitic East. The Romans themselves spoke with wonder of the fertility of African and Egyptian women ; but Egypt was very full under the Ptolemys, and the high birth-rate was probably balanced by a high death-rate. The regions where the numbers increased were, it seems, those inhabited by Jews and other Semites, and those colonised by Germans. The steady influx from these fertile races seemed at times to have stopped the decline, so that Tertullian and Aristides speak in exaggerated language of the great abundance of population. The multiplication of the Jews, in spite of frequent massacres,[1] is one of the problems of history. Germans penetrated everywhere, and were not kept down by massacre ; they probably formed a large proportion of the serfs who were beginning to take the place of rural slaves in many parts. The army was chiefly composed of them : the fact that the minimum height for the infantry was fixed, in 367, at 5 feet 7 inches, and 5 feet 10 inches for crack regiments, shows that recruits were no longer expected or desired from the Mediterranean races.[2]

The general result of these changes was that in the third century the traditions and civilisation of Greece and Rome were guarded almost entirely by a population of alien origin. One curious difference was that while the old Romans were almost vegetarians, and temperate wine-drinkers, the new Romans lived by preference on beef, and swilled great quantities of beer. In more important matters there was a great change from the second to the third century. Till the period of the Antonines ancient morality shows an unbroken con-

---

[1] The figures given for these massacres are in my opinion quite worthless. Harnack thinks that there may have been great numbers of proselytes among those killed ; but after Bar Cocheba proselytism was severely repressed, and the figures given (e.g.) for the massacres in Cyprus are ridiculous.

[2] The Roman foot was about $\frac{1}{80}$ less than the English ; but even so, no modern nation is able to exact so high a standard.

tinuity, and in certain respects differed widely from our own. The most remarkable instance is the toleration extended throughout antiquity to the love of boys, which was practised openly and with hardly any sense of degradation in most parts of the Græco-Roman world. This vice was not imported from the East, but spread to the Persian empire from Greece. It appeared later than the Homeric Age, 'quite recently,' according to Plato, and fell into complete discredit only after Christian and Northern ethical ideas made themselves felt. Not to linger over a disagreeable subject, I will only call attention to the contrast between the pious thanksgiving of Marcus Aurelius, that he 'touched neither Benedicta nor Theodotus,' making no difference between mistress and minion, and the angry disgust of Plotinus, when a paper justifying this practice was read in his presence. In some respects the change was for the worse. The barbarisation of the empire is shown by the increasing brutality of the criminal law. Torture became the commonest mode of examining witnesses, even free men. The 'avenging flames,' a penalty almost unknown to pagan antiquity, became the prescribed punishment for every offence which the government found inconvenient or difficult to stop. The advent of the Dark Ages was deferred only by the amazing cast-iron despotism of Diocletian and his successors, which saved the empire from a welter of savagery at the cost of establishing a bureaucratic caste-system which bound every man to his father's calling, and gradually sucked the life-blood of the people by insatiable and unscientific taxation. Throughout the storms of invasion, revolution and civil war, the large landowners somehow maintained their colossal fortunes. The *latifundia* rivalled in extent the largest *haciendas* and *estancias* in Mexico[1] and the Argentine Republic. The six magnates who in Nero's

---

[1] The largest landowner in the world is said to be a certain Mexican general, whose estates are about as large as Scotland—twenty million acres.

time owned half the province of Africa must have had millions of acres apiece. These vast estates were very carelessly farmed, and as the depopulation advanced land became almost valueless. An astonishing decree of Pertinax (A.D. 193), which applied to Italy as well as the provinces, allowed anyone to ' squat ' on uncultivated land, whether in private ownership or belonging to the *fiscus*, and to acquire complete proprietary rights on condition of farming it. The senatorial class, forbidden to govern, to trade, and finally even to fight, were condemned to a life of useless dilettantism. They read and wrote, or looked after their property in an easy-going fashion. The main part of their capital consisted of slaves, whose labours supplied all the needs of the great house, and who could be let out to various employers ; and of flocks and herds, which roamed over the vast sheep-runs in charge of slave herdsmen and shepherds. New fortunes were acquired chiefly by inheritance from wealthy bachelors, by usurious money-lending, or by the pickings of office, which for an unscrupulous official might be very large. The small proprietors were easily bought out, and the luckless middle-class were the chief victims of the *fiscus*.

The decay of culture in the third century is even more deplorable than the disappearance of the old races. The barbarians brought new blood into the empire, but literature, art, and science, which were born with the Greeks, died with them. After the death of Hadrian, ' a Sahara of the higher intellect spreads its dreary wastes over the empire.'[1] Under the enlightened rule of the Antonines law and grammar alone seem to flourish. Suetonius is an entertaining gossip who in an affected age has the sense to attempt no style at all. Aulus Gellius, the epitomator, is a typical product of an age of timid pedants. With him ends classical Latin. The historian of Latin literature now turns his eyes to Africa, where the accomplished rhetorician Fronto is attempting to

[1] Dill.

l.—D

regenerate the language by reviving the prose of the second century B.C., and to the ' barbarous jewellery ' of the decadent Apuleius, the Huysmans of the ancient world, in whom the *elocutio novella,* that strange mixture of pre-classical Latinity and medieval sentiment, reaches its highest excellence. The swan-song of Latin poetry is the *Pervigilium Veneris,* with its singularly pathetic close, in which the Muse bids her tearful farewell to the language of Ennius, Lucretius, and Virgil.

> ' Illa cantat ; nos tacemus ; quando ver venit meum ?
> Quando fiam uti chelidon, ut tacere desinam ? '

There was no second spring for Latin poetry, though Ausonius and Claudian were to make the first renaissance not undistinguished. In the third century the chief writers in Latin are Christians, some of them, like Tertullian and Cyprian, followers of the African tradition, others, like the feebler Minucius Felix and Lactantius, would-be Ciceronians. Tertullian, in spite of his unquestionable power, is a sinister figure, with his gloomy ferocity and scorn of the old civilisation. After reading him we can understand, what sometimes seems hard to account for, the extreme unpopularity of Christianity at a time when the moral condition of the Church was only a little below its best. Cyprian was an able administrator, with a comparatively chastened style. Commodian, though hardly a poet, had the courage to write as he talked, in a Latin which is beginning to pass into the language of medieval Italy. The great lawyers remain ; and we must not forget that ' the first half of the third century is the golden age of Roman law.'[1] The names of Ulpian and Papinian do honour to their time, and their work marks a real progress in justice and humanity, before the barbarism of the later empire set in.

The list of Greek writers is far longer and more respectable than of Latin. A revival of Hellenism had been one of the most prominent facts of the second century. The

[1] Réville.

victory of Vespasian with his Syrian legions over his western rival was perhaps an early indication that the centre of gravity was soon to pass eastwards, though the roll of eminent Spaniards closes only with Trajan. Plutarch, Dion Chrysostom, Herodes Atticus, Maximus of Tyre, Arrian, and Lucian, are among the chief names of a real though rather superficial Greek revival. It bears all the features of a revival, in its artificiality, its conscientious imitativeness and reliance on authority, and in its short duration. But the achievement of Athenæus, Dion Cassius, and Pausanias, followed by Herodian, Longinus, and Philostratus, is by no means contemptible, and Christianity now contributes its share to literature in Clement of Alexandria, Origen, and Methodius. In spite of political disturbances, a cultivated society existed in the capital. It included *littérateurs* of all kinds, poets or poetasters, rhetoricians, grammarians, critics, philosophers. There were also numerous portrait-painters, and architects and engineers capable of undertaking large works. The art was imitative, but of a fair quality till the middle of the century, when the coins begin to show a strange deterioration. The bas-reliefs in the arch of Septimius Severus are vigorously executed. But, speaking generally, there was stagnation or retrogression everywhere, except in law, religion, and religious philosophy.

The Religious Revival

The revival of the religious sentiment, which Augustus had desired in vain to see and had laboured in vain to encourage, was now a swiftly rising flood.[1] Lucian's Voltairean impiety was a belated product even under

---

[1] It rose much higher after our period. Civil functionaries tended more and more to be priests. Among the 164 decurions of Canusium in 223 not one priest is found ; but out of 91 names of the Album of Thamugas (about 365) there are 2 *sacerdotes*, 36 flamens for life, 4 *pontifices*, 4 augurs (Duruy, *Rom. Hist.* (English Ed.), Vol. 6, p. 149). The titles of emperors, such as ' Pius,' which after Macrinus becomes a regular title like *fidei defensor*, and *sanctissima*, officially applied to empresses, mark the growth of the theocratic idea.

the Antonines ; he would have been impossible half a century later. The causes are obscure. Chief among them was probably the consciousness of spiritual sickness and alienation from God, which made men and women feel the ' need of a physician.' As Kirchner says, ' the rich fullness of the world of appearance had lost its charm ; men now cared only for the pure universal and the pure individual.' The movement took many forms. There was a sheer conservative reaction, which looked back to the gods of Olympus. There was a turning towards a religion of pure inwardness ; there was also a growth of theosophy and magic. Above all, the religion of the Hellenistic period found its characteristic expression in the cult-brotherhood (θίασος). The oracles, too, were no longer dumb. Communion with God in some form or other was desired by all. A very prominent feature in the religion of this period was the deliberate mixture of cults originally quite distinct. It was taught that the gods of different nations are all manifestations of the same Divine principle. In many cases the confusion of races, each with its own religious traditions, made interdenominationalism not only easy but necessary, as we observe in some parts of the United States in our own day. Toleration and fusion were the result, all the more readily because most of the old cults, in their traditional forms, were by no means adequate to the higher religious and moral needs of the age.

It is not easy in this period to separate the religious syncretism from the philosophic, for philosophy had now become the intellectual expression of personal religion. But it will be most convenient to consider the philosophical genesis of Neoplatonism in a separate chapter, and to give here a brief sketch of the religious condition of the empire.

The Roman pantheon was densely populated before the immigration of Oriental deities began. ' There are more gods than human beings,' as Pliny the Elder and Petronius[1] assure us in the first century. But the Roman

---

[1] Petronius, however, refers to Capua, not Rome.

gods were invertebrate creatures, shadowy abstractions which had not enough flesh and blood to make a mythology. No one ascribed any definite personality to Domiduca, Volupia, or Pertunda. But the feast-days, which were as numerous as the *festas* of Catholicism, gave abundant opportunities for little pious functions, with prayer and sacrifice, followed by a meal on the sacred flesh. Rome was full of dignified ecclesiastics, with ancient titles, and revenues sufficient to allow of frequent and sumptuous banquets. The numerous benefit-clubs and trade-unions had a religious basis, and the members attended a periodical ' church-parade ' in honour of the deity who was the special protector of their calling. Private and domestic piety flourished in well-ordered households, and the time-honoured religious ceremonies no doubt filled an important place in the country life which Pater describes in *Marius the Epicurean*. This piety was prompted by very different feelings from those which dictated conformity with the established and official cult of the reigning emperor, who could make it more dangerous to swear falsely by his genius than by all the other gods in the pantheon.[1] There was nothing revolting either to Greeks or Asiatics (except Jews) in paying Divine honours to a man. The apotheosis of the ruler of the civilised world was a matter of course. Vespasian no doubt had been conscious of the comic side of his approaching deification (*vae ! puto deus fio*) ; and Caracalla, after murdering his brother Geta, could jest upon the promotion which he had secured for him.[2] This complimentary worship of dead Cæsars was so little serious or so little religious that the Christians must have seemed to their contemporaries merely obstinate or unpatriotic for objecting to it. But recalcitrance was always dangerous, and the living emperor was now beginning to collect the insignia of a real theocratic ruler.

[1] Tertullian, Apol. 28. 'Citius per omnes deos quam per unum genium Cæsaris peieratur.'
[2] Spartianus, Geta 2. ' Sit divus dum non sit vivus.'

Diocletian compelled those who had interviews with him
to prostrate themselves as before a god.[1] Long before
this, each divinised emperor and imperial family had
their own association of worshippers, and membership of
these guilds added interest and a sense of importance to
the life of a middle-class citizen. Paganism, like Catholicism, knew how to make religion pleasant and interesting.

Strictly, it was not the emperor, but his genius or
guardian-angel, who must be propitiated and by no means
blasphemed. Every man had a ' genius,' every woman
a ' Juno.' This piece of old Roman folk-lore was now
so much mixed up with speculation about disembodied
souls and spirits that the fuller consideration of it must
be postponed to a later chapter. Apuleius is a valuable
source of information on the spiritualistic beliefs which
were now becoming almost universal. Christianity was
not unaffected by them, but it did a great service by
discountenancing magic and theurgy. The school of
Plotinus was less successful in resisting the popular
craving : it was at last deeply infected by this kind of
superstition, which Plotinus himself disliked but could
not wholly repudiate, since nature, for him, was a web of
mysterious sympathies and affinities. The ' genius ' was
properly a man's higher self, his spiritual *ego*. It is therefore significant, as showing how fluid was the conception
of personality at this time, that families, cities, trades,
had their ' genius,' much as the individual soul might be
held to be subsumed under a higher unit, and ultimately
under the universal Soul. This vagueness about personality made the notion of a celestial hierarchy easy and
acceptable. Maximus of Tyre is fond of regarding the
spirits as messengers and interpreters between earth and
heaven, and Celsus, the Roman official, compares them
to proconsuls or satraps, deputy regents of the supreme
ruler. Plotinus himself believed in these intermediate
beings, and so did the Christians, for whom the ' dæmons '
of paganism became demons in our sense.

[1] Aurelius Victor, Cæs. 39, 4.

In an age when the Semitic element in the population was gaining every year on the Mediterranean stocks, the East, always the cradle of religions, was certain to have a great influence both on belief and worship.[1] Rome was almost equalled in population, wealth, and culture by Alexandria and Antioch, and a considerable fraction even of the Roman population came from Syria and Egypt. In the army the Eastern gods were the most popular objects of worship; inscriptions in their honour are found in the military stations of England, Germany, and North Africa. The Eastern religions brought with them their priests, not state-officials like the higher Roman ecclesiastics, who might hold many secular posts in combination with their *sacerdotium*, but a dedicated caste with no other interests except the service of their god, and a recognised obligation to proselytise. These priests ranged from the often saintly servants of Mithra or Isis to the disreputable charlatans who perambulated the country-side with an image, a donkey, and a band, and collected coppers from the gaping crowd.

The four countries from which the most important Oriental religions came were Egypt, Syria, Phrygia, and Palestine. We will consider them in turn.[2]

The Egyptian Religion

At Rome, the cult of Isis was the most important among the foreign religions. Even in the first century her worship was widespread in Italy, as is testified by numerous inscriptions at Pompeii. For Minucius Felix the Egyptian gods are already 'Roman.' At first looked down upon, the Egyptian goddess had become fashionable long before the arrival of Plotinus at Rome. Commodus, while emperor, took part with shaven head in her cere-

---

[1] Cumont says truly that the East was far more civilised in religion than the West. 'Never did any highly cultured people have a more infantile religion than the Greeks and Romans.'

[2] It will of course be understood that only a very cursory summary of a subject on which much new material has come to light, and on which valuable books are being written every year, is here possible.

monies, and carried the image of Anubis. Caracalla
showed special favour to the Egyptian rites, and built
splendid temples to Isis at Rome. The eclectic Alexander
Severus was as learned in the theology of Egypt as in
that of other countries.

As the goddess of fertility, Isis combined some of the
attributes of Venus, Ceres, and other Roman deities ;[1]
she was also in a special degree the protectress of com-
merce and navigation. Sailors and women were equally
devoted to the goddess who brought ships safe into port,
and children into the world. But she was also the vision
of the initiated mystic. The *Metamorphoses* of Apuleius,
full of foulness as it is, leads up to a passionate prayer of
devotion to her, as she reveals herself to her pious votaries.

In earlier times the shrines of Isis had an equivocal
reputation.[2] The goddess was popular with the demi-
monde, and her worship can have had little connection
with moral purity. But such scandals are not recorded in
the third century, when indeed they would have hardly
have been tolerated. In our period the worship of Isis
was organised in a manner very like that of the Catholic
Church. There was a kind of pope, with priests, monks,
singers, and acolytes. The images of the Madonna were
covered with true or false jewels, and her toilette was
dutifully attended to every day. Daily matins and even-
song were said in the chief temples. The priests were
tonsured and wore white linen vestments. There were
two great annual festivals, in the spring and autumn.
The autumn festival was the occasion of public grief and
joy over the death and resurrection of Osiris-Sarapis. The
processions and ceremonies described by Apuleius and
others were ingeniously contrived to excite curiosity,
stimulate devotional feeling, and gratify the æsthetic
sense. For the mystic, Isis represented the deepest mys-

[1] Plutarch, *De Iside et Osiride* 53. ἡ Ἶσις μυριώνυμος κέκληται, διὰ τὸ
πάσας ὑπὸ τοῦ λόγου τρεπομένη μορφὰς δέχεσθαι καὶ ἰδέας.
[2] Cf. e.g. Tibullus 1.3.23 ; Ovid, *Ars Amat.* 1.77 and 3.393 ; Juvenal
6.489 ; Josephus, *Ant.* 18.3.4.

teries of life. Proclus makes her say, 'I am that which has been, is, and will be. My garment none has lifted.'

The worship of Isis was closely connected with that of the dog-headed Anubis, long popular in Egypt ; of Harpocrates the son of Isis and Osiris, and above all of Sarapis, who more and more took the place of the old Egyptian god, Osiris. Sarapis was a deity of many attributes ; he had a great reputation for miraculous cures, and invalids often slept in his temples. He ended as a solar deity of omnipotent majesty,[1] and as the great god of Alexandria threw Isis somewhat into the shade. Caracalla paid him the compliment of dedicating to him the sword with which he had killed his brother Geta, as South-Italian assassins have been known to offer to the Virgin the knife which they have used successfully on a private enemy.

Isis was a suffering and merciful mother-goddess, who longed to ease human troubles. Her worship had a miraculous element for the vulgar, a spiritual theology for the cultured, and an attractive ritual for the average worshipper. No other religion practised faith-healing, by passing the night in temples ($\dot{\epsilon}\gamma\kappa o i\mu\eta\sigma\iota s$), on so large a scale. This Egyptian religion never inculcated a very robust or elevated morality. Its power lay in its charm, and in the hope of immortality which was always strong in the Egyptian religion. 'There is a famous passage in an ancient Egyptian text relating to the worship of Osiris, which speaks of the loyal votary of the god after death. " As truly as Osiris lives, shall he live ; as truly as Osiris is not dead, shall he not die ; as truly as Osiris is not annihilated, shall he not be annihilated." The initiate is to share eternally in the divine life ; nay, he does already share it. He becomes Osiris.'[2]

---

[1] 'Sarapis alone is Zeus,' came to be a sort of watchword in the Alexandrian religion. Legge, *Forerunners and Rivals of Christianity*, Vol. I. p. 55. The μυστικὴ θεοκρασία of the age enabled Sarapis to unite almost every divine attribute in his own person.

[2] Kennedy, *St. Paul and the Mystery-Religions*, p. 99. An admirable book.

Phrygian Cults

The worship of the *Magna Mater* had been known and recognised in Attica as early as the fourth century B.C., and at Rome as early as the second Punic war, and was patronised by the aristocracy, though no Roman was allowed to enrol himself among the eunuch priests of the Asiatic goddess. King Attalus at this time presented the senate with the black aerolite, formerly kept at Pessinus and then at Pergamum, which was supposed to be the abode of the Idæan Mother. The grateful Romans, at last rid of Hannibal, erected a temple to her on the Palatine, and ordained an annual holy week in her honour. The Phrygian religion was wild and violent, as befitted a climate which produces extremes of heat and cold. It included such primitive elements as the worship of stones and trees, and at once horrified and fascinated the West by its wild orgies at the spring festival, which culminated in the self-mutilation of devotees. But it had also an ascetic order of mendicant friars, and 'mysteries,' of which little is known. Till the beginning of the empire, the Phrygian worship was kept under strict control, and attracted little notice except on the festival days when the foreign priests marched in procession through the streets. But Claudius, according to a second-century authority, removed the restrictions on the worship of Cybele and Attis, and Roman citizens began to be chosen as *archigalli*. Henceforth the Phrygian worship received a measure of official support not extended to other Oriental religions. The festal processions were very imposing, and the death and resurrection of Attis was regarded as a sacrament and pledge of human immortality. The worshippers sang, ' Take courage, ye initiated, because the god is saved : to you also will come salvation from your troubles.'

Cumont thinks that in the worship of Sabazius, the Phrygian Jupiter or Dionysus, closely connected with

Cybele, some Jewish influence may be traced. The
religion of the *Magna Mater* was certainly changed by
partial fusion with the Persian cult, of which more will
be said presently. The baptism of blood (*taurobolium*)
was, according to some, introduced into the Mithraic
worship from the cult of the Great Mother ; though it is
perhaps more probable that it belonged originally to the
cult of Anahita, a Persian goddess. In the sacred feasts
of Attis we can trace the familiar change from an *agape*
to a sacrament in which the flesh and blood of the god
were consumed.[1] In the fourth century this plastic cult
even tried for a *rapprochement* with Christianity. Augustine tells that priests of Cybele (or Mithra) used to say,
Et ipse pileatus Christianus est, ' even the god with the
cap (Attis or Mithra) is a Christian.'[2]

Mithra

Lucian, in one of his Voltairean Dialogues of the Gods,
makes Momus ask contemptuously, ' Who is this Mithra,
with the sleeves and tiara, who knows no Greek and cannot even understand when one drinks his health ? ' But
in point of fact Mithra was a parvenu only in the West.
He was a very old god of the rising sun, who had been
degraded to a subordinate place by the worshippers of
Ahuramazda, but who refused to remain in the shade,
and advanced rapidly in popular favour among the
Persians.[3] The Persian religion was always disliked by
the Greeks ; the deadly rivalry of the two races is enough
to account for this. The West was less prejudiced. And
Mithra acquired characteristics which made him as wel-

---

[1] Cumont, *Oriental Religions*, p. 69.

[2] Cumont thinks that the god referred to is Attis ; Legge that it is
Mithra.

[3] Mithra is also one of the gods of the Vedic pantheon, where he
represents the light of day, the all-seeing witness. Zarathushtra seems
to have attempted, without permanent success, to discourage Mithra-
worship (H. S. Jones in Hastings' *Dict. of Religion and Ethics,* ' Mithra-
ism '). Sun- and star-worship was not a feature of primitive Iranian
religion.

come in Europe as in Asia. As god of the sun, he claimed
affinity with the nature-deities with whom the Greeks
and Romans were familiar, and as patron of life and
giver of immortality he appealed strongly to the harassed
subjects of the empire. While Isis attracted chiefly
women and peaceable citizens, Mithra was the god of
soldiers and adventurers. Plutarch says that the Romans
first became acquainted with this religion through the
Cilician pirates whom Pompey subdued in 67 B.C. For
Plutarch, Mithra is still a barbarian god. It was in the
time of the Antonines that he gained recognition as a
deity of importance at Rome. Marcus Aurelius installed
him on the Vatican, where St. Peter's now stands. From
this time he became a favourite of the legionaries, who
have scattered votive monuments in his honour over
every province where they encamped, and also of the
slave-class, for reasons less easy to determine.

The Mithraic symbol is familiar to all frequenters of
sculpture museums. The god, in the guise of a young
Phrygian wearing the national cap, a short tunic, and a
mantle floating in the wind, plunges his dagger into the
neck of a bull. The scene is complete only when several
other figures are present ; two young Phrygians, each
holding a lighted torch, the one upright and the other
reversed ; five symbolic animals—a crow or owl, a scor-
pion gripping the bull from beneath, a dog lapping the
blood, a serpent, and a lion. The sacrifice is represented
as taking place in a cave or grotto. The details, however,
differ a good deal, and the meaning of the symbols is,
perhaps always was, obscure. In some representations
the signs of the Zodiac are introduced. This is part
of the process by which Mithra, now identified with
Shamash, the Chaldean sun-god,[1] became *sol invictus*.
The worship passed direct from the Parthian and Persian
empires to Italy, for the Greeks never worshipped the

---

[1] On a tablet from the library of Ashurbanipal. Herodotus (1.131)
is clearly wrong in identifying Mithra with the ' Assyrian ' Mylitta
(Ishtar).

god of their old enemies, the Persians. In the West its progress was rapid, especially after Commodus was initiated into its mysteries.

All through the third century its influence increased, till in 307 Diocletian, Licinius, and Galerius dedicated a sanctuary at Carnuntum on the Danube to Mithra, 'the protector of their empire.' In order to understand this phenomenon, we must remember two things—first, the great prestige of the revived Persian empire in the third century; and secondly, the dualism of the Persian religion, which introduced a new and, to many minds, an attractive explanation of the evil in the world. Plato, towards the end of his life, was supposed to have dallied with the idea of an evil world-soul; Plutarch adopted it more decidedly. But Hellenism knew of no anti-gods, such as were a prominent feature in Mazdeism, and disliked the whole type. Ahriman is identified with Satan by Theodore of Mopsuestia, and the attributes of the two are almost the same. Neoplatonism made room for maleficent agents, but not so easily as Christianity. Porphyry gives us a demonology which he says that he took from 'certain Platonists,' but which looks like pure Mazdeism. The medieval hell, with its denizens, is a legacy from Persian thought, partly direct, and partly through Judæo-Christian literature.[1] The obstinate persistence of Manicheism[2] in the Middle Ages is another proof of the attractiveness of dualism. The popularity of Mithra-worship in the army is easy to understand on other grounds, for the Persian religion was one of strict discipline and military ethics. It regarded lying as the basest of sins, and loyalty to comrades as the chief of the virtues. Soldiers would also readily understand that the moral life is a state of war against 'ghostly enemies.' It was indeed a fine and manly religion, spurring men to action, guiding them by its discipline, and teaching them to live

[1] And yet we must not forget the dualism of (e.g.) Empedocles, nor the influence of Plato and Virgil.

[2] The dualism of Manicheism is more uncompromising than that of the old Persian religion.

honourably, cleanly, and often holily. Some writers
have even speculated as to what the consequences to
civilisation would have been if this cult, instead of
Christianity, had become the state-religion of the Roman
empire. The answer probably is that it would have
become very much what Christianity became in the
hands of the same population. The religion of the fourth-
century Pagan was nearer to Christianity than to the
paganism of the first century. The genuinely Persian
element would have decayed in Europe, as the Jewish
element in Christianity decayed. But such speculations
are of small value. Harnack, who takes a less favourable
view of the Persian religion than Cumont, calls it a
' barbaric cult,' and reminds us that it hardly touched
the Hellenised (i.e. the most civilised) parts of the empire.
It was favoured by the court and popular in the army,
but never made much way among either the intellectual
class or the free populace.

Nature of the Religious Syncretism

The syncretism of the later Roman empire differed
widely from the older polytheism, in that formerly the
gods had their several functions and lived together more
or less amicably as fellow-citizens of Olympus under the
limited sovereignty of Zeus or Jupiter. It differed from
the identification of Greek with Roman gods, which was
only the recognition of a bilingual religion. But now
Sarapis, the Great Mother, and Mithra all claimed to be
the supreme deity. We should have expected, from our
later experience, to see furious jealousies and bloody
persecutions of the weaker religion by the stronger. But
nothing of the kind occurred. On the contrary, the
temples often stood side by side in the same city, and little
or no friction is recorded. The religious condition of a
great city in the third century must have presented a
strange spectacle. ' Let us suppose,' says Cumont, ' that
in modern Europe the faithful had deserted the Christian

churches to worship Allah and Brahma, to follow the precepts of Confucius or Buddha, or to adopt the maxims of the Shinto ; let us imagine a great confusion of all the races of the world in which Arabian mullahs, Chinese scholars, Japanese bonzes, Tibetan lamas, and Hindu pundits would be preaching fatalism and predestination, ancestor-worship and devotion to a deified sovereign, pessimism and deliverance through annihilation—a confusion in which all these priests would erect temples of exotic architecture in our cities and celebrate their diverse rites therein. Such a dream would offer a fairly accurate picture of the religious chaos of the ancient world before the reign of Constantine.' In a modern city thus divided, every pulpit would thunder with denunciations of the soul-destroying errors taught in the next street, and the old state church, if there was one, would be most bitter of all. But at Rome the new gods fused easily with the old ; no difficulty was felt in identifying a virgin goddess with the Mother of the gods. Isis could be adored as Venus, Minerva, Ceres, Diana, according to the pleasure of the worshipper. Wendland prints at the end of his book an extraordinary statuette of Fortuna Panthea, who is loaded with the characteristic emblems of Fortuna, Isis, Nike, Artemis, Asclepius, and the Dioscuri ! The Oriental cults were not quite so complaisant to each other ; but even in them there was borrowing, as when the lore of the Chaldæans mingled itself with the Persian religion. Paganism had no horror of heresy. The deity, said Themistius, takes pleasure in the diversity of homage. Paganism had no dogma and no church. It showed a kind of wisdom in tolerating Lucian, who made few disciples, and persecuting the Christians, who made many. There never was *one* pagan religion. The common folk maintained their simple sacred holidays through all changes till the victory of Christianity—and long after ; the philosophers turned the myths into allegories and so speculated without restraint. The official religion was really dead, as dead

as the republican magistracies, the titles of which were
kept up for the sake of old associations. The Romans
had no objection to make-believe of this kind, and distinguished men were quite ready to accept dignified
priesthoods without believing anything. We must not
form our ideas of paganism from the rhetorical polemic
of Christian men of letters. Augustine probably got his
list of absurd little Roman gods from Varro, not from his
own contemporaries. The real rivals of the Church were
the Oriental deities, who are for the most part ignored
by the Christian Fathers. The paucity of allusions to
Mithra-worship in Christian literature is as strange as
the silence of the Pagan authors about Christianity.
The Church stood outside the zone of mutual tolerance ;
for the rest, a cult was only disliked if it seemed to be
unmanly, immoral, or anti-social.

Plutarch is for us the chief mouthpiece of the theory
that all religions are fundamentally one, under different
names and with different practices. For him and Maximus of Tyre ' the gods ' are symbolic representations of
the attributes of a Deity who is in his inmost nature
unknowable. Maximus and Dion Chrysostom are
' modernist ' in their views about myth and ritual;
Philostratus and Ælian are genuinely superstitious. The
Hermetic writings are good examples of the Plutarchian
theory. They show, however, that the combination of
philosophic monotheism with popular polydæmonism
was becoming difficult, though the writers are equally
anxious to retain both, as indeed the Neoplatonists were.
Syncretism was easier when the gods were regarded as
cosmic energies, or when their cults were fused in the
popular worship of the sun and stars.[1]

In the third century, and indeed earlier, educated men
were no longer ashamed of being superstitious ; the one
unpardonable thing was to be an atheist. There was no
reluctance to believe in miracles. Galen, the great

[1] Dill, *Roman Society from Nero to M. Aurelius*, p. 435. Otherwise
Cumont, p. 163.

physician, is still a Stoic ; but in the third century magic played havoc with medical science. Charlatans of every kind found a ready market for their wares. At the same time, the Stoic faith in an unbroken order of nature was too deeply rooted to be at once abandoned. While in the lower intellectual strata sorcery and magic were allowed to run riot, the more philosophical writers tried to combine belief in a predetermined and inviolable order with the patronage of popular superstition. The most acceptable theory was that what Carlyle called a natural supernaturalism is the law of the universe. Mysterious correspondences, sympathies, and antipathies pervade the whole of nature. There is a divine science which enables men to turn to their advantage, though not strictly to control, these spiritual agencies, which form a celestial hierarchy of dæmons, gods, and the supreme Being, the Author of the whole scheme, in whose mind all discords are harmonised. But the distinction between utilising occult forces and controlling them was too subtle for the popular mind. The dæmons became the faithful servants of the magician, and the old oracles, which had been almost abandoned, once more did a lively trade.[1] Artemidorus, at the end of the second century, writes a quasi-scientific and quite serious treatise on the principles of interpreting dreams. Every variety of divination was practised, and few enterprises were attempted without consulting those who knew or could influence the will of the higher powers. Tertullian even speaks of child-sacrifice as still carried on secretly in Africa ; ' in the proconsulate of Tiberius ' (seemingly lately) several priests had been crucified for this crime.[2]

But of all the superstitions which flourished rankly at this time, astrology was by far the most important. It was spoken of as ' the queen of the sciences,' ' the

[1] See the passages quoted in Cumont's note, p. 271.
[2] For table-turning, telepathy, and other superstitions common to the third and the twentieth century, see Bigg, *Christian Platonists of Alexandria*, p. 248 n.

most precious of all arts,' and was almost universally believed in. The learning of the Chaldæans influenced all the Eastern religions, even that of Egypt. It had taken firm root at Rome as early as the second century before Christ, and gained greatly in authority by the advocacy of Poseidonius, the learned teacher of Cicero, whom Cumont and Wendland have shown to have been one of the most influential thinkers of his time. All through the first century A.D. the folly was growing, not at first among the vulgar so much as in fashionable society, where the makers of horoscopes practised their art for high fees. Their calculations were supposed to be so difficult that an occasional mistake might be confessed without loss of reputation. The immense popularity of this pseudo-science has left its mark upon modern languages. When we speak of jovial, mercurial, or saturnine tempers, or of lunacy, we are using the language of astrology. The curious figures which cover old-fashioned celestial globes, and the names which the constellations still bear, are direct survivals of the same science. It was easy, by the theory of universal sympathies, to give a plausible justification of belief in astrology, and the art was so much connected with religion that scepticism could be represented as impious. It directly favoured fatalism, and so tended to paralyse energy as well to crush the mind under a load of gloomy and absurd superstitions. It drove men to sorcery and magic, as the only hope of combating the direful influences of the stars. It was in vain that the government, while encouraging astrology, condemned magicians to the cross. The severity of the punishment only emphasised the malignant power which adepts in the black art were supposed to exercise.

We probably realise very inadequately the pernicious effects of astrology and magic in the last age of pagan antiquity. These superstitions were all-pervading, and except for accidentally stimulating interest in the heavenly bodies and, to a less extent, in physics, they did unmitigated harm. Christian apologists might well claim more credit than they have done for the Church, as the liberator of Europe from these two causes of human wretchedness. Astrology no doubt lingered on, though no longer sheltered by religion; and magic survived as 'the black art' in spite of fierce attempts at repression; but Christianity may take at least some of the credit for reducing a permanent nightmare of the spirit to a discredited and slowly dying superstition.[1]

Beliefs about the Future Life

Eschatology is always vague and contradictory. The human mind tries to envisage the 'ought to be'—the not-given complement of our fragmentary and unsatisfying experience—under various forms borrowed from finite existence. There are three types of formulated eschatology, which present these hopes or beliefs under the forms of place, time, and substance respectively. The better world is either not here but elsewhere, or not now but sometime, or it is the reality which lies behind illusory appearance. In the higher religions, and in the faith of educated individuals, two of these, or even all three, are often combined or confused, the whole subject being admittedly so obscure that even manifest contradictions are tolerated. It is impossible to estimate what proportion of the population at the present time really believes in human immortality, or to determine whether there have been great fluctuations in the diffusion and intensity of the belief at different periods. In dealing with an age long past, it is hopeless to attempt an answer to such questions. Inscriptions on tombstones, as we know, are not trustworthy evidence either for the charac-

---

[1] We must not, however, forget the appalling witch-trials of the Middle (rather than of the 'Dark') Ages, to which there is no parallel in antiquity. This phenomenon is a measure of the barbarisation of religion in the so-called ages of faith, and it is a saddening reflection that the enlightenment of the Renaissance could not expel the evil.

ter of the deceased or for the real beliefs of his surviving relations.[1] And the tone of polite literature is not good evidence for the beliefs of the masses.

So far as we can form any opinion, belief in immortality was less general in the first century than it is among ourselves, and decidedly less general than it became two hundred years later. Those who rejected the doctrine, like Pliny the Elder, sometimes avowed their incredulity with contemptuous frankness.[2] But for the most part the Romans were disposed to believe in some sort of shadowy survival, which justified family meetings at the grave and the customary tributes to the departed spirit. Here it is difficult to distinguish belief in personal survival from the natural desire to be remembered and honoured after death. But the belief in ghosts and apparitions (in spite of Juvenal's emphatic testimony to the contrary) seems to have been almost universal in the second century, except among the ' godless Epicureans.' Plutarch, Dion Cassius, the younger Pliny, and Suetonius all believed in spiritualism; and Neoplatonism, with its doctrine of dæmons, did nothing to discourage it. The decay of Aristotelianism removed obstacles to free belief in immortality, for in this school the later teachers had taken up a more distinctly negative position than the earlier.[3]

Religious and philosophical faith in immortality subsisted quite independently of spiritualistic superstition. Orpheus and Pythagoras, the former a purely mythical character, the latter a historical figure embroidered with legend, were regarded as the first teachers of the true

[1] The commonest of the conventional dedications on tombs is, ' Dis Manibus '; the commonest aspiration, ' Eternal Rest.' Others cynically avow (through their friends) their disbelief in any hereafter, in such words as ' non fui, fui, non sum, non curo.' Some mottoes are frankly jocular, as ' Dum vixi, bibi libenter ; bibite vos qui vivitis.' Ancient sentiment about the grave, as Friedländer says, differed from ours. Comic and even indecent sculptures on a sarcophagus are not unknown.

[2] Pliny, *Nat. Hist.*, 7, 188–191.

[3] Alexander of Aphrodisias rejected human immortality.

doctrine about the Soul. These two traditions blended almost completely into one, and in the third century it was the Neopythagoreans, with their spiritual kinsfolk, the Neoplatonists, who practised and preached the 'Orphic' religion. The main doctrines of Orphism were the probation of the Soul in this life as a preparation for eternity, the need of purification and sacramental initiation as the condition of a blessed immortality, and the rebirth of Souls in higher or lower forms, determined by the merits or demerits of the subject in its previous state of existence. The philosophical side of Neopythagoreanism will be discussed in a later lecture ; its religious aspect is our present concern. It was conservative and eclectic, uniting a devout reverence for traditions and beliefs hallowed by antiquity with a genuine zeal for moral reform and spirituality. It taught that the Soul is linked to the Divine by a chain of spiritual agencies, which form a ladder of ascent for it. We are undergoing a probation here on earth ; and our salvation consists in liberating the Soul from contamination by the gross vesture of decay which now surrounds it, and in allowing it to emerge into the pure air of the spiritual world. The destiny of the Soul is determined in accordance with the most rigorous retributive justice. We choose our company and consort with our likes. Death is only the transit to that environment which we have made our own. The higher part of the Soul is by nature indestructible ; but its immortality may be an immortality of degradation, or of blessedness. Such a theory of retribution, which resembles the Karma-doctrine of Oriental religions, could dispense with any clear pictures of the future state, when the Soul shall have finally escaped from the 'grievous circle' of births and deaths. Speculation about the condition of beatified spirits was discouraged. According to Philostratus, the spirit of Apollonius of Tyana, the idealised prophet and saint of the school, appeared in a dream to a doubter and said to him, ' Thou shalt know all when thou art dead ; why dost thou enquire about these things when thou art still among the living ? ' Imaginative pictures of future bliss and torment were for the most part lightly sketched and, unlike the lurid creations of medieval Catholicism, they were, by the educated at least, not taken literally. For it was the Soul only which was represented as in paradise, purgatory, or hell, and a disembodied spirit cannot be susceptible to physical delights or torments.[1]   Immortality was an axiomatic truth ; if we are in any degree sharers in the Divine nature, a fact which is proved by our capacity of holding spiritual communion with the Deity, there must be a divine and imperishable element in the human Soul.   On the other hand, the survival or resuscitation of the earthly self was neither to be expected nor desired.   The category of personality, in the modern sense, hardly existed for ancient thought.   Few troubled themselves with the problem how the self could persist in a totally different environment.   ' Thou shalt be a god (i.e. an immortal) instead of a mortal,' was enough. Nevertheless there were many who pictured beatified spirits as enjoying themselves in a rather gross fashion ; ' the shout of them that triumph, the song of them that feast ' was no Christian invention.   Even Plato jested upon the ' everlasting drunkenness ' ($\mu \epsilon \theta \eta$ $\alpha \iota \omega \nu \iota o s$) of the Orphic heaven.   These notions are entirely absent from Plotinus and his school.   In fact, Neoplatonism is open to the charge of considering the tastes of the philosopher and the saint rather too exclusively in its scheme of salvation.   The popular teaching was at once more attractive and more terrifying.

The doctrines of the evolution of Souls, and their reincarnations, do not agree well with the belief in rewards

[1] Plutarch (in *De Sera Numinis Vindicta*) gives us a vision of judgment decidedly less fierce than Dante's, which nevertheless it resembles in many ways.   His Inferno is tenanted only by a few desperately wicked persons.   In his essay on the dæmon of Socrates there is a more philosophic vision, in which the so-called Neoplatonic Trinity appear in charge of their several spheres.   In his treatise on Superstition he complains, like Lucretius, of the terror caused by stories of torments in hell.

and punishments in a supra-terrestrial world. But attempts to combine incompatible theories are character- istic of all eschatology. Another favourite notion was that the spirits of the just live the life of the blessed dæmons, who people the intermediate spaces between heaven and earth, and may aid the living in their earthly difficulties and trials.

The Oriental religions which were now gaining ground everywhere owed a great part of their attractiveness to their definite teaching about a future life. If Judaism ceased to make numerous proselytes in the third century, the cause may be not only the persecution and unpopu- larity to which the Jews were exposed, but the absence of 'other-worldliness' from 'their religion. The popular cults, those of Isis, Sarapis, and Mithra, resembled Christianity in incorporating with their moral teaching symbolical mysteries representing a dying and resusci- tated God, whose victory over death contained a promise of human deliverance from the power of the grave. The old classical legends of Heracles, of Alcestis, of Perse- phone, of Ariadne, were now invested with allegorical significance, like the more obviously eschatological myths of Adonis and Osiris. Whatever myths were made the medium of the teaching, the aim and the method were similar—namely, to stimulate faith in atonement, for- giveness, and eternal salvation by means of symbol and sacrament. The dramatic representation of the Soul's deliverance by divine interposition was the central act of religious worship. Curiosity was also excited by throw- ing a veil of mystery over all the higher teaching. It was held that 'mysterious concealment gives dignity to the divine' (ἡ κρύψις ἡ μυστικὴ σεμνοποιεῖ τὸ θεῖον). Philosophers made genuine efforts to prevent their theories from being made public, and sometimes exacted a promise of secrecy from all who attended their lectures. We find traces of this esotericism even in the Christian school of Alexandria.

The old mysteries, such as the Eleusinian, naturally profited by this new tendency. These strange institutions combined ritual tradition and mystical theology,[1] the realism of a legendary divine drama and philosophical idealism, the religion of the senses and that of the heart. They were the embodiment of the whole syncretistic movement, in which nearly all who felt religious needs could find what they wanted. They are the great enemies of such Christian apologists as Arnobius, Clement, and Lactantius, just because in them genuine religion sheltered itself under the forms of paganism.

Although the secrets of the mysteries were supposed to be kept as carefully as those of freemasonry, Christian writers like Clement and Arnobius knew something about them, and enough has been gathered from them and other sources, some of them very recently discovered, to give us a general idea of the character of these ceremonies. They contained much that to an unsympathetic observer would seem grotesque and not a little that was really revolting. It is a very primitive idea in religion that union between man and God is sacramentally effected in two ways, by eating the flesh of a god or goddess, and by becoming his or her mate. The former notion rests on the superstition, almost universal among savages, that we acquire the qualities of whatever we eat. Much cannibalism has this origin ; and among ourselves many persons still eat large quantities of beef ' to make them strong,' like oxen. In preparing for the mysteries long fasts were enjoined, especially from flesh-food, the idea being that no impure animal spirit should be allowed to enter the body soon to be honoured by the reception of the god. Continence was practised for the same reason, when the sacrament was to take the form of a mystical marriage. This latter mode of union with the Deity was enacted only symbolically in

[1] Rohde appears to me to be wrong in minimising the mystical and moral elements in the older mysteries. I agree with Wobbermin and Kennedy (*St. Paul and the Mystery-Religions*, p. 84).

the mysteries, but, as Seeck shows, the symbolism was probably of an unpleasant kind. Besides this ceremonial purity, moral innocence was insisted on at all the more reputable mysteries. At Eleusis the herald issued the invitation to 'whoever has clean hands and sincere tongue.' In other mysteries the call is addressed to him 'who is holy from all guilt and is conscious of no evil in his soul.' This formula is probably Orphic. There is no reason to doubt that the mysteries helped many persons to live pure and dutiful lives. The original myths were not very edifying, especially when they concerned the Olympian gods and goddesses ; but a bold use of the allegorical method could smooth away almost every offence. The device was not wholly unscientific, since myth is often naïve allegory ; but the beliefs which the ancient myths may have been invented to signify were very different from the religion of the third century. The old mythology was a heavy weight for the Pagan revival to carry.

Dionysus and Orpheus were two nearly connected forms of the Sun-god, and the worship of both was influenced by the rites of the Thracian Sabazius. The central act of both mysteries was the rending in pieces of the god or hero, the lament for him, his resurrection, and the communion of his flesh and blood as a ' medicine of immortality.' The Egyptian Osiris had also been torn in pieces by his enemies ; his resemblance to Dionysus was close enough to tempt many to identify them. In the Egyptian worship the doctrine of human immortality had long been emphasised, and this was now the most welcome article of faith everywhere. It was easy to fuse these national mystery-cults with each other because at bottom they all symbolised the same thing—the hope of mystical death and renewal, the death unto sin and the new birth unto righteousness, based on the analogy of nature's processes of death and rebirth. The æsthetic and orgiastic side of these rites was attractive to a population now largely Oriental by extraction, and too little cultivated to appreciate the idealism which the philosophers offered them. The ritual was much more exciting than anything which Christianity had to offer. We can fancy the emotion of the neophytes when the priest of Isis in his linen vestments drew the curtain and displayed them to the assembled throng, standing with blazing torches in their hands and crowns of palm on their heads, in all the glory of their new initiation. The sacred robes alone must have been an attraction to women. Tertullian tells us how some chose Demeter for her white robes, others Bellona for her dark colours and great black veil, others Saturn for his purple and red. The proceedings were made more impressive by mysterious and half unintelligible verbal formulas, to be learnt by heart and on no account repeated to profane ears ; by weird scenes in dark chambers, representations of souls in torment, followed by a sudden blaze of light in which the statue of the goddess, surrounded by attendant deities, was suddenly disclosed ; by songs and by dances ; by the sacred meal of the brotherhood ; and by solemn processions in which each participant felt the dignity and holiness of his position.

Apollonius of Tyana

The life of Apollonius of Tyana, by the elder Philostratus, is one of the most important documents for the history of religion in the third century. The subject of the biography was a contemporary of Christ, a Pythagorean and a religious reformer. In the early years of the third century the Empress Julia Domna requested Philostratus to write a life of him. The work is a highly apocryphal gospel, in which the hero is almost divinised. Many have thought that there was a deliberate attempt to set up Apollonius as a rival to the Founder of Christianity. But there is no trace of rivalry in the details. Apollonius is turned into a sort of Pagan Christ because the age craved for a historical object of reverence. The picture is in part noble, but the discourses are very frigid, and there are masses of silly thaumaturgy, which it has been reserved for our contemporary theosophists to treat seriously. The feebleness of the whole production is apparent when we compare it with the canonical Gospels. The chief interest in it is the evidence which it gives of Pagan ideals of saintliness at the time when it was written. Apollonius, we are told, tried everywhere to restore religion to its pristine purity, without attempting to alter any man's manner of worship. He hated bloody sacrifices, and would eat nothing that had lived. He condemned war, holding that we have no right to shed blood in any circumstances. Much stress is laid on the 'science' of prayer and sacrifice. The piety of Apollonius, or rather of Philostratus, is on the whole of the Indian type ; the hero is recorded to have travelled through India as far as the Ganges valley.

Judaism in the Third Century

After the edict of Antoninus Pius, which forbade under the severest penalties the circumcision of any Gentile, proselytism must have almost stopped, and it is not unlikely that a good many half-proselytes at this time came over to Christianity. Judaism until the last revolt under Hadrian had been a strong rival of Christianity ; some may even have dreamed that it might become an universal religion. But the savage reprisals which followed this fanatical outbreak drove the Jews back upon themselves, and compelled them to preserve their faith and nationality by returning to the exclusiveness of an earlier period. Philo and Josephus had claimed that Judaism was a 'philosophic' religion[1]—that is, it was

---

[1] Some great writers in Greece and Rome admitted as much, 'Aristotle (according to Clearchus), φιλόσοφοι παρὰ Σύροις; Theophrastus (according to Porphyry), ἅτε φιλόσοφοι τὸ γένος ὄντες; Strabo (16.2.35), Varro (in Augustine, De Civ. Dei, 4.31).' Harnack, Expansion of Christianity, Vol. I. p. 338. Kennedy (St. Paul and the Mystery-Religions) has a valuable account of the affinities of Hellenistic Judaism to the mystery-religions.

compatible with Greek culture. At Antioch and
other places large numbers of 'Greeks' had been bap-
tized into Judaism, if not circumcised. But this policy
was gradually abandoned in the second and third centuries. It must be remembered that in the first century
the profession of Judaism (not of course by a Roman
citizen) carried with it certain political and commercial
advantages. Even in the third century the Jews were
still a privileged class.[1] But the periodical Jew-hunts
must have been a formidable set-off against such im-
munities as they enjoyed, and the Pagan revival greatly
increased the unpopularity of a sect who were accused
not only of unsociability and want of patriotism but of
atheism, from their insulting attitude towards the
religion of their neighbours and the absence of any visible
objects of adoration in their rites.

Christianity in the Third Century

While Judaism was purging itself from its Hellenistic
element and relapsing into an Oriental religion, the bond
of union in a people who were determined to remain
aliens in Europe, Christianity was developing rapidly
into a syncretistic European religion, which deliberately
challenged all the other religions of the empire on their
own ground and drove them from the field by offering
all the best that they offered, as well as much that they
could not give. It was indeed more universal in its
appeal than any of its rivals. For Neoplatonism, until
it degenerated, was the true heir of the Hellenic tradition,
and had no essential elements of Semitic origin. Christianity had its roots in Judaism ; but its obligation to
Greek thought began with St. Paul, and in the third
century 'philosophic' Christianity and Platonism were
not far apart.

A great change came over the Christian Church between

[1] Compare Origen's account of the power of the Ethnarch in Palestine.

the death of Marcus Aurelius and the middle of the third
century. In the second century the Christians had
appeared to their neighbours 'a benighted, hole-and-
corner tribe' (*tenebrosa et lucifugax natio*). The type to
which they seemed to belong—that of a semi-secret society
for mutual help, with a mystical religious basis, was
familiar enough to their neighbours, but they were looked
down upon—so much despised indeed that no trouble
was taken to gain accurate information about them.
The apologists—Justin and his successors—were contemptuously ignored. Fronto, who in the time of Antoninus Pius wrote the first polemic against Christianity,
could set down in all seriousness the old scurrilities about
cannibalism and incest which Jewish hatred had circu-
lated. The apologists of this and the next two generations
—Theophilus, Tertullian, Clement, Minucius Felix, the
writer to Diognetus, are all occupied in defending the
Christians against the three charges of immorality,
atheism, and misanthropy. The government, till the
reign of Decius, was not afraid of the Christians, nor did
the educated and official classes feel any special hostility
towards them. It was the mob who hated them. This
feeling was perhaps strongest among the free or freed
lower class, who, imbued with intense conservatism and
jealousy, disliked the position which Christianity gave
to slaves and women, and the condemnation which it
pronounced upon their cruel and immoral amusements.
The martyrs before Decius were few in number, and
belonged almost exclusively to the *humiliores*, whose
lives were held in small account. They were even sacri-
ficed to make the shows in the amphitheatre more popular, as in the case of Perpetua and her companions. There
was no systematic effort to destroy the Christians ; we
never hear of a congregation being netted in a church,
though there could have been no difficulty in discovering
where they met for public worship. Nevertheless there
was no disposition on the part of the government to
make Christianity a tolerated religion. From the Pagan

point of view, the existence of an 'atheistical' sect,
which mocked at the recognised rites, and regarded itself
as a spiritual nation within the secular state, was an
offence if not a danger. The tests which were employed
at the trials of Christians were the simplest tests known
to be effective, and were selected as such. The Christians
could easily clear themselves of disloyalty ; they were
always willing to pray for the health and safety of the
emperor ; but they objected to offering sacrifice. This
accordingly was the test chosen to convict them, though
the Jews were not compelled to sacrifice. The Jews were
recognised as 'the second race' ; the Christians were
'the third race,' and not licensed. This nickname
(though Harnack thinks that it may have originated
among the Christians themselves) seems to have suggested
something unnatural and monstrous—as we might speak
of a third sex, and not merely another type by the side
of Pagans and Jews. The third race had their own laws
and customs ; they recognised each other by masonic
signs, and 'loved one another at sight.' It was a secret
society, and as such odious to a despotic government.

But already in the time of Commodus, according to
Eusebius, many noble and wealthy men at Rome became
Christians. They were protected no doubt by Marcia,
the devout concubine ($\phi\iota\lambda\acute{o}\theta\epsilon o\varsigma$ $\pi\alpha\lambda\lambda\alpha\kappa\acute{\eta}$)[1] of the emperor.
Tertullian himself was a distinguished lawyer at Rome
before he became a Christian. Some of the old family
of the Pomponii were converted before the end of the
second century. There were many Christians at the
court of the tolerant Alexander Severus. By this time
Rome was full of churches, and of schismatical chapels
for Montanists, Modalists, Marcionites, and Gnostics of
different sects.[2] The capital of the empire, in the
multitude of its competing places of worship, must have
resembled an English or American city. But the Catholics were by far the most powerful of these bodies, since
Decius, according to Cyprian, made the surprising state-

[1] Hippolytus.   [2] Harnack, *Expansion of Christianity*, Vol. 2, p. 385.

ment that he would rather have a rival emperor at Rome than the pope.[1] The extreme hostility of the great church to heretics was noticed as early as Celsus, and exhibited a striking contrast to the brotherly feeling which united the orthodox.

The unpopularity of the Christians among the vulgar was diminishing during the first half of the third century, though the alarm of the official class was now beginning to be excited; after 250 the conditions which, after a fierce struggle, led to the recognition of Christianity as the religion of the State, were already in process of being realised.[2] The Church was approximating to the hier- archical organisation of contemporary society; and it was drawing support from all classes in fairly equal propor- tion. It had shed most of its Jewish severity. In its sacramental doctrine, its encouragement of relics and charms, its local cults of saints and martyrs, it met paganism more than half-way. Its annual festivals became more and more like the *festi dies* of the old worship. These accommodations were indeed too facile, inasmuch as many now joined the Church without under- standing what Christianity really meant, and fell away at the first threat of persecution. The differences which remained between Christianity and its rivals were never- theless considerable, and all of them marked the superiority of the new religion. The absence of bloody sacrifices was a pure gain. Apart from the unseemliness of making a piece of common butcher's work the central act in a religious rite, the distribution of the flesh among the worshippers must have been an undignified finale. Far more important was the entire exclusion of the sex- element from Christian worship. The dissociation of religious rites from impurity is to us a matter of course; but most of the other popular religions had at any rate traditions of an undesirable kind. Other advantages which helped to give Christianity the victory were that

---

[1] Cyprian, *Ep.* 55, 9.
[2] Geffken, *Der Ausgang des Griechisch-Römischen Heidentums* (1920) proves by a wealth of evidence the decay of paganism all over the Empire about 250.

the Christian Founder was a historical person who had lived comparatively recently ; and above all that in its response to the most vital needs of the human heart its superiority was one of kind rather than of degree.

The silence of Plotinus about Christianity certainly cannot be set down to ignorance. While at Alexandria he must have known of the famous Catechetical School, and its distinguished heads, Clement and Origen. The latter of these was one of the most celebrated scholars of his time, whose adhesion to Christianity made it henceforth impossible for educated men to sneer at the Church. At Rome the philosopher could not have walked far without passing a Christian church or dissenting chapel, nor mixed in society without encountering Christians. In fact we know that he did meet them. In the middle of his residence at the capital came the persecution under Valerian, which was chiefly directed against converts in the upper class. His friend and patron, Gallienus, restored the churches which Valerian had destroyed, and gave back to the Christians their confiscated property. We may even conjecture that Plotinus advised this act of justice and toleration. His silence, then, is deliberate. He attacks at great length the heretical Gnostics, as bad philosophers. They attended his lectures and unsettled some of his pupils. Their arrogant tone about Plato angered him. Nevertheless he speaks of them with gentleness, and wishes not to hurt the feelings of those who were Gnostics 'before they became our friends.'[1] As for the Catholics, religion, apart from philosophy, does not come within the scope of the Enneads. Plotinus had a good deal in common with the Christian Platonism of Alexandria, and, like Amelius, could have admired the prologue of the Fourth Gospel.[2] But Roman Christianity, already stronger in administration than in

---

[1] 2, 9, 10.

[2] Amelius, writing by order of Plotinus against the Gnostics, quotes from the prologue of the Fourth Gospel, the author of which he designates (without disrespect) as the ' barbarian,' Eusebius, *Præp. Evang.* 2, 19.

thought, had little to attract him ; he was probably not aware how far the Gnostics diverged from the orthodox Church ; and he was definitely on the side of those who wished to maintain the old culture and the old philosophy. He combated the Gnostics, on grounds which will be more fully explained later ; the controversy with Christianity he left to his disciple Porphyry. It is interesting to compare the attack of Porphyry with that of Celsus, about a hundred years before. Celsus is most concerned at the indifference of the Christians to the welfare and security of the empire, in which he perceived a public danger. Porphyry has no political cares. His polemic is thoroughly modern. He has not much quarrel with Christian ethics, nor (except in certain points) with the Christian philosophy of religion. He objects to the doctrine of the creation of the world in time, and its future destruction in time, as separating God from the world. The doctrine of the Incarnation seemed to him a clumsy attempt to reunite what had been falsely dissevered. The resurrection of the body he spurned as an impossible and objectionable doctrine. ' In every other respect,' as Harnack says,[1] ' Porphyry was entirely at one with the Christian philosophy of religion, and was quite conscious of this unity.' Christian thinkers were even anxious to satisfy the Platonists on the points where they differed, with the exception of the Incarnation-doctrine, which they rightly perceived to stand on a different footing from the others, and to constitute a real cleavage between the two creeds. Porphyry on his side was ashamed of the theurgy which Neoplatonism—never quite having the courage of its disbeliefs—had first tolerated and then sheltered. Augustine was ready to seize the advantage thus offered him. ' Porphyry,' he says, ' holds out the prospect of some kind of purgation for the Soul by means of theurgy, though he does so with a certain hesitation and shame, denying that this art can secure for anyone a return to God. Thus you can detect

[1] Harnack, *Expansion of Christianity*, Vol. 2, p. 138.

his judgment vacillating between the profession of philosophy and an art which he feels to be both sacrilegious and presumptuous.'[1] Augustine elsewhere[2] speaks of Porphyry with great respect ; and Porphyry pays the most respectful homage to the Founder of Christianity, though not to His followers. This respectful tone was not altogether new ; for Numenius is credited with the strange statement that Plato is simply Moses talking in Attic Greek ; and 'a certain Platonist,' according to Augustine, used to say that the prologue of St. John ought to be inscribed in golden letters. There were in fact honest attempts at a *rapprochement* from both sides.

The real quarrel between Neoplatonism and Christianity in the third century lay in their different attitudes towards the old culture. In spite of the Hellenising of Christianity which began with the first Christian missions to Europe, the roots of the religion were planted in Semitic soil, and the Church inherited the prejudices of the Jews against European methods of worship. Hellenism was vitally connected with polytheism, and with the sacred art which image-worship fostered. These things were an abomination to the Jews, and therefore to the early Christians. We, however, when we remember later developments, must take our choice between condemning matured Catholicism root and branch, and admitting that the uncompromising attitude of the early Church towards Hellenic polydæmonism was narrow-minded. Porphyry made a very dignified protest against the charge that the Pagans actually worship wood and stone. ' Images and temples of the gods,' he says, ' have been made from all antiquity for the sake of forming reminders to men. Their object is to make those who draw near them think of God thereby, or to enable them, after ceasing from their work, to address their prayers and vows to him. When any person gets an image or picture of a friend,

---

[1] Augustine, *De Civ. Dei*, 10, 9.
[2] *De Civ. Dei*, 19, 22. ' Philosophus nobilis, doctissimus philosophorum, quamvis Christianorum acerrimus inimicus.'

he certainly does not believe that the friend is to be found in the image, or that his members exist inside the different parts of the representation. His idea rather is that the honour which he pays to his friend finds expression in the image. And while the sacrifices offered to the gods do not bring them any honour, they are meant as a testimony to the good-will and gratitude of the worshippers.'[1] The early Christian horror of idolatry was a legacy from the Jews, who were, on the æsthetic side, too unimaginative to understand a mode of worship which for other nations is natural and innocent. Some of the Christians also used insulting language about the great names of Greek and Roman history. Minucius Felix calls Socrates 'the Athenian buffoon' (*scurra Atticus*) ; Tatian speaks of 'the wretched Aristotle'; and Cyprian calls the heathen 'dogs and swine.'[2] Nor was the charge of unpatriotic sentiment without some justification. Tertullian, among other protestations of crass individualism, says, '*Nec ulla magis res aliena quam publica.*' Commodian gloats over the ravages which he hopes to see the Germans perpetrate in Italy. The Pagans on their side were both indignant and contemptuous. 'Barbarous' and 'insolent' were their favourite adjectives in speaking of the Christians.[3] If Tertullian and (later) Jerome surpassed them in scurrility, we must remember that Pagan prejudice was not vented in words alone. The Christians would not have hated the empire if they had been treated with common fairness. And so the blame must be divided. We must bitterly deplore that Catholicism took over from paganism what was most barbarous in it—sacerdotal magic—while destroying the masterpieces of sculpture and suffering much of the literature to be lost. But on the other hand, Catholicism extirpated what was worst in paganism—

---

[1] Quoted by Harnack, *Expansion of Christianity*, Vol. 1, p. 376.
[2] Duruy, *Roman History*, Vol. 6, p. 215.
[3] e.g. Iamblichus reproves Porphyry for introducing 'archangel' into his writings: οὐδὲ φιλόσοφος ὁ τρόπος οὗτος ἀλλὰ βαρβαρικῆς ἀλαζονείας μεστός. Proclus, *in Tim.* 47.

its licentious rites ; it greatly diminished the gravest
moral scandal of the ancient world ; and it quietly conveyed into its hive, and so preserved, the philosophical
tradition, in which the succession failed more from the
barbarisation of the empire under the devastating inroads of the northern tribes than from the hostility of
the Christian emperors. After Porphyry there was more
sound philosophy in the Church than in the Pagan
schools. Unhappily the time came when priestly tyranny
destroyed the philosophy of religion, or drove it, under
the reign of scholasticism, into bondage as the *ancilla
fidei*. With the modern period, the emancipation of
science and philosophy from religion began, and Europe
retraced, in the reverse direction, the steps by which the
independent science of Ionia developed at last into the
Neoplatonic philosophy of faith and devotion. The
severance was complete in the materialism and agnosticism of the nineteenth century ; there are signs that the
tide has now begun to turn again.

Moral Reformation

The ethical reformation under the empire was not less
conspicuous than the religious revival. We must of course
be on our guard, in studying an age of rhetoricians,
against accepting literally either the denunciations of
satirists or the edifying language of moralists. There was
indeed far too much talk about justice and temperance,
and too little practice of those virtues. But we find, from
the second century onwards, a general acceptance of the
conviction that man is sinful, and needs moral discipline
and reformation (θεραπεία and διόρθωσις). The religious
guilds for the most part, though not always, insisted on
purity of life as a condition of membership. And in the
growth of asceticism we find a new element in morals.
Its characteristic Greek form was Cynicism, which was
revived as the perfection of Stoicism, and sometimes as
a rival to it. The new Cynics were the begging-friars of

antiquity. They were recognisable by their long beards and coarse mantles, which sometimes masked idle impostors. The modern clerical profession had its origin in our period ; the private chaplain, the sermon, and the pious tract were all familiar to the subjects of the Pagan empire. The Hebraic and Hellenic ideas of morality influenced each other, and in Christianity were combined, without anything like perfect fusion. On the whole, the Hebraic element receded, and the Greek advanced. Clement's ethics are mainly Greek, though he is an orthodox believer. Rather later, the moral teaching of Ambrose is mainly Stoical, that of Augustine mainly Neoplatonic. The moral type, however, was changing. There was less public spirit than formerly, and what there was chiefly took the form of ostentatious civic munificence. The personal rights of the individual were better recognised. The treatment of slaves was less harsh, and Dion Chrysostom has a fine protest against the degradation of young slaves in the service of vice, which had always been regarded as a regular part of the slave-system, in spite of some legislative efforts to check it. The moral influence of Christianity was probably considerable among the adherents of other religions. It tended to make social intercourse more sympathetic, more cheerful (the happiness of the early Christians was one of their most obvious characteristics), and more democratic. Pagan civilisation had no greater fault than its neglect of, and contempt for, women, slaves, and handworkers, that is to say, for the large majority of the human race. It was aristocratic in a bad sense, and it paid the penalty. The masses allowed culture to perish, partly because they had never been allowed to share it.

Conclusion

Some writers, like Seeck, who perhaps exaggerates the importance of the racial factor in history, and certainly exaggerates the dysgenic effects of racial admixture, have treated the third century as a period of senile decay, without qualification. From the standpoint of art, literature, and science the decay is unquestionable, but not from that of religion or of psychology. Here, on the contrary, there was progress. The groundwork of religious thought was laid; the problems of religious thought were set and answers attempted. The so-called Alexandrian philosophy of religion was a great achievement of still unexhausted richness. Its characteristics have been summed up by Schmidt as 'the union of philosophy and religion, a strong trend towards system and dogma, mistrust of arid intellectualism, consciousness of the need of revelation, aspirations after the spiritual life, thoughts of immortality, inwardness, purity, mysticism.' The three protagonists were Plotinus, Origen, and the successors of Valentinus; representing respectively Greek philosophy, Hellenised Christianity, and Hellenised Orientalism. The common debt to Greece prevented these three parties from being wholly alien to each other, though the fact that they responded to the same needs, and often in a similar manner, brought them into strong rivalry. Greek Christian theology, and the Augustinian theology, were alike the heirs of the first two. In East and West alike the influence of Plotinus on Catholic dogma, and on the whole intellectual life of the Church, has been enormous, and is still operative. The emergence of a philosophy which has had an abiding influence on the religious thought of the whole civilised world is enough to acquit the third century on the charge of complete sterility.

LECTURES IV, V

FORERUNNERS OF PLOTINUS

THE philosophy of the third century is more closely linked to the intellectual tradition of the past than to the social conditions of the time. It is impossible to expound Plotinus without saying something of Plato, and of the vicissitudes of the Platonic school during the six hundred years which divided them. So cursory a treatment of great subjects must seem unsatisfactory, at any rate to a scholar ; I must ask such to consider these lectures only as a necessary introduction to the subject of my book.

We have lately been bidden to see in Plato a kind of brilliant digression from the main current of Greek thought.[1] Plato, we are told, was not a representative Greek thinker. The Hellenic spirit is concrete and definite, mundane and unmystical, open-minded and liberty-loving. Plato, on the other hand, is as, Nietzsche says, ' a Christian before Christ.' His view of love is romantic and mystical ; he distrusts the natural instincts and scorns the flesh ; he is afraid of poetry and the arts ; he wishes to ' make life a long study for death ' ; and finally he is willing to enforce the acceptance of his views by persecution. ' The legislator has only to find out what belief will be to the greatest public advantage, and then use all his efforts to make the whole community

[1] This view is advocated by Rohde, and also by Nietzsche. It has recently been defended in this country by Mr. Livingstone, in his very able and interesting essays on *The Greek Genius.*

utter these words and no others all their lives.'[1] Heretics
are to be locked up for five years, with the option between
death or submission at the end of them ; atheists are to
be executed at once.

These characteristics of Plato must certainly be taken
into account in any estimate of his work and influence.
But the writers whom I have mentioned have, I think,
overstated their case. The author of the *Symposium*
was surely a Greek to the finger-tips. The famous myths
may be unlike anything else in Greek literature ; but
they would be much stranger in any other. They are
quite unlike the bloodless mythologies of the Gnostics.
The harsh regimenting of men and women appears no
doubt in the *Republic*, but the passage quoted above is
from the *Laws*, the work of Plato's old age. There is no
lack of fresh air and free talk in the dialogues generally.
The qualities which are said to separate him from Hellenism are un-Attic rather than un-Greek. Plato, in fact,
was politically a pro-Spartan ; just as we can imagine an
Englishman, in despair of the undiscipline and inefficiency
of English democracy, praising German institutions, without altering his distaste for some features in the Prussian
character. As a natural result of his leaning towards
military discipline and iron bureaucracy, he turns his
eyes back to the philosophy which seems most in harmony
with such a state-organisation—the philosophy of stable
equilibrium as taught by the Eleatics. This is not un-
Hellenic ; it is, so far as it goes, a recognition of an early
and very characteristic tendency of Greek philosophy.
Above all, it seems to me, those critics go wrong who
talk of Plato's ' otherworldliness ' as a departure from
the genuine Greek view of life. It is true so far as this—
that the ' intelligible world,' or spiritual world as I have
called it in these lectures—the κόσμος νοητός—is in a
sense the Hellenic ideal of existence, banished from earth
by hard experience and now transported to heaven. But
it is not true that Plato abandons the directness and

[1] Plato, *Laws*, 664.

concreteness of Greek thought, and prefers the nebulous region of dreams and hypostatised abstractions. The true account is rather different. When Pater speaks of a ' sensuous love of the unseen ' as a characteristic of Platonism, he indicates a rare quality of mind which Plato seems to have possessed in an eminent degree. He *saw* his generalised Ideas[1]—saw them as the great Greek sculptors saw their ideal types of beauty and copied them in marble from the mental picture. They were for him so clear and concrete that they made the visible world pale and dim by comparison. This again is not un-Hellenic. The world of the Ideas was a very Greek world, in its order, symmetry, beauty, and clear outlines. Only it was not the world which the ordinary man sees clearly and calls the real world. Lastly, those who rebel against Greek ways of thinking generally dislike mathematics, or at least the application of mathematical methods to other sciences. Plato, as is well known, had an exaggerated reverence for geometry, and came to hold (in the Laws) that without mathematics ' no one could be a god or a demigod or a hero to mankind.'[2] In this he resembled Leonardo and Spinoza. It is true that much in Plato's ideal state could only be realised, if at all, under conditions resembling those of medieval Catholicism, and quite unlike those of ancient Greece. But Hellenism was itself an ingredient of Catholicism. In short, I feel sure that we cannot separate Plato from his nation, and that we must not suppose that there was any very deep difference between his view of life and that of Pindar or Sophocles, for instance. It is, as Reitzenstein says, only when two distinct nationalities clash, that profound conflicts in religion and philosophy take place.

The real Plato has been obscured behind Platonism, as the real St. Paul behind Paulinism. Plato was not a

[1] Professor Stewart brings out this characteristic of Plato's mind in his book on Plato's Ideas. ' Plato was a visualiser.' This does not mean that he saw the Ideas clothed in sensuous forms.
[2] Plato, *Laws*, 818.

mere professor of philosophy, and no 'system' can be
found in his writings. He was a poet and prophet; and
his true followers are those whom Professor Stewart[1] calls
'personal Platonists.' The true Platonist is he who sees
the invisible, and who knows that the visible is its true
shadow. The man Plato was of course many things
besides a poet of Divine beauty, and he was many things
at different periods of his life. In his early works we find
a sunny light-heartedness, combined with much reserve;
there is little exhortation, sentiment, or emotion. In the
Gorgias there appears for the first time the Pythagorean
influence, and a deep moral seriousness. He has also
begun to distrust and dislike the vulgar commercial
prosperity which he saw around him, and he despises the
democracy, though rather from the standpoint of an old
Whig family than from that of an extreme Tory. 'What,'
asks his Socrates, 'would be the fate of a physician accused by a confectioner before a jury of children?'

To touch upon the famous doctrine of Ideas in a single
paragraph is a rash proceeding;[2] but introductory
lectures can hardly escape rashness and its penalties.
The doctrine seems to spring from three sources—the
gift of abnormally clear spiritual vision above mentioned,
which caused Plato to *see* concepts more clearly than
material objects; a real confusion caused by the habit
of human speech, which clothes abstractions in the same
dress as percepts, so that forces, qualities, and relations
were treated as things, sometimes even as persons; and
the strongly mathematical bent of Plato's mind, a habit
which always tempts a thinker to assign constant values
to the fluid images of thought and the changing processes
of nature.[3] That these tendencies caused Plato to give

---

[1] J. A. Stewart, *Platonism in English Poetry*, in the volume called
English Literature and the Classics. This short essay is a perfect gem,
and should be read by all lovers of Pláto and of pure English.

[2] The doctrine of Ideas in Plotinus is dealt with in another chapter.

[3] An unknown hand has added to Alexander's Commentary on
the Metaphysics of Aristotle (A.S. 985 b.), that Plato κατεμαθη-
ματικεύσατο τὴν φύσιν. The *Philebus*, as Prof. Stewart says, aims
at establishing a mathematico-scientific method which will apply to all

a handle to his critics is not to be denied ; but he has
suffered injustice both from his own disciples, who tried
to systematise his doctrine without sharing anything of
the poetical imagination and the *amor intellectualis* which
are its primary sources, and from opponents who are
debarred from sympathy with or understanding of
Platonism by the same defects in their own minds.
Platonic generalisation, as Pater truly says, is a method,
not of obliterating the concrete phenomenon, but of
enriching it with the joint perspective, the significance, the
expressiveness of all other things beside. It is applied
chiefly (in the *Phædrus*, *Phædo*, and *Republic*) to spiritual
values, such as the Good and the Just, and to such mathematical universals as equality and similarity. These
spiritual values are fully known only when they are
perceived to put forth ' organic filaments ' everywhere.
These values are seen by Plato and all Platonists to be
also creative forces.

> ' General truths, which are themselves a sort
> Of elements and agents, under-powers,
> Subordinate helpers of the living mind.'[1]

Nor must we forget that for Plato exclusion or distinction
(διαίρεσις) is as essential to the clarifying of thought as
combination (συναγωγή). To idealise is to essentialise
—to eliminate non-characteristic elements. The Platonic
Socrates is largely occupied in trying to elicit the exact
meaning of ethical terms ; vague ' generalities ' are just
what he desires to hunt and slay. Aristotle is probably
right in saying that the quasi-personification of the Ideas
as separable (χωριστά) from particulars is the doctrine
of Plato, not of Socrates.[2] It was the natural way for

branches of knowledge, to ethics and æsthetics among others. Kant
declares that ' Nothing has been more injurious to philosophy than
mathematics.' The school of Bergson has pressed home this criticism
with much exaggeration.

[1] Wordsworth, *Prelude*, Bk. 1.

[2] But he is wrong in making Plato's Ideas separate *things*. They are
(in themselves) eternal truths of the spiritual world, and formative
principles in the world of appearance. In the *Sophist* (p. 248) he

Plato to think ; he does not wish us to picture anything like an extraction of the ideal element from a concrete compound. These transcendental Ideas are the contents of the creative mind of God,[1] the final causes of the world and the inspirers of our thoughts, not the products of our speculation or imagination. They are ' that which really is '—they are reality ; whereas sensible objects are only imperfect reproductions of reality. All philosophy is a quest of reality ; this is the wisdom, to love which makes a man a philosopher (φιλό-σοφος). To love the Ideas, then, is virtue and wisdom ; and it is in natural beauty that the spiritual world is most clearly revealed to our senses. ' Beauty alone has had this fortune [to reveal the Ideal to sight] ; so that it is the clearest, the most certain, and the most lovable of all things.' In the *Sophist* the *dynamic* character of the Ideas is strongly insisted on ; whatever truly *is*, must be active and creative. The argument of this dialogue would almost satisfy modern ' activists ' ; but the genuine Platonist must feel that the ' vision splendid ' of the earlier prose-poems has faded into the light of common day. The famous *Timaeus*, which had an immense influence on later religious philosophy, teaches

argues against the ' friends of the Ideas ' who deny to the Ideas active and passive qualities. These friends of the Ideas have been identified with the Megarian School, with Plato himself at an earlier stage of his philosophy, and with Plato's ' muddle-headed disciples ' (Stewart) from whom Aristotle can hardly be excluded. Proclus (in *Parmenidem*, p. 149, Cousin) identifies them with ' the wise men of Italy '—i.e. the Pythagoreans, and this must have been the accepted view in the Academy. Plotinus, we may say parenthetically, gives his Ideas ποιεῖν, but not πάσχειν. It is, I am convinced, a useless attempt to make the Platonic νοητὰ depend for their existence on the αἰσθητά (Natorp and Stewart). Stewart even holds that the ψυχὴ alone is real, and that Plato always held this view. This is modernising Plato with a vengeance. I have no wish to explain away the definition of Being as Power in *Sophist*, 247 ; but for all that, the Ideas are not ' simply force,' but eternal fountains of force. In no sense whatever are they the products of our thought ; our thoughts conform to them. Modern psychologism must not be read into Plato, or into any Greek philosopher.

[1] This phrase is not Platonic. The Idea of the Good is the ground of all that exists ;' but Plato is not at pains to connect this with the mind of a personal Deity. See Vol. II, p. 29, where the subject of the Ideas is further discussed.

that the supreme Deity, the Demiurge, creates a universal World-Soul, through which the universe becomes an organism. The World-Soul bears the image of the Ideas, and the World-Body was fashioned after the same pattern. The Creator desired all to be good, and ' as far as possible ' ordered the world accordingly ; but ' necessity ' impedes the full power of the good. This ' necessity ' seems to reside in an intractable material, which was in ' disorderly motion ' before the Creator imposed form upon it. It is hard to reconcile this notion with the doctrine that time came into existence with the world-order, and I believe that the whole passage is intended to be myth rather than science. We must remember that for a Platonist a science of the phenomenal, the half-real, is impossible, precisely because Platonism is not dualistic. Plotinus, as we shall see, teaches that there was never a time when the universal Soul was not present in the universe. Plato in this dialogue seems for a moment to dally with the dualistic solution, which has been so unjustly imported into his philosophy as a whole. As soon as the beneficent creative power is personified, there is, no doubt, a danger that the force, whatever it is, which prevents or retards progress in the world of time and space, may also be personified. The evil World-Soul threatens to appear for a moment in the *Laws*. But Plato shrinks from making the powers of evil too powerful ; he is no Manichean. And so man himself must have the seeds of degeneracy within him : the brutes, he suggests, are degenerate men. I think that we may regard as typical the gradual change in Plato's mind in the direction of definite theism. I will even risk the epigram that pantheists generally become theists if they live to be seventy.

The evolution of thought in Plato's mind was a curious foreshowing of what happened at last to his school. Whether we consider the Pythagoreanising tendency, with its devotion to mathematics and astronomy, or the growth of religious interest, of solemnity and devoutness, or the increase in ethical severity, especially as regards sex-matters, or the deepening pessimism about politics and human society, we find the whole history of Platonism anticipated in Plato himself. But before the partial fusion of Greek philosophies in Neoplatonism could take place there had to be a new development and transformation of all the older schools. Heracleitus and the Cynics had a new life in Stoicism ; the Atomists and Cyrenaics joined to produce Epicureanism ; the Eleatics and Megarians, and the Socratic Plato, on one side, lived on, to some extent, in the Scepticism of the post-Aristotelian period. Plato, the many-sided, influenced them all, except perhaps the Epicureans ; and at last seemed to be the inspired prophet under whose mantle all Hellenism might find a shelter against the storm. And it was the author of the *Timaeus* whom the dying Hellenism chiefly meant by Plato, while it was preparing to bequeath its treasure to enrich another creed.

We could not expect that the most inspired part of Platonism—its spiritual vision—would be preserved intact when its custodians became endowed professors at the University of Athens. The intellectual atmosphere of Athens for a long period must have been too much like that of the German universities, at the time when new systems were appearing every other year. The school of Plato was not content with mere commentatorship, like many of the Peripatetics, and in spite of their loyalty to their master, which was a tradition among them, the Academics diverged from his teaching more widely than they knew. After Polemo, the mathematical or Pythagorean element, which had for a time been emphasised, receded, and the rest of the speculative side in Plato was also neglected. The doctrine of Ideas was practically abandoned as unintelligible, but great attention was paid to ethics. This decay of speculation may be compared with the collapse of Hegelianism in Germany, and was due to the same causes. On the one hand, Plato's logical structure seemed to be out of relation to the facts of experience and human needs ; and on the other, the natural materialism of the ordinary man reasserted itself against the exalted idealism of the master. During this phase, the Academy devoted itself to a rather arid and timorous moralising.

At the beginning of the third century before Christ there existed at Athens four schools, all firmly established, the Academics, the Peripatetics, the Stoics, and the Epicureans. It was inevitable that free interchange of views should result in free borrowing of ideas, and in breaking down the dogmatism which was characteristic of all alike when left to themselves. Hence arose the kindred movements of Scepticism and Eclecticism. Scepticism not only had a flourishing school of its own in the third century—the disciples of Pyrrho, but it almost completely captured the Academy. From merely ignoring theoretical knowledge, the school of Plato at this period came to preach its impossibility. Arcesilaus, the founder of this movement, accepted from the Stoics their theory that no knowledge can come to us except through the senses, and then attacked the validity of sense-impressions. Having thus destroyed the possibility of knowledge, he taught that probability is enough for practical purposes. The Sceptics even claimed that they were more invulnerable than the adherents of any system which left objective reality standing over against our views about it. Carneades followed the same path, which leads towards what is now called pragmatism. But every attack upon the possibility of knowledge is foiled by the impossibility of finding a ground on which to fix its batteries. If we try to plant them on anything within the intelligible world, we assert the knowableness of that world in the act of denying it ; and there is no place outside the intelligible world on which they can be fixed. The Academics were too acute not to see this ; and before long the sceptical development of Platonism gave way to frank Eclecticism. Doubt was no longer a dogma.

Greek thought was now fast entering upon a long period of comparative barrenness. From the early part of the third century before Christ till the rise of Neopla-, tonism no new system arose ; men were content to choose what suited them best among the doctrines of their predecessors. Eclecticism is closely akin to sceptical pragmatism, and naturally follows it. For when scepticism refers us to practical utility as the test of truth, we are bound to ask what is the end towards which action should be directed in order to be useful ; and the answer to this question, if any answer can be found, takes us beyond scepticism. Though each individual must answer the question for himself, and with reference to his own character and circumstances, this much at least is implied, that each man has within him the means of distinguishing truth from error. Thus the Academic sceptic was brought back to a position nearer Plato's own. For Plato had taught that the soul possesses, by recollection of its experiences in a previous state, an innate consciousness of the Ideas, which only needs to be elicited by scientific and moral training. The eclectic Platonists, however, had begun by denying the value of dialectic for acquiring a knowledge of truth. They were therefore obliged to rely more upon the inner light ; they now taught that truth is given intuitively to our consciousness. This ' ontologism ' is philosophically objectionable ; it is often the last resource of the confused thinker who cannot make a rational defence of his convictions ; but it had the double advantage of once more finding within the individual the ground of a higher knowledge than can come through the senses, and of perceiving that this higher knowledge, if it is genuine, must be communicated to the soul by some kind of divine inspiration. Thus eclectic Platonism began to display a new feature ; it became a philosophy of revelation. The earliest philosophies had been cosmocentric ; the later anthropocentric ; the last phase (foreshadowed no doubt in Plato) was to be theocentric. This tendency was destined to dominate the whole of the last period of Greek philosophy. It grew out of the Scepticism of the New Academy ; but was none the less a revulsion from it ; and by insisting once more on the supersensual as alone real, and on divine inspiration (' enthusiasm ') as alone blessed, it made a return to the true Plato. There was a slight recrudescence of scepticism under the influence of Ænesidemus (first century B.C.) ; but the whole trend of thought under the empire was towards belief and piety.

Meanwhile, the Peripatetics also were becoming eclectic. Antiochus tried to read Stoicism into Aristotle, making the Deity a kind of World-Soul ; while Alexander of Aphrodisias, in spite of his polemic against Stoicism, deviates from Aristotle in the direction of materialism. After Alexander we hear of no more distinguished Peripatetics, and this school, like the others, was at last absorbed by Neoplatonism.

But the cradle of Neoplatonism was not Athens but Alexandria. The official Academy, with its διάδοχος or professor at Athens, fell into an insignificance which continued until, about the beginning of the fifth century, it was captured by the school of Plotinus, or rather of Iamblichus, and remained Neoplatonist until the edict of Justinian in 529 closed the roll of Platonic professors who had taught at Athens for more than eight hundred years.[1] Alexandria had been ever since its foundation an important centre of learning and cultivation, and it was as cosmopolitan as Rome itself. The East and West met in its streets, its lecture-rooms, and its temples. It was there that first Judaism and then Christianity became Hellenised ; the writings of Philo and of the Christian Platonists remain as memorials of these transformations. If we may believe the emperor Hadrian, even the exclusiveness of Christianity broke down here, and the same persons worshipped Christ and Sarapis. It was no doubt inevitable that Oriental ideas should also mingle with European ways of thinking. The wisdom of the East was held in high repute at Alexan-

---

[1] It is significant that Plotinus, Porphyry, and Iamblichus wished to be called Platonists, not Academics. Augustine *De Civ. Dei*, 7, 12.

dria. But those who have sought Asiatic elements in the philosophy of Plotinus are, I think, in error.[1] The whole system may be accounted for without leaving the lines of genuine Greek philosophy. In spite of the affinity between some parts of Buddhism—'Boutta' is named by Clement—and the later Platonism, it is not necessary to infer direct influence ; and it is doubtful whether Philo found many readers outside the Jewish body. But the affiliation of ideas is, on the whole, a tiresome and unprofitable quest.

Neopythagoreanism

The Pythagorean school, as a theoretical philosophy, almost disappears from view during the fourth century before Christ ; but as a mystery-cult, in connection with the so-called Orphic discipline, it was full of life. It represents the main stream of the mystical tradition in Greek religion. The Pythagoreans were strict vegetarians ; they also abstained from wine, from marriage, and (their enemies said) from washing.[2] They were in a word ascetics of a familiar type. In Aristotle's time there was little or no dogmatic teaching. The initiate 'was not expected to learn or understand anything, but to feel a certain emotion and get into a certain state of mind, after first becoming fit to have such an experience.'[3] The only doctrine was the history of the god—that is, the dramatised experience of the soul's redemption. After a long interval we find a Pythagorean lecturer, Nearchus, at Tarentum in 209 B.C. ; and Ennius translated Epicharmus. About 100 B.C. a number of pseudo-

---

[1] I do not wish to be too dogmatic about this. The contrast between Form and Matter is Greek, that between Light and Darkness is Oriental. Both are prominent in Plotinus. It is also alleged that in the later books of the Enneads Plotinus shows more interest in theodicy, and that there are traces, here and there, of Persian dualism.

[2] Athenæus, 4, 161, ἔδει δ'ὑπομεῖναι μικροσιτίαν, ῥύπον, ῥῖγος, σιωπὴν, στυγνότητ', ἀλουσίαν. (From a comic poet.) They also inculcated a number of very absurd taboos, quite worthy of the Rabbis. Burnet, *Early Greek Philosophy*, p. 104.

[3] Aristotle, Frag. 45, 1483, a. 19.

nymous Pythagorean treatises began to appear, among
which the ' Golden Verses '—excellent moral precepts
in hexameters—are well known.   Bloody sacrifices are
prohibited, and all oaths—we ought so to live that all
men will believe our bare word ; we ought to make
friends of enemies, and never enemies of friends ; we
are to destroy no animal that is not harmful to mankind.
The learned P. Nigidius Figulus, a friend of Cicero,
tried to found a Pythagorean club at Rome ; but in
Seneca's time the school was unpopular and could find
no professor to guide them.[1]   The condition of the sect
at Alexandria, from which the gnomic literature probably
emanates, was no doubt better.

The Pythagoreans of the first two centuries after
Christ were so decidedly the precursors of Neoplatonism,
that we must give some account of this eclectic system.
It was indeed an attempt to fuse into one whole all the
most acceptable doctrines of Plato, Aristotle, and the
Stoa. The Pythagorean tradition supplied the fantastic
number-symbolism, very popular at this time, the insistence on divine revelation as the source of faith, and
the bodily discipline which had always been the chief
external mark of the brotherhood. The members of the
confraternity believed themselves to be true to the
teachings of Pythagoras, and defended their loyalty to
him partly by the assumption of an oral tradition handed
down from the Samian philosopher, and partly by forged
documents. The arithmetical symbolism of the older
school was now given a deeper metaphysical meaning.
The Monad and the Indefinite Dyad became metaphysical
categories of wide scope. By the name of the One, the
ground of all good, of all perfection and order, and of all
imperishable and unchangeable being was indicated.
The Dyad was the ground of all imperfection and bad-
ness, of disorder and change. The Monad was the sign
of the Godhead, of Spirit, of Form ; the Dyad of Matter,

---

[1] Seneca, *Nat. Quæst.* 7. 32. 2.   ' Pythagorica illa invidiosa turbae
schola praeceptorem non invenit.'

as the root of all evil.   Such, we are told, was the metaphysical dualism taught by the Pythagoreans.   But the
Pythagoreans were really eclectics, and they produced
no master-mind to harmonise their contradictions.   Some
of them, in whom the Stoic influence predominated,
identified the Monad with the Godhead, which duplicates
itself in order to form the Dyad, and is the active force
which penetrates down to inert Matter.[1]   Others, following the *Timaeus* and Aristotle, taught that the Godhead
is the First Mover,[2] who brings together Form and
Matter, the Creator who gives the Ideas a visible shape.
They were not strict monotheists, speaking freely of a
plurality of gods beneath the Godhead, and paying special
honour to the heavenly bodies.   They conceived of God
as both immanent and transcendent, wishing to combine
what was true in Stoicism and Platonism.   Perhaps, in
the absence of any great thinkers among them, the two
ideas are rather intertwined than harmonised.   The
Godhead, they said, is something higher than Intelligence ;[3] he is to be honoured not by sacrifices but by
spiritual worship.   The World-Soul, as in Neoplatonism,
occupied the third rank, next after the Intelligence.
They held with Plato that the phenomenal world is
unsubstantial and constantly changing, the intelligible
or spiritual world being alone truly real and eternal.
The visible world derives all the reality which it possesses
from the divine Ideas, in which it ' partakes.'   But here
came in with a full flood the fantastic lore of numbers
which captivated even Plato at one time of his life.
Number is the original picture of the world, the first
thought of the Godhead, the determining principle of
forms and ideas, the instrument in the creation of the
world, the ground of all things.   ' Number ' was personi-

[1] Nicomachus is quoted as saying that the Monad is νοῦς, εἶτα καὶ
ἀρσενόθηλυς καὶ θεὸς καὶ ὕλη δέ πως.
[2] Windelband points out that the ' Idea of the Good ' and the
' First Mover ' have very much the same attributes.
[3] When we come to Plotinus, I shall always translate νοῦς by
' spirit.'

fied and apostrophised as the father of gods and men.[1]
But this deification of Number brought them into conflict with the dogma that the Monad, not plurality, must
be the highest principle. The Monad must be the source
of the other numbers, or of ' Number ' in the abstract ;
and so they appear to have taught. Number is the source
of all things, in the same sense in which the Platonic
Ideas are the types and sources of all things ; but whereas
Plato, in his writings at least, had not clearly envisaged
any principle prior to the Ideas, and supreme over them,[2]
the Neopythagoreans were compelled to give this position
to the Monad, as the creator of Number. The wing of
the school which set God and Matter dualistically over
against each other was equally obliged to transcend this
dualism by postulating an unknown principle higher than
either. This strange metamorphosis of arithmetical symbols into creative types of objects deprived ' the One '
of its mathematical meaning ; it became a mystical
symbol. The number ten was also invested with
peculiar sanctity, as the perfect number, embracing the
whole ' nature ' of Number. They swore by Pythagoras
as the god who had left them the ' tetractys '—a symbol
consisting of a pyramid of ten units, tapering to its apex
from a base of four.[3] This symbol, they held, contained
the ' fountain and root of ever-springing nature.' It was
a picture of the processional movement ($\pi\rho o\pi o\delta\iota\sigma\mu\delta s$)
of life, out of unity into plurality.[4] The tetractys was
a figure both of the Orphic ' cycle of birth,' by which
souls proceed out of their perfect state of union with
God, and at last find their way back, and of the ' processional' movement just mentioned. Pythagoras found

---

[1] Simplicius, *Phys.* 453, 12. κέκλυθι, κύδιμ' ἀριθμέ, πάτερ μακάρων,
πάτερ ἀνδρῶν.
[2] It is difficult to say how much importance we should give to the
isolated passage of the *Republic*, in which he speaks of the Good as
' beyond Being.'
[3] Porphyry, *Vit. Pyth.* 20. Theon of Smyrna quotes the oath :
οὐ μὰ τὸν ἀμετέρᾳ ψυχᾷ παραδόντα τετρακτύν, παγὰν ἀενάου φύσεος ῥίζωμά
τ' ἔχουσαν.
[4] Cornford, *From Religion to Philosophy*, p. 209.

this movement in the procession of numerical series, which he originated. A progression like those contained in the tetractys of Plato's World-Soul (in the *Timaeus*)— the series 1, 2, 4, 8 ; 1, 3, 9, 27—is what the Pythagoreans called a *harmonia* : it is a continuous entity knit together by a principle of unity running through it, namely, the *logos* or ratio which links every term to its predecessor by the same bond. Both series, moreover, radiate from the One, the source in which the whole nature of all numbers was gathered up and implicit. The sanctity attached to the number 3, as the first number which has beginning, middle, and end, has lasted on and has had a very remarkable history. But the number 4 was regarded as even holier than 3.

It is not necessary to describe their theory of knowledge, in which they followed Plato, helped out by the use of the Aristotelian categories. In cosmology they taught that the world is eternal, and that the human race will never perish.

They laid great stress on human immortality. The original doctrine was that souls are reincarnated in each generation, passing through the ' wheel ' of alternate life and death for ever. This doctrine has no moral significance. But it soon came to be modified by another view, really quite distinct from it, according to which the Soul falls through error from its state of purity, undergoes a long purification from its sins both here and in a purgatorial state hereafter, and at last returns to heaven. With this was combined the doctrine of transmigration or rebirth, incorrectly called metempsychosis.[1] Thus the older idea was moralised, but at the same time changed, since now the individuality of the Soul persists from one life to another. And since reincarnation is always for the sake of punishment or discipline, the ' weary wheel ' of existence is regarded as something to be escaped

---

[1] *Metensomatosis* or *palingenesia* are the right words, since it is the bodies, not the souls, that are changed at rebirth.

from, a notion which was far from the view of those who, like Heracleitus, maintained the older doctrine.

They were ascetics on principle. The 'Pythagorean life' was a recognised discipline, which involved the observance of many excellent and some unwise precepts. They were also stern guardians of purity in family life.[1] Iamblichus represents Pythagoras himself as preaching against the loose manners of Croton. We have three lives of Pythagoras, by Diogenes Laertius, Porphyry, and Iamblichus. They are of little value as history; but they are accurate portraits of what the ideal Pythagorean was expected to be. The life of Apollonius of Tyana, already referred to, is another valuable document of the same kind. The Pythagorean sage regarded the Sun as the highest revelation of the supreme Being; but he took part in almost every pious rite, and was initiated into all the great mysteries. In spite of his austerity, he eschewed the coarseness and brutality of Cynic asceticism.

Pythagoreanism, as Mr. Cornford says, was an attempt to intellectualise the Orphic religion, while preserving its social form. It was also an attempt to moralise it; more importance is attached to purity of life, and less to ceremonial. We can trace three strata in this complex product. The oldest was that which taught the unity of all life, the unending cycle of births and deaths, and the conception of a common Soul of the group. The more definitely Orphic element is the doctrine of the fall of the Soul, and its return by means of purifying discipline. But Orphism also valued the passionate emotion aroused by sacramental participation in the sufferings of the god. This kind of communion was what Orphics meant by contemplation—*theoria*. The Pythagorean influence, as distinct from the two factors just mentioned, tended to

---

[1] The Pythagorean philosopher, Theano (for women were prominent in this school), says that an adulteress must be permanently excommunicated from the temple worship; and Phintys, another female Pythagorean, says the same. Farnell, *Higher Aspects of Greek Religion*, pp. 38, 41.

intellectualise *theoria*. It now meant that free exercise
of the Soul's highest faculties which leads to spiritual
enlightenment.[1] The excitements of emotional religion
are merely a hindrance to the attainment of this calm
wisdom. Nor should the mortification of the flesh be
carried too far ; its object is merely to liberate the mind
from the importunities of the body.

In almost all its teaching, the resemblance of Pythagoreanism to the later Platonism is very close.

Plutarch

Plutarch is an important and interesting figure for us,
because his voluminous writings have survived. He gives
us a vivid picture of the intellectual life of his time. But
he was not a great philosopher, and the eclectic Platonism
which he expounds in numerous pleasantly written essays
marks no epoch in the history of thought. His main
interests were religious and ethical, not speculative ; and
he was a religious conservative of a familiar modern type.
His reverence for Plato is such that when he finds (to his
surprise) that according to that inspired man liquid
food descends not into the stomach but into the lungs,
he says : ' the truth in such matters is perhaps unascer-
tainable ; and it is not right to take a presumptuous
attitude towards a philosopher of the highest reputation
and genius in a matter so obscure and so disputable.'[2]
In dealing with religion, he is equally deferential to
authority. The following utterance, which he gives as
his father's, is characteristic. ' You seem to me, Pemp-
tides, to be handling a very large and dangerous question—or rather you are disturbing subjects which ought
to be left alone,[3] when you question the opinion we hold
about the gods, and ask reason and proof for everything.

---

[1] Philosophy, as Iamblichus says in his life of Pythagoras, is ἡ τῶν
καλλίστων θεωρία.   [2] Plutarch, *Qu. Conviv.* 7.1.3.24.
[3] τὰ ἀκίνητα κινεῖν, a proverbial expression, from the old oracle
about Camarina. A late Neoplatonist complains that the glorious art-
treasures of Greece have been removed or destroyed by οἱ τὰ ἀκίνητα
κινοῦντες—in this case, I suppose, meaning the Christians.

For the ancient and ancestral faith[1] is enough, and no
clearer proof could be found than itself—"not though
man's wisdom scale the heights of thought"[2]—but it is
a common home and established foundation for piety ;
and if its stable and traditional character is disturbed
and unsettled in any one place, it becomes insecure and
distrusted by all.'[3] It is the argument of ecclesiastical
orthodoxy in every age. But as Paganism had no dogmatic theology, he will not quarrel with any religion or
philosophy that puts God and man in their right relation
to each other. There are parts of Stoicism which he dislikes, but Epicureanism is the only irreconcilable enemy.
What he chiefly objects to in the Stoics is their cold
rationalism. Like Alexander Knox, he could not ' cordial-
ise with an *ens rationis*.' He loves religious ceremonies,
which helped him to banish care and feel joy, ' not by the
abundance of wine and roast meat, but through good
hope, and belief that the god is present and gracious.'[4]

[1] ἀρκεῖ ἡ πάτριος καὶ παλαιὰ πίστις. The use of πίστις by non-
Christian writers might be made the subject of a very illuminating
study. Plutarch, who distinctly regards philosophy as *ancilla fidei*
(θεολογία τέλος φιλοσοφίας, *De Defectu Orac.*), uses ' faith ' in the
Catholic-Christian sense, as does Philo: ἀληθὲς μέν ἐστι δόγμα τὸ
πιστεύειν θεῷ, ψευδὲς δὲ τὸ πιστεύειν τοῖς κενοῖς λογισμοῖς. Reitzenstein
(*Die Hellenistischen Mysterien-religionen*, p. 85) quotes instances
from ' Zauber-papyri,' in which πίστις is deified. Plotinus returns
to the Platonic use of the word, in which it is opposed to ' demonstra-
tion.' Of the Christian writers of this century, Clement is the most
interesting upon faith. He defines it as σύντομος γνῶσις, whereas
γνῶσις is πίστις ἐπιστημονική. Proclus, deserting Plato and Plotinus,
but in agreement with the ' Zauber-papyri,' puts faith above reason.
' Those beings,' he says, which are not enlightened by reason are
necessarily deprived of faith, which is above reason,' *In Alcib.* 3, p. 10 ;
Theol. Plat. 1.1.26. This last passage is of great interest and importance. τρία μέν ἐστι τὰ πληρωτικὰ ταῦτα τῶν θείων διὰ πάντων πληροῦντα
τῶν κρειττόνων γενῶν, ἀγαθότης, σοφία, κάλλος. τρία δὲ αὖ καὶ τῶν πληρούντων
συναγωγά, δεύτερα μὲν ἐκείνων, διήκοντα δὲ εἰς πάσας τὰς θείας διακοσμήσεις,
πίστις καὶ ἀλήθεια καὶ ἔρως. The influence of the three is distinguished
in *In Alcib.* 2, p. 141 ; faith is ἡ ἑδράζουσα τὰ πάντα καὶ ἐνιδρύουσα τῷ
ἀγαθῷ. Faith, for Proclus, is the state which admits us directly to
the beatific vision. This is not the Christian doctrine, which teaches,
on the contrary, that faith is the beginning, and love the crown, of
the devout life. For proof of this, see my *Faith and its Psychology.*
[2] From Euripides, *Bacchæ*, 203.
[3] Plutarch, *Amatorius*, 12.
[4] Plutarch, *Non suaviter*, 21. (Quoted by Glover, *The Conflict of
Religions*, p. 77.)

To a religious mind like his, the most pressing of philosophical problems is the origin of moral evil. Plutarch comes nearer to the Manichean solution than any other Greek thinker. The imperfection of the world cannot come from God ; for to make God the author of evil is to contradict the idea of God. We must therefore assume two principles, hostile to each other ; this hypothesis alone can account for the strife and confusion which we find everywhere in the world. The evil principle cannot be Matter, for we find evil to be a positive, active thing, such as could not proceed from anything so characterless and indeterminate as Matter. There must be a spiritual power of evil, which may best be designated as an evil World-Soul. From this evil principle proceeds all that is destructive in nature and all that is perverse in man. Matter is only reluctantly overcome and dominated by the evil spirit ; in itself it aspires after the good and would fain come into contact with the divine. Matter, says Plutarch, is the Egyptian Isis, the ' Poverty ' of the Platonic myth. The moral dualism which Plutarch finds in the constitution of the world is reflected in the individual soul. We are ' double ' ; and the two parts of us are sharply opposed to each other.[1] Like St. Paul, he is aware of a law in our members warring against the law of our mind. Like Victor Hugo, he could say :

Si j'écoute mon cœur, j'entends un dualogue ;
Nous sommes deux au fond de mon esprit.[2]

The higher part (νοῦς) is not properly speaking a part or function of the Soul, but something above us and rather outside than inside us.[3] Our Spirit (νοῦς) is not what we are, but our dæmon. Spirit is immortal, Soul is not.[4]

[1] De Virt. Mor. 3. αὐτῆς ἐστι τῆς ψυχῆς ἐν ἑαυτῇ σύνθετόν τι καὶ διφυὲς καὶ ἀνόμοιον. De Anim. Procr. 28. τὴν ψυχὴν σύμφυτον ἔχουσαν ἐν ἑαυτῇ τὴν τοῦ κακοῦ μοῖραν.

[2] L'Année Terrible.

[3] Plutarch, De Gen. Socr. 22. οἱ πολλοὶ νοῦν καλοῦντες ἐντὸς εἶναι νομίζουσιν αὐτῶν . . . οἱ δὲ ὀρθῶς ὑπονοοῦντες, ὡς ἐκτὸς ὄντα, δαίμονα προσαγορεύουσι.

[4] Plutarch, De Sera Num. Vind. 17. There is a higher, rational soul, which does not die.

Plutarch fathers his theory of the evil World-Soul on Plato, appealing to the Politicus, the Timæus, and the Laws. Xenocrates and Chrysippus had distinguished good and bad spirits, as did the Christians, who identified the bad spirits with the Pagan gods. In Plutarch's time, therefore, the idea of malignant powers was more familiar than it was to Plato; and this hypothesis enabled Plutarch to rescue Matter from the aspersions which popular Platonism cast upon it, and to claim that Matter ' has a share of the first God, and is united to him by love of the goodness and beauty which surround him.'[1]

Plutarch knows of the Persian doctrine about Ormuzd and Ahriman, and speaks of it with respect. But his evil World-Soul is no rival of the supreme God. The Godhead, in his system, is an emperor who rules through deputy-governors. These subordinate gods and dæmons are not (as the Stoics thought) natural forces or laws; they are personal rulers. There is a hierarchy of them; the gods are the superior class, the dæmons the inferior. Some of the dæmons are disembodied human spirits, delivered from the cycle of births and deaths. Each person has one (or more probably, as Empedocles suggested two) dæmons in attendance upon him. One of these two may be the evil genius (κακὸς δαίμων), such as appeared to Brutus at Philippi. It is evil dæmons, sometimes gathered up into the evil World-Soul, who are responsible for the sin and sorrow of the world.

It is characteristic of Plutarch that he cannot make up his mind about superstition. He cannot bring himself to condemn outright any practice or belief which stimulates religious emotion. If superstition is a rheum in the eye of faith, it is better to leave it there than to risk putting out the eye in removing it.[2] On the other

---

[1] Plutarch, De Is. et Osir. 58. It is not easy to see how Matter can be too characterless to be the evil principle, but definite enough to ' desire God and be ever in his presence, and be filled with the most powerful and purest parts of him '—words which follow the passage quoted in the text.

[2] Plutarch, Non Suaviter, 21.

hand, superstition is one of the main causes of human
misery, and it encourages all kinds of impious and
unworthy beliefs about the gods. ' The atheist thinks
there are no gods ; the superstitious man wishes there
were none.'[1] So he leaves the door wide open for superstition to enter, and hopes that she may be willing to
remain outside.

Departing from the best Platonic tradition, Plutarch
holds that the world was created in time, though he also
says that time is the form of the world-order, and began
with it. It is unnecessary to follow further his utterances
on anthropology, psychology, and ethics. They all
present the same features—a combination of Plato,
Aristotle, and the Stoa, dominated throughout by a
religion of feeling and emotion. In all this he is very
modern ; but since he does not place the knowledge
of truth first in his enquiries, he cannot claim to be
treated very seriously as a philosopher.

Maximus of Tyre

This rhetorical writer, who flourished under Antoninus
Pius and Marcus Aurelius, is a pleasing example of a
religious teacher rather than a deep philosopher. He
works out his theory that myth and legend are the
philosophy of the unlearned, enshrining the same truths
which philosophers teach under a higher form. The
ancient poets, whose prophetic inspiration it would be
impious to question, taught the same truths as later
philosophers, in a symbolic manner. He also thinks
much of the beneficent dæmons, the guardian angels of
Paganism. He says that 'he who has heard Plato and
yet needs other teaching is like a man who cannot see the
sun at noonday.' And yet, in his admiration for the
Cynic life, he puts Diogenes above Socrates and Plato.
He is an eclectic, like Plutarch.

[1] Cf. Glover, *The Conflict of Religions*, p. 109. So Clement of
Alexandria, speaking as a true Platonist, says, ἀκρότητες ἀμαθίας ἀθεότης
καὶ δεισιδαιμονία. (*Admon. ad Græcos*.)

Apuleius

This licentious African novelist was also a capable
thinker, keenly interested in philosophy, and like many
decadent ritualists in our time, religious after a fashion.
His voluminous writings supply much information about
the welter of religious and philosophical beliefs in which
the civilised world then lived. Apuleius believes in a
transcendent, impassible and inaccessible God; in the
Ideas, which he at one time describes correctly as *formae
simplices et aeternae*, at another, by an amazing blunder,
as *inabsolutae, informes, nulla specie nec qualitatis significa-
tione distinctae*.[1] He is attracted by the superstitious
side of the Pagan revival; spirits and ghosts, sacraments
and oracles, white magic and divination, make up the
larger part of his religion. The end of the *Metamorphoses*,
where queen Isis appears in glory to Lucius, and claims
him as her pious servant for the rest of his life, is justly
famous. Apuleius may here be describing his own
experience, but we could believe more readily in the
genuineness of his conversion if it had led him to expur-
gate the earlier parts of his novel.

Numenius

More important in the history of the later Platonism
is Numenius of Apamea, who so far anticipated Plotinus
that Amelius, a favourite pupil of the latter, was commissioned to write a treatise to vindicate the originality
of his master's teaching. Numenius wished to go back
from Platonism and Pythagoreanism to Plato and Pythagoras; but he also wished to sweep into his net the wisdom of the Magi, Egyptians, Brahmins, and even the
Jews. The respect which he showed for the Hebrew
religion is something quite new in Greek philosophy.
He is said to have referred to Moses as 'the prophet,'[1]

---

[1] Apuleius, *Dogm. Plat.* 1.5 and 6.
[2] Cf. Zeller, p. 236.

and, which is still more astonishing, to have called Plato
'a Moses speaking in Attic.' Origen tells us that he also
referred to Jesus, respectfully, it would appear, but without naming Him. Here for the first time we come across
a very probable trace of Philonic influence in a Pagan
thinker. He separated the 'second God'—the Demiurge
or Creator, from the supreme Being, thereby gathering
together the crowd of inferior gods, to whom Platonism
entrusted the part of administering the universe, into
one divine Being, with attributes like those of the
Christian-Alexandrian Logos. He may have borrowed
something here from the half-Christian Gnostics. The
supreme Godhead he called in so many words a *roi
fainéant* (βασιλεὺς ἀργός).[1] The second God, though
all his divine qualities are derived from the First Principle, is the active power for good in the world. The
'First God' is concerned only with the spiritual world
(τὰ νοητά) ; the Second with the spiritual and phenomenal both. He is double (διττός) in nature, in accordance
with this double interest. The Neoplatonists would say
that he is related to the spiritual world by his essence,
and to the phenomenal world by his activity. Our
world, says Numenius, is the 'Third God.' There are
therefore three divine hypostases—The Godhead, the
Creator, and the Created ; but these three are not equal
in glory. Just as the Demiurge is double, so the Soul is
double ; or rather there are two Souls, the rational and
the irrational Soul.[1] This division in the human Soul is
the common property of the later Greek philosophy,
and we shall find it in Plotinus. But Numenius, according to our authorities, taught that there are two World-
Souls, one good, the other bad ; and identified the
second with Matter. This last seems hardly credible.
Other dualistic interpreters of Plato, such as Plutarch,
had made the evil World-Soul a principle acting upon
Matter from without ; Numenius, we are told, invested

---

[1] Chalcidius (*in Timaeum*, §295) says : ' Platonem idem Numenius
laudat quod duas mundi animas autumet, unam beneficentissimam,
malignam alteram, scilicet silvam, quae fons malorum est.'

Matter itself with a spiritual activity, as a living and recalcitrant power in opposition to the good World-Soul. In the world and in man these two souls are in conflict.[1] Apparently human souls may be good or bad souls, and at death these are united each to its own principle. But Numenius also believes in reincarnation.

On the whole, Amelius cannot have had a hard task in proving that the philosophy of Plotinus differed substantially from that of Numenius.[2]

Ammonius Saccas

Ammonius, called 'The Porter,' was, according to Porphyry, born of Christian parents, but reverted to the Greek religion.[3] He must have been a very remarkable man, since Plotinus was contented to be his scholar for so many years, but the scanty and untrustworthy notices that we have of his oral teaching (he committed nothing to writing) do not enable us to say with certainty whether he deserves to be called the founder of Neoplatonism. Hierocles affirms that his object was to reconcile the philosophies of Plato and Aristotle. Nemesius, at the end of the fourth century, reproduces two arguments which he attributes to Ammonius, one on the immateriality of the Soul, the other on the union of Soul and Body. The former he attributes to 'Ammonius and Numenius the Pythagorean.' These pieces of information would be more interesting if we knew where Nemesius found them ; but they are probably a genuine tradition.[4]

The Hermetic Writings

The *Corpus Hermeticum* is composed of various strata. The collection of these writings probably belongs to the

---

[1] Iamblichus (in Stobæus, *Ecl.* 1, 894) quotes Numenius on this 'battle.'

[2] For an estimate of the differences between them, cf. Zeller, p. 470.

[3] Eusebius and Jerome, who say that he remained a Christian, have confused him with another Ammonius.

[4] Wundt and Heinemann are disposed to minimise the influence of Ammonius on Plotinus ; this naturally follows from their theory of development in the views of Plotinus. These writers rather exalt his obligations to Numenius.

last quarter of the third century, and is therefore later than Plotinus.[1] They show no trace of his influence, and most of them may have been written earlier. The *Poemander* is remarkable for its 'activist' theory of God's existence. 'His energy (or activity) is will ($\theta\epsilon\lambda\eta\sigma\iota\varsigma$), and his being is in willing all things to be.' 'Spirit ($\nu o\hat{\upsilon}\varsigma$) is the Soul of God.' The second and third hypostases are Spirit and Soul, as in Neoplatonism. A curious innovation is the doctrine that the world was created in time, but will last for ever. To the Greek mind immortality in the future implied immortality in the past ;[2] if the human soul is to survive death, it must have existed before birth.

The Hermetic writings are the surviving fragments of a mass of literature, vaguely attributed to Hermes Trismegistus, and claiming inspiration. They show an acquaintance with Greek philosophy down to the time of their appearance, with the Septuagint, and with the New Testament. Some kindred spirits have found much to admire in them. But they are of no philosophical value, since they swarm with flagrant contradictions. The world is the Son of God, and also the sum of all evil ($\pi\lambda\dot{\eta}\rho\omega\mu\alpha\ \tau\hat{\eta}\varsigma\ \kappa\alpha\kappa\dot{\iota}\alpha\varsigma$). Space is incorporeal, but also body. Human souls can and cannot pass into the bodies of animals. If we were to collect the passages which define the attributes of the 'Son of God,' or of the origin of evil, we should be left in hopeless bewilderment. The main interest of *Poemander* is as an illustration of the boundless hospitality of Alexandrian religion, and of the extreme looseness of its texture. The Hermetic writings are authorities for what has been called vulgar Gnosis.

---

[1] Reitzenstein believes that an Egyptian priest, about A.D. 300, collected eighteen sacred documents, to prove that the Hellenised religion of Egypt was uniform with that of the Empire as a whole. Those documents belong to various dates, some of them to the first century. Cumont and Zielinski think that Reitzenstein has exaggerated the Egyptian element in these writings.

[2] There were of course legends of mortals who were granted immortality by the Olympians ; but I am speaking of serious thinkers.

Jewish-Alexandrian Philosophy

It will not be necessary in these lectures to give a detailed account of Philo, because there is no evidence of any direct influence upon Plotinus proceeding from his writings.[1] At the same time, he is so characteristic a product of the developments in Platonism which prepared the way for the great philosopher of the third century, that a brief survey of his views can hardly be omitted. Philo is for us the representative of a type of thought which was widely diffused, and which was fundamentally the same in Pagans, Jews, and Christians who belonged to what is called the Alexandrian school.

Philo, a contemporary of Christ, believed himself to be an orthodox Jew of the dispersion ; the fact that his orthodoxy was apparently accepted is strong evidence how far the Judaism of the dispersion differed from that of Palestine. He is an upholder of the verbal inspiration of the Old Testament, which nevertheless he turns into a moral and metaphysical romance by his theory of allegorism. Philo himself calls this the method of the Greek mysteries. It is in fact the only method by which the sacred books of a primitive race can be made edifying to a highly civilised society, when the doctrine of development is wholly ignored.

Philo's theology is a curious blend of Platonism and Judaism. The two creeds were drawing together. The Alexandrian Jews worshipped a Jehovah who was far more than the tribal God of the Hebrews ; and the Greeks of Alexandria were no longer content with Stoical doctrines of immanence, and were willing to believe in a transcendent Deity. Philo, like the Neoplatonists, taught that we cannot know the Godhead as He is, while we live on earth. ' In order to comprehend God, we must

[1] Heinemann (p. 189) says that no direct or indirect influence of Philo on Plotinus can be traced in the earliest books of the Enneads, but that it is very probable in his ' second period,' especially in 6. 9. Cf. also, Gujot, *Les reminiscences de Philon le juif chez Plotin*, 1905.

first become God, which is impossible.'[1] Strictly, we can know nothing of God except His bare existence[2] (ψιλὴν ἄνευ χαρακτῆρος ὕπαρξιν). But we are safe in ascribing to Him attributes which can belong only to the supreme Being, and such attributes as goodness, which can be fully realised only in God. The Platonic doctrine of Ideas enables him to enumerate other qualities of which only the copies or images exist here below. The archetypes may be said to exist in God.[3]

Philo is a child of his age in assigning the administrative work of the Deity to subordinate ' Powers.' These Powers are the divine Ideas in action ; or they are ' Logoi ' proceeding from the Ideas.[4] They are distinct from the angels (in spite of Zeller and others) ; they are personified only as countless other abstract ideas are personified by Philo, for whom ' all the virtues are virgins.' The criticisms which have been passed on this part of Philo's doctrine seem to me beside the mark. The ' Powers ' are not invented to bridge over an impassable chasm between God and the world ; nor are they the officials of a sultan who is too exalted or indolent to do anything for himself. Such notions of the Deity were never far away from religious speculation in this period ; but Philo does not appear to me to have adopted them. The transcendent Godhead must reveal himself through something ; and the ' Powers ' are his thought and will taking the form of creative forces. Drummond quotes a very close parallel from Athanasius. ' The Logos is, as it were, in all creation, outside the whole in his essence, but in all things by his powers . . . containing the whole of all things and not contained, being wholly and in all respects within his own Father, and him only.' In the hierarchy of ' Powers,' the Logos of God

---

[1] Philo, *Fragm.* 2, 654.   [2] Philo, *Quod Deus*, 11.

[3] Heinemann says that this identification of the Platonic Absolute with the God of the Hebrews is very important. It definitely makes the Ideas the thoughts of God. Cf. Vol. II, p. 57. The Ideas are the Logoi of the one Logos.

[4] The ' Logoi ' of the later Platonism are rather like the ' Idées-forces ' of Fouillée.

is supreme. Philo invests his Logos with the attributes
of the Platonic *Noûs*, though he combines with these the
all-penetrating activity of the Stoic Logos. He gathers
up all the inferior ' Powers ' into the Logos, in whom
' are inscribed and engraved the constitutions of all other
things.' The doctrine naturally follows, that the Logos
is ' double '—it is eternal archetype and also eternal
activity. The Logos in Philo is not a personal being.

Philo, in spite of his isolation, as a Jew, from the
comity of Greek and Roman philosophers, is directly
in the line of development which ended as Neoplatonism.
The main difference, as Heinemann shows (*Hermes*,
January 1926) is that in Philo, though God sends his
' Powers ' into the world, the world is always outside
God, and as such deprived of value. ' God is the only
citizen in his State.' There is no hierarchy of creative
powers, as in Plotinus. His theory of ecstacy prepared
the way for Neoplatonism. ' He first recognised ' (says
Caird) ' the two great needs of the religious consciousness
—that of rising from the finite to the infinite, and that of
seeing the Absolute as mediated in the finite.' As a
thinker, he seems to me to have been considerably under-
estimated by his German critics. Geffken has lately
called him ' ein wahre Proteusgestalt,' borrowing succes-
sively from many schools of thought.

Christian Platonism at Alexandria

Clement and Origen were fellow-townsmen of Plotinus,
and Origen is said to have attended the lectures of
Ammonius Saccas. It will be interesting, before passing
to Plotinus himself, to show (as far as can be done in so
very brief a summary as the limits of an introductory
lecture prescribe) what form the Platonic tradition
assumed when it was taken up into the Christian religion.

It was in the latter half of the second century that the
famous Catechetical School was established at Alexandria.
It was modelled, perhaps, on the Gnostic schools for the
study of religion, and its avowed object was the attain-

ment of 'Gnosis,' which meant any kind of esoteric knowledge of Divine things, whether imparted by metaphysical learning, or by sacramental rites, or by mystical intuition. Biblical studies were seemingly the centre of the teaching given in the School; but all the Greek philosophers except the Epicureans, who were branded as atheists by all outside their own sect, were read and lectured upon. For us, the two representatives of the movement are Clement and Origen, the second and third heads of the School.

Clement tells us plainly that he admitted only the more popular part of his doctrine into his books. The suppressed doctrines probably consisted mainly of a bold allegorising of Scripture, and perhaps contained also certain mystical experiences, not easily described. He is concerned to defend Christian philosophy, which many Christians feared and distrusted as much as the orthodox in our day dread science and criticism. 'Philosophy is not a goblin who wants to run away with us.' He has to support his position by appealing to an oral tradition handed down from the apostles. His theology is mainly Platonic. God is above space and time, 'above even the One'; but He is a moral Being, whose will is only to do good. The Second Person of the Trinity, the Logos-Christ, has much the same attributes as in the Prologue to the Fourth Gospel. Clement is not at pains to identify him with the Platonic Noûs;[1] and he never speculates about the relation of the Holy Ghost to the universal Soul of Platonism. His interests are throughout more ethical than metaphysical, and for this reason he has considerable sympathy with the Stoics. He dwells at length on the 'Two Lives,' the natural and the spiritual, the characteristics of which are faith and knowledge. Faith is a 'voluntary anticipation of things unseen,' 'an uniting assent to an unseen object,' 'the foundation of rational choice.' Thus he emphasises the co-operation

[1] This had been done as early as the Gnostic Saturninus, who makes the Aeon Noûs (=Christ) deliver even the Demiurge (the God of the Old Testament) from the power of Satan.

of the will in faith, while insisting that in its progress it must go hand in hand with enquiry (ζήτησις). The goal of the journey is to become a true ' Gnostic '—a word which Clement will not abandon to the heretics. The Gnostic ' trains himself to be god ' (μελετᾷ εἶναι θεός) ; a phrase which was not shocking to Greek theology, since ' god ' meant simply an immortal being. But Clement also says, in more Christian language, that knowledge of God is inseparable from likeness to Him. The Gnostic is distinguished especially by two qualities —freedom from all passions (ἀπάθεια), and love, which is the hierophant of all the higher mysteries. In Clement, says Dr. Hort, ' Christian theology in some important respects reaches its highest point.'

Origen was the first great scholar whom Christianity produced.[1] He strongly combats the Stoical materialism, from which writers like Tertullian were by no means free, and insists that God is incorporeal Spirit, ' everywhere and nowhere,' ' natura simplex et tota mens.' His doctrine of the Son resembles that of Clement ; but he distinguishes more carefully those attributes which have belonged to the Second Person of the Trinity from all eternity, from those which were assumed at the Incarnation. He attempts, as Clement did not, to determine the special office of the Holy Ghost in relation to the world.

God created the world out of nothing. Our world had a beginning ; but it is only one in an innumerable series of worlds, which had no beginning in time. All things began in unity, and will end in unity. The first creation was of innocent spirits, some of whom fell by their own fault from the ' first estate of good.' Others—the good angels and the stars (for Origen endows the heavenly bodies with Souls) did not fall. The world which we know was made to be the scene of suffering and discipline for guilty Souls, who are here expiating their ante-natal sin. Thus Origen holds the Platonic doctrine of the Soul's

[1] I do not think, however, that he was well acquainted with Greek philosophy. He knows the Stoics fairly well, Plato a little, Aristotle perhaps not at all. He is strictly a Biblical student.

fall, though he does not believe in reincarnation. Soul
is Spirit in process of redemption. ' Spirit has somehow
become Soul, and Soul when it is restored to its right
condition becomes Spirit.'[1] But during the process of
restoration ' the Spirit is with the Soul as a master and
director, associated with it to remind it of the good, and
to accuse and punish it for its faults.' If the Soul be
disobedient and obstinate in revolt, it will be divided
from the Spirit after it leaves the body.[2] The Soul which
is exalted by following the Spirit must put off its nature
as Soul and become spiritual.[3] God never speaks to us
from outside ; [4] what we regard as a ' divine sensation '
(θεία αἴσθησις) is only externalised by our minds. The
real agent in sanctification is the indwelling Logos, who
reveals himself both in history and in the inner life of
the individual, as men are able to receive him.

It is well known that Origen deviated from ecclesiastical orthodoxy in teaching, or rather hoping, that all
men will be saved at the last. He was led to this opinion
partly by the argument that God cannot hate any one,
or render evil for evil ; and partly by the purely Platonic
doctrine that man is a ' spiritual nature ' (νοερὰ φύσις),
and that spiritual natures cannot perish everlastingly.
He is aware that this view comes into conflict with the
New Testament. But who, he asks, can interpret the
eschatology of the Gospels literally ? How can Spirits
' gnash their teeth ' ? How can the stars, which are
much larger than the earth, ' fall from heaven ' upon it ?
It is not the empirical self which survives, but the Soul
become Spirit, which will make a new house for itself,
the resurrection-body.[5] But the purification is not complete at death ; even the holiest saints, such as Peter and
Paul, must pass through purgatory. At last, he hopes,
though he will not speak positively, the promise that

---

[1] Origen, De Princip. 2, 8.   [2] Origen, in Rom. 2, 9.
[3] De Orat. 10.   [4] In Psalm. 27, 1.
  [5] This resembles the Pauline view of the resurrection, which differs
widely, as every candid and attentive reader must acknowledge, from
the later Catholic orthodoxy.

'God shall be all in all' (i.e. fully present in every individual)—will be fulfilled, and all alike will find salvation in being made like God.

Origen extends to the popular, half mythological beliefs of the uneducated Christian the same tolerance which the Platonists allowed to vulgar paganism. The Logos teaches men in various manners, according to their capacities ; some must be fed with milk, others with strong meat. The Gnostic knows that there is a mythical, symbolic element in the New Testament as well as in the Old.[1]

The fortunes of Origenism in the Christian Church do not fall within the subject of these lectures. But it may be said here that Origen attempted to do for Christianity very much the same that Plotinus attempted to do for paganism. He destroyed Gnosticism by giving the Church a Christian Platonism which was in every way superior to the barbaric and Orientalised Platonism of the Gnostics. But the price had to be paid, by accepting the Hellenic compromise of a spiritual, idealistic religion for the educated, with a superstitious and half-paganised Catholicism for the masses. And the fate of the two enterprises was the same. Christianity was degraded into a religion of cultus, and Neoplatonism (in the hands of Iamblichus[2] and others) into a philosophy of theurgy and white magic. The idealistic and mystical tradition was not destroyed, but was suspected and sometimes condemned, or driven underground. In the Christian Church it has never been lost. Gregory of Nyssa is an Origenist (in many of his doctrines) who has never been condemned.

The Gnostics

The word 'Gnosticism' is modern : the adjective 'Gnostic' appears first in the latter half of the second

---

[1] Origen, *in Joh.* 1, 9.

[2] Prof. Taylor, however, has shown that this element in Iamblichus has been exaggerated. He says, ' Unless Iamblichus wrote the Abammon treatise, which is impossible, there is no theurgy in him.'

century. ' Gnosis,' however, in its technical sense was
already familiar a hundred years earlier. ' Knowledge '
and ' Faith ' had become catchwords of parties in the
Church when the Fourth Gospel was written, which must
be the reason why the evangelist carefully avoids both.
Gnosticism is the name not of a sect but of a tendency.
It was a large and many-sided movement,[1] which was
continually changing. Its distinguishing feature was,
as I have said, its claim to esoteric knowledge, to be
gained either by sacramental and magical rites, with
their appropriate discipline, or by secret teachings, or by
divine inspiration. It was not, as Harnack says, ' an
acute Hellenising of Christianity.' ' Hellenism ' at this
period is only another name for European culture, and
Gnosticism certainly does not represent European culture. When real Hellenism came into contact with
Gnosticism, it felt itself strongly repelled, as by an alien
and hostile influence : there is no more earnest polemic
in the Enneads than the chapters in which Plotinus
denounces the Gnostics. Gnosticism sprang up first in
Syria, and through its great period, in the second century,
it bore the signs of an Eastern movement, and was
marked by characteristics which belonged to no Greek
philosophy. It was not Greek to allow the mythological
imagination to run riot in serious thinking. Greece had
a mythology, but the philosophers did not invent it.
Plato created myths, but did not present them as science.
The Greeks sought for pure concepts, which could be
used as symbols having a fixed connotation in philosophical discussion. The Gnostics turned abstractions
into spirits, and created a quite peculiar transcendental mythology, which blossomed out into the wildest
luxuriance.[2]

[1] E. F. Scott, article ' Gnosticism ' in Hastings' *Dict. of Religion
and Ethics*.
[2] This statement is in formal contradiction with Mr. Scott, who
says that in Gnosticism ' personal names are replaced by terms of
philosophy.' He is probably thinking of the treatment of historical
dogmas by the Gnostics.

Reitzenstein has shown that there was a pre-Christian Gnosticism in the Levant, from which in fact the Hermetic writings had their origin. But the movement acquired a new impetus by its contact with Christianity, and it is convenient to treat it as a half-Christian development of Babylonian, Persian, and Egyptian religious ideas, blended in very various proportions.

The Gnostics were free-thinkers as compared with the great Church, refusing to be fettered by a ' tradition ' which was really the average Christian consciousness. They had no wish to make their doctrine acceptable to everybody ; they recognised unalterable differences in the moral and intellectual status of believers, who were not all capable of acquiring ' Gnosis.' On the other hand they were not votaries of pure science or philosophy. Their professed aim was the liberation of the spirit from the trammels of the flesh, that it might enjoy communion with God and knowledge of Him.

Their speculation was a barbarised Platonism, in which all history is sublimated into a dramatic poem, describing allegorically the fortunes of shadowy personifications.[1] All real history is supramundane ; the historical Jesus disappears with the rest of past events. These dramas of the invisible were sketched according to taste ; there were no schisms among the Gnostics, for whom, according to Tertullian, *schisma est unitas ipsa*. They mostly agreed in holding that below the supreme God, the Father, there are numerous spiritual beings who are arranged in pairs, male and female.[2] These are the manifestations of the unknowable God, and taken together they constitute the Pleroma, or totality of the divine attributes. Valentinus, the most influential of the Gnostic teachers, called these beings Æons. They fill in his system the place of the Platonic Ideas. One of these Æons, Sophia, fell, and thereby called this lower world into being, the agent in

---

[1] Blake's fantastic treatises present a modern parallel.

[2] Plotinus protests that in heaven they neither marry nor are given in marriage—ὅτι μηδὲ ἐν οὐρανῷ γάμοι, 3. 5. 2.

creation being the Demiurge, the son of Sophia, a blind though not intentionally malignant being, who is strangely identified with the God of the Jews. The great object of the soul is to escape from the tyranny of this unintelligent power. The Pleroma has been broken up by the lapse of one of its members, and the loss can only be repaired by the redemption effected by a superior Æon, Christ. This Æon, in the character of ' Saviour,' comes down like a knight-errant to rescue the truant Sophia and restore her to her home.

The worship of the Gnostics was highly ritualistic, and was allied with magic and freemasonry. In morals they were generally ascetic, but sometimes antinomian, like other ' despisers of the flesh ' in the history of religion. The nearest parallel perhaps is the ' Brethren of the Free Spirit ' and similar heretical mystics of the Middle Ages. The Gnostic associations took every imaginable form of union—churches, mystery-cults, strictly private philosophical schools, free unions for edification, entertainments by charlatans and deceived deceivers, and attempts at founding new religions based on Christianity. This is not the place to estimate the debt which the Church owed to the movement, especially in the field of Biblical scholarship. It quarrelled with the Gnostics mainly on the Old Testament, the creation of the world, the unity and equality of the human race, and the historical Christ. The contest was severe enough to oblige the Church to stiffen her organisation, which was on the whole a misfortune. In the time of Plotinus, Gnosticism was a spent force. Its last teacher of note, Bardesanes, died about 240. But Plotinus would not have paid so much attention to condemning their attitude towards the visible world, if their opinions had not been widely held among those with whom he associated. Plotinus disliked them for caricaturing his own creed. There was much similarity between parts of his teaching and theirs, but their arrogance and perversity were intolerable to him. They claimed a superior science, transmitted mysteriously, and chiefly through secret tradition. This 'science' concerned only God and the invisible world. Like Justin Martyr, they turned impatiently away from teachers who wished to make them learn the exact sciences. They threw Aristotle aside, and revered the *Phaedrus* and *Timaeus*. Like the Neoplatonists, they taught that the Soul, which has lost its way in the dark, must return to God. Like them, they believed that there is a divine spark in the Soul which can light us through the gloom. Like them again, they held that this desire to return to God is not an individual affair only, but a cosmic movement. They also spoke of the Godhead as beyond existence.[1] Plotinus falls foul of them mainly for their pessimism about the visible world,[2] and for their impiety in not recognising the sun and stars as the abodes of Deity. Campanella makes exactly the same complaint against the despisers of the visible world in his day.

> ' Deem you that only you have thought and sense,
>   While heaven and all its wonders, sun and earth,
> Scorned in your dullness, lack intelligence ?
> Fool ! what produced you ? These things gave you birth :
>   So have they mind and God.'[3]

But no doubt he also disliked their Christology, which must have held a larger place in their teaching than their orthodox opponents would lead us to suppose ; otherwise they would not have considered themselves Christians. It may be that the extant *Pistis Sophia* gives us a fair notion of the kind of Gnosticism which Plotinus encountered at Rome. This curious treatise teaches that the child takes in evil with its food, which is ' material.' Jesus bids us ' say good-bye to the world and all its associations, lest we acquire more Matter ($\H{v}\lambda as$) than that which we have in us.' But the book also recognises a ' necessity,' which forces men to sin. The remedy is by means of sacraments.

---

[1] Pseudo-Basilides in the *Philosophumena*.
[2] ' Il se souvient qu'il est Grec,' says De Faye, *Gnosticisme*, p. 437.
[3] Symonds' translation, quoted by Whittaker, p. 199.

Plotinus also objects against the Gnostics that they intercalate unnecessary grades in the spiritual world; that they exclude divine influence from part of nature, viz. the material world; that they ascribe the existence of the phenomenal world to the fall of the Soul; and that they call the vilest of men their brothers, while denying the divinity of the heavenly bodies.[1] He speaks bitterly of their arrogant disrespect for the great masters of Greek philosophy; and in one place alludes to ' the fraud which at present invades mankind ' : this can hardly be anything else than the Christian religion. The Gnostics also, he says, attempt to account for the creation of the world in time, ignorant that it has existed from all eternity. Again, they deny the plurality of gods: Plotinus attempts a defence of polytheism.[2] They practise absurd magical arts, and claim without justification that they can cure diseases by these means. They are lifted up with ridiculous pride;[3] and, lastly, they presume to speak of God, without possessing true virtue.

Many of the writers whose views have been cursorily summarised in this chapter are known to us only from fragments quoted by later writers, or from *ex parte* statements about the opinions which they held.[4] We cannot

[1] Bentley, in his Boyle Lectures, thus states the doctrine which moves the anger of Plotinus. ' Nor do we count it any absurdity, that such a vast and immense universe should be made for the sole use of such mean and unworthy creatures as the children of men. For if we consider the dignity of an intelligent being, and put that in the scales against brute inanimate matter, we may affirm without overvaluing human nature that the soul of one virtuous and religious man is of greater worth and excellency than the sun and his planets and all the stars in the world.'   [2] 2. 9. 9.

[3] Compare Irenæus's description of a Valentinian Gnostic: ' The fellow is so puffed up that he believes himself to be neither in heaven nor on earth, but to have entered within the Divine Pleroma, and to have embraced his guardian angel. On the strength of this he struts about as proud as a cock.'

[4] Such statements are more unreliable in the mouths of ancient critics than when we have to deal with the more sensitive literary conscience of modern times. Some of the Christian Fathers thought that any stick was good enough to beat a heretic with; and many students of Plato and Aristotle have been astonished at the superficiality of the latter's criticisms upon the former.

be sure that we have the means of doing them justice.
But it is probably safe to say that between Aristotle[1] and
Plotinus no thinker quite in the first rank attached himself to the school of Plato. The only two who may claim
to have anticipated Plotinus in some of his distinctive
doctrines are Numenius (according to some third-century
students who knew his writings) and Philo. Philo is a
very interesting figure; but he suffers from the almost
inevitable contradictions which lie in wait for all who try
to square an idealistic philosophy with a dogmatic
theology. His God, though exalted above existence,
must preserve some of the attributes of Jehovah; his
Logos must not be too personal; his dæmons must be
something like angels. It remains for us to consider
briefly the relation of Plotinus to his predecessors.

Plotinus has often been called an eclectic. By some,
like Jules Simon, the word has been used as a compliment; eclecticism for him consists in harmonising and
combining the best that has been said by different schools.
Others have used it as a reproach; an eclectic philosopher
is one who clothes himself in a patch-work mantle. But
Plotinus was not consciously an eclectic in either sense.
He wished to be a Platonist, and indeed a conservative
Platonist. Nothing would have pleased him better than
the encomium of Augustine, who finds in Plotinus nothing
less than Plato himself come to life again.[2] But though
he wished to go back from the Platonists to Plato himself, and for this reason was unwilling to be called an
Academic, his reverential temper made him reluctant to
acknowledge any serious errors in other 'ancient philosophers of blessed memory,'[3] even when they seemed to
be at variance with each other or with his master. This
deference to antiquity, always prominent in classical

[1] Aristotle himself, though the founder of a distinct school, several
times says 'we,' meaning the disciples of Plato. References in Ross's
edition of the *Metaphysics*.

[2] Augustine, *c. Acad.* 3, 18. Quoted above, p. 21.

[3] 3.7.1, οἱ ἀρχαῖοι καὶ μακάριοι φιλόσοφοι; 4.3.25; 6.4.16; 6.8.19,
οἱ πάλαι, οἱ παλαιοί; 5.1.6, οἱ πάλαι σοφοί.

literature, was very strong in the third century, when
creative genius was at a low ebb. Thinkers under the
empire felt it to be incumbent on them to harmonise
differences as far as possible, as though the divergent
views of the ancients were but superficial discrepancies
covering a fundamental unity. Plotinus even maintains
that his three Divine hypostases, the One, Spirit, and
Soul, are to be found not only in Plato but in Parmenides,
Anaxagoras, Heracleitus, and Empedocles, though in the
case of Anaxagoras he admits that ' in consequence of his
early date he has not treated the question thoroughly.'[1]
But to Plato alone he attributes plenary inspiration. He
will not admit that he ever differs from his master's
teaching. Again and again we find such protestations
as this : ' This doctrine is not new ; it was professed from
the most ancient times, though without being developed
explicitly. We wish only to be the interpreters of the
ancients, and to show by the evidence of Plato himself
that they had the same opinions as ourselves.'[2] Plotinus
himself, as I have said, was treated with almost equal
reverence after his death. The epithet, ' most divine '
($\theta\epsilon\iota\acute{o}\tau\alpha\tau os$), was reserved for him, and occurs often
in Proclus and Simplicius.[3] Next to Plato, and not much
behind him, is Pythagoras, from whom Plotinus never
consciously differs. Pythagoras is only named thrice ;[4]
but this is no token of neglect, since even Plato is rarely
mentioned by name.[5] However, Plotinus admits very
little into his system from Pythagorean sources that had
not been admitted by Plato himself after he came under
Pythagorean influences. The symbolism of numbers,
which played an important part in the writings of the

---

[1] 5.1, τὸ ἀκριβὲς δι' ἀρχαιότητα παρῆκε.

[2] 5.1.8.   See also 6.2.1. and 6.3.5.   This extreme reverence for Plato
was characteristic of the school.   Compare the language of Plutarch
and Maximus of Tyre, quoted by Zeller, p. 179.

[3] Julian alone (Ep. 29) gives this title to his master, Iamblichus.

[4] 4.7.8. ; 4.8.1. ; 5.1.9.   The Pythagoreans are named three times ;
5.5.6. ; 6.6.5 ;   6.6.9.   In the second passage he differs from them
about the lore of numbers.

[5] Opponents too are seldom named ; we have φησί, λέγουσι,
τινές, etc., in introducing their views.

later Neoplatonists, is touched upon by Plotinus in a slight and almost perfunctory way. Aristotle is treated with less deference. Plotinus regards him as an ally against the materialism of the Stoics and Epicureans; but he frankly criticises his categories, and hardly does justice to the considerable obligations which a modern reader readily observes in the Enneads. Some of these obligations are of great importance. For instance, the fundamental distinction of δύναμις and ἐνέργεια, which he owes to Aristotle, is as essential to the philosophy of Plotinus as the Platonic distinction of unity and plurality. The One is defined, in Aristotelian rather than Platonic fashion, as absolute activity.[1] It is an Aristotelian doctrine that no potentiality can achieve potency without a previously existing activity.[2] The world of Ideas is alive for Plotinus, since each Idea is an ' activity.' Every Idea is the original type of a definite individual. All general Ideas betoken something qualitative or quantitative, and in so far, are characters of particulars. The eternity of the world was a Peripatetic dogma, on which the later Platonists had wavered. There are also several points in psychology, in which unacknowledged obligations to Aristotle can be traced. The Enneads give one the impression that Plotinus knew Aristotle as well as he knew Plato.[3] Although he is not much interested in biological speculation as such, he shows intimate knowledge of nearly all the most important works of Aristotle, and has welded much of his thought firmly into his own system. If these obligations are too scantily acknowledged,[4] we must remember that there had been a very active interchange of ideas between the Academy

[1] i.e. as not merely an αἰτία εἰδική, but an αἰτία κινητική and τελική for all things.

[2] It is of course true that Plato is nearer this position in his later than in his earlier dialogues.

[3] Bouillet shows that Plotinus was acquainted with all the following Dialogues of Plato : Theaetetus, Phaedo, Republic, Phaedrus, Philebus, Symposium, Politicus, Timaeus, Laws, Cratylus, Parmenides, Sophist ; also with the Second Epistle and the Alcibiades.

[4] Aristotle is named four times only : 2.1.2 ; 2.1.4 ; 2.5.3 ; 5.1.9.

and the Peripatetics before Plotinus, and also that Plotinus was probably anxious to vindicate his orthodoxy as a Platonist in face of the jealousy of the Athenian school, who were the established church of Platonism and had the Diadochus over them.[1]

The attitude of Plotinus towards Stoicism was in the main hostile. One of the main objects of his life was to combat materialism in all its forms, and to establish on a firm basis the spiritual nature of reality. The Stoics were not among the ' ancients of blessed memory ' whose dogmas it is impious to attack. And yet Plotinus owes a great debt to them—only less than his debt to Plato and Aristotle. The so-called dynamic pantheism of Plotinus (the name is not very happy)[2]—the doctrine that the living forces of the Deity permeate the whole of nature—is Stoical. It was the Stoics who taught him that ' Matter,' so far as it exists, is the creation of God. Perhaps, as De Faye says, the Stoa helped him to reject Gnostic dualism and pessimism. The terms λόγος and πνεῦμα, the former of which is used very freely, the latter

[1] To later generations (and even to Porphyry, Life, §14) it appeared as if Plotinus had set out to reconcile Plato and Aristotle, explaining away the differences between them. So Augustine (Contra Academ. 3, 19) says : 'Quod autem ad eruditionem doctrinamque attinet, et moribus quibus consulitur animae, quia non defuerunt acutissimi et solertissimi viri, qui docerent disputationibus suis Aristotelem ac Platonem ita sibi concinere, ut imperitis minusque attentis dissentire viderentur, multis quidem saeculis multisque contentionibus, sed tamen eliquata est ut opinor una verissimae philosophiae disciplina.' Porphyry asserts that the metaphysics of Aristotle are all contained in the Enneads. But there is much truth in what Arnou says, that the Neoplatonists invented a religious and mystical Aristotle, and made him a good Platonist. Porphyry certainly attempted this very task in his treatise, περὶ τοῦ μίαν εἶναι τὴν Πλάτωνος καὶ 'Αριστοτέλους αἵρεσιν; and Boethius, at the beginning of his De Interpretatione, promises to harmonise the doctrines of Plato and Aristotle ' after the example of Porphyry.' Hierocles (Photius, Biblioth, p. 127, 461) says that Ammonius Saccas achieved this reconciliation, thus leaving philosophy in peace for Plotinus and Origenes, his disciples, and their successors. Simplicius too, on the Categories of Aristotle, says that Iamblichus has proved the agreement of the doctrine of Archytas (a Pythagorean) with that of Aristotle. Themistius (Orat. 20) has 'Αριστοτέλει προθύσας εἰς τὴν Πλάτωνος ἔλησεν ἱερουργίαν.

[2] The phrase is Zeller's. It is incorrect because in Plotinus the world is immanent in God, not God in the world, and the supreme principle is transcendent.

only in two or three places in the Enneads, belong to Stoical nomenclature. The Neoplatonic ethics, in their indifference to external interests and concentration upon the subjective condition of the individual, are Stoical, and also in their very close connexion of theory with practice. These obligations to the Stoa were not direct borrowings. The eclectic Platonists, as we have seen, had already adopted Stoical doctrines, and Plotinus was probably hardly aware that not much sanction could be found for them in Plato. He sums up his quarrel with Stoicism and kindred theories in the seventh book of the Fourth Ennead. It is a radical mistake, he says, to explain the higher by the lower, and to suppose that the merely potential can of itself develop actuality.

Can we trace any debts in Plotinus to the sceptical developments of Platonism, of which a short sketch has been given earlier in this chapter, or does he reject the agnosticism of the Academy as an aberration and a misunderstanding of Plato ? The answer is that there is indeed a sceptical element in Plotinus ; but it is like the so-called scepticism of Bradley, of which Höffding speaks in words which are helpful also to the understanding of Plotinus. ' Scepticism is hardly the correct expression for Bradley's point of view. He does not rest content with a cleft between the labour and the goal, between appearance and reality. The highest is present at every step, and every step has its truth. There are many grades and stages, but all are indispensable. We can find no province of the world so unimportant that the Absolute does not dwell therein. Rather he should be called a mystic ; and that he certainly is, when his thought comes to rest, and when he enters upon a polemic against the concept of time and the importance of activity. Here he passes over to undisturbed contemplation, to a settled view, to a treatment *sub specie aeterni*.'[1] The complete experience is beyond our grasp,

[1] Höffding, *Modern Philosophers*, p. 68.

just as we cannot get beyond the strife between good and evil. 'The standard is the same for reality and value. Every unsatisfied impulse is an ineffectual thought : in all pain there is expressed a disharmony, and there is an incitement to do away with this conflict. Our thought is always aspiring to something which is more than thought, our personality to something more than personality, our morality to something higher than all morals.'[1] Even the highest that we can discover implies as its logical *prius* something unknown to us. Scepticism has thus a partial justification, in that we come to recognise the inadequacy of every synthesis except the last. It is used, not to destroy absolutism, but to establish it.

Life of Plotinus

Our chief authority for the life of Plotinus is the short biography written by his disciple Porphyry, who knew the philosopher intimately during the last six years of his life. He was an enthusiastic admirer not only of his master's teaching but of his character, and we may suspect some tendency to portray Plotinus as the typical philosopher - saint. But in spite of a few legendary details, in which miraculous powers are attributed to his master, Porphyry gives us the impression of being a conscientious and accurate biographer, and his picture of the personality of Plotinus is clear and convincing as well as attractive.

The name Plotinus is Roman. It is possible that the philosopher was descended from a freedman of Trajan, who on his emancipation called himself after the empress Plotina. But this is mere conjecture ; an Egyptian with a Roman name in the third century may have belonged to any of the numerous races which made up the population of Egypt. Plotinus would never talk about his family or his country. He seemed, says Porphyry, to be ashamed of being ' in the body.' His birthplace is

---

[1] Höffding, *Modern Philosophers*, pp. 64, 65.

uncertain. Porphyry did not know it ; Eunapius says that he was born at ' a place called Lyco ' ; Suidas calls him ' a Lycopolitan ' ; the empress Eudocia (eleventh century) says that ' some say he was born at Lyco, a *nome* of Lycopolis in Egypt.' He was born in A.D. 204 or 205, in the reign of Septimius Severus. Plotinus would not allow his portrait to be painted. When Amelius came to him with a request that he would consent to sit to a painter, the philosopher replied : ' Is it not enough to have to bear the image (εἴδωλον—the mere simulacrum of reality) in which nature has wrapped me, without consenting to perpetuate the image of an image, as if it were worth contemplating ? ' His friends had to resort to stratagem. A skilful portrait-painter attended his lectures, and watched the professor's face under pretence of listening. With the help of Amelius he afterwards worked up his recollections into an excellent likeness, without the knowledge of Plotinus. We are told that his countenance reflected the sweetness and beauty of his character.

From chance words let fall by his master, Porphyry learned that he attended an elementary school at his birthplace, and then followed the usual course of liberal education at Alexandria. It is plain that from an early age he determined to devote his life to the search for truth, for he remained at Alexandria making trial in turn of all the philosophical teachers who were most in repute, till he reached the age of twenty-eight. Depressed at finding no guidance in any of them, he took the advice of a friend and went to hear Ammonius Saccas. ' This is the man I was looking for ' (τοῦτον ἐζήτουν), he exclaimed after listening to a discourse of Ammonius, and from that time became his disciple. Ammonius, whose name is not mentioned in the Enneads, nor by Iamblichus nor Proclus, was a self-taught[1] philosopher like Böhme, the cobbler of Görlitz. Plotinus attended his lectures for

---

[1] The laudatory title θεοδίδακτος, applied to Ammonius, probably indicates that he had no instructor in philosophy.

ten years. I have already said that scarcely anything is known about the doctrine of Ammonius, who was a lecturer, not a writer, and wished his teaching to be kept secret. He must have been a remarkable man to have retained such a hearer as Plotinus till the age of thirty-nine.

The wisdom of the East exercised a great attraction upon the students of Alexandria, and there was nothing unprecedented in the desire of Plotinus to consult the Magi, and perhaps even the Brahmans, in their own homes. An opportunity seemed to be presented by the military expedition of the Emperor Gordian against Sapor, King of Persia. Plotinus accompanied the army to Mesopotamia, where Gordian was assassinated, and the philosopher made his way back to Antioch with difficulty. Thence, in 244, he went to Rome, which was to be his home for the rest of his life. He may well have felt that Ammonius (if he was still alive) had taught him all that he had to teach ; he would not wish to open a school at Alexandria as his rival ; and he could hardly have lived at Athens, which was the seat of the Diadochus, the official professor of conservative Platonism. Rome, the capital of the empire and an important intellectual centre, had obvious advantages.

On his arrival at Rome, he opened a school which from small beginnings soon became popular and even fashionable. The emperor Gallienus and his wife Salonina showed him great favour, and consented to a scheme which, like the Persian expedition, must be regarded as a foolish episode in an otherwise wisely ordered career. Plotinus applied for leave to found a city, to be called Platonopolis, on a deserted site in Campania, which was to be governed on the principles of Plato's Republic. The site was probably malarious, and the project would certainly have ended in a fiasco, had not the emperor withdrawn his consent, probably in order to save his friend from so great a blunder. The chief interest of the story is in the light which it throws on the character of

Plotinus. He is frequently reproached for building a philosophy in the clouds and leaving the Empire to its fate. But it is plain that he had his plans for the reconstruction of society, and courage to carry them out. The scheme was after all no wilder than some modern attempts to found socialistic communities.[1]

One of the most devoted disciples of Plotinus was Amelius, who had previously studied at Athens, and was a great admirer of Numenius. Hearing that the Athenian students regarded Plotinus as a mere echo of Numenius, Amelius wrote an essay, in the form of a letter to Longinus, to explain the differences between the two teachers. He was the first editor of Plotinus' lectures, and the author of rhetorical and wordy commentaries on Plato. Plotinus commissioned him to convince Porphyry on an important point of Neoplatonic philosophy—ὅτι οὐκ ἔξω νοῦ τὰ νοητά:[2] and after a friendly controversy Porphyry accepted his master's view, and abandoned his belief in a spiritual world which exists independently of the spirit which knows it.

Porphyry was about thirty years old when he came to Rome and joined the school of Plotinus, who was now in his sixtieth year. Unlike his master, he was an industrious writer, and produced numerous treatises, including a short but very clear summary of the philosophy of Plotinus, which he entitled Ἀφορμαὶ πρὸς τὰ νοητά, a title which is nearly equivalent to ' The Pathway to Reality.' After some years of arduous work Porphyry fell into a state of melancholy, and meditated suicide. Plotinus discovered the conditon of his mind, and advised him to take a holiday in Sicily. The depression was thus remedied, but Porphyry missed the privilege of attending his master in his last illness. Among less

---

[1] Examples are numerous. In 1670 an attempt was made in North Carolina to introduce a new government called the ' Fundamental Constitution,' drawn up by John Locke. This project was soon abandoned. William Penn's experiment in Pennsylvania, modelled partly on Harrington's ' Oceana,' was very successful. Berkeley and Coleridge both dreamed of similar schemes.

[2] See p. 138.

notable members of the school we hear of two physicians, Paulinus and Eustochius, Zoticus, a critic and poet, Zethus, another physician, Castricius Firmus, Serapion, and some senators, one of whom, Rogatianus, renounced the world to live the philosophic life in poverty and austerity. The circle included some ladies, one of whom, named Gemina, gave Plotinus rooms in her house.

Porphyry tells us something of the manner of teaching which Plotinus employed. The works of the great philosophers, especially the Platonists, but also the Peripatetics, were diligently studied, and a frequent correspondence was kept up with Athens and other intellectual centres. In these letters differences were freely discussed, and Plotinus would instruct his disciples to write essays against astrology, magic, and the errors of the Gnostics. But like a true Greek, he did not devote himself so completely to intellectual speculation as to have no leisure for other things. Not only was much time given to private devotion and meditation ; we hear that he studied art and music, though he was not personally much attracted by them ; and he allowed himself to be appointed guardian and trustee to several orphans of good family, to whom he was like a father, listening to their childish compositions and managing their property with as much skill as integrity. He was also in request as an arbitrator, since he had a high reputation for perspicacity as well as for absolute fairness. During all the years of his residence at Rome he made no enemy, except for the jealousy of some rival teachers.

For several years, we are told, the instruction given by Plotinus was purely oral and professedly an exposition of the teaching of Ammonius. We are told that he had made an agreement with Erennius and Origenes, not to divulge the doctrine of Ammonius by publication. He was fifty years old before he began to write anything. It was Porphyry who persuaded him to throw his lectures into a more or less orderly and regular form. Hitherto he had allowed his auditors to interrupt by raising questions which sometimes broke the thread of the discourse. Much of the Enneads was written before Porphyry joined him, but his writings were not widely known, partly from the difficulty of copying them. Plotinus wrote badly, and took no pains about composition ; he was even guilty of misspellings and mispronunciations.[1] Porphyry very oddly refers to these first-written parts of the Enneads as the work of the philosopher's ' early youth ' ; they were written, as we have seen, between the ages of fifty and sixty. Porphyry professes to find far greater maturity of genius in the other half of the work, which was written in the six years when Porphyry lived with him. The latest portion of the Enneads was sent in manuscript to Porphyry in Sicily. The pupil thinks that these chapters show traces of failing powers, due to the illness which was wearing out his master's constitution. These judgments do not commend themselves to a modern reader : Porphyry seems to think that Plotinus was at his best only when Porphyry was with him ! The whole of the Enneads was written by a man at the summit of his powers ; there is no sign anywhere either of immature crudeness or of senile decay.[2]

Porphyry, following, as he tells us, the example of Andronicus of Rhodes in his editions of Aristotle and Theophrastus, tried to arrange the scattered lectures of Plotinus according to their subject-matter. He further made a capricious division of the whole into six books, each containing nine chapters, an arrangement for which only Pythagorean reasons can be found. The plan of gathering together all discussions of the same subject is by no means consistently followed. But in fairness to Porphyry we must admit that few editors have had a more difficult task. Plotinus had weak eyes ; he disliked the trouble of writing, and never corrected his manu-

[1] Some have supposed that he spoke Greek like a foreigner ; but this is impossible in an educated Alexandrian.

[2] I therefore disagree with Heinemann. Cf. my preface to this edition.

script, which was composed hurriedly, amid constant interruptions. His style in lecturing is said to have been pleasing and eloquent. But his writing seemed ' enigmatic ' even to Eunapius ; it is so concise as to demand constant effort from his readers, who, as Macaulay said of Montgomery, ' must take such grammar as they can get and be thankful.' There are many very beautiful passages in the Enneads, but these are admirable for the sublimity and deep sincerity of the thought, not for the style. It is necessary to emphasise these unfortunate characteristics of the Enneads, not at all in order to disparage the transcendent value of the contribution which Plotinus has made to the philosophy of religion, but to account for the widespread misunderstanding of his teaching, which is mainly the result of laziness on the part of his critics, who have shrunk from the labour of reading a very difficult author. If Plotinus had been studied with half the care that has been bestowed on Plato and Aristotle, the continuity of philosophical and religious thought in the early centuries of the Christian era would be far better understood, and the history of Greek philosophy would not be habitually deprived of its last chapter.

We should misconceive the whole character of Plotinus and his circle if we did not recognise that the intellectual discipline was throughout subsidiary to holiness of life. The main object of Plotinus was to bring back souls to ' their heavenly Father.' The philosopher himself lived the life of a saint. Austerely simple in his habits, though without any harsh asceticism, he won all hearts by his gentle and affectionate nature, and his sympathy with all that is good and beautiful in the world. His countenance, naturally handsome, seemed (so Porphyry tells us) to radiate light and love when he discoursed with his friends. He was almost too patient of interruption, and would not cut short any honest objector who propounded a difficulty. He was a shy man, and signs of nervousness were frequently observed while he lectured. This diffidence led

him to mask his own originality, and sometimes fettered
his freedom, since his reverence for authority was extreme.
But in another way his modesty stood him in good stead.
He never presumed upon the favour of heaven, or supposed that private revelations had been made to him.
He had, as he believed, experienced the beatific vision
of the all-transcending Godhead several times ; but such
privileges were, according to his conviction, very rare
exceptions ; they were to be waited for, not sought ; he
never tried to throw himself into an ecstatic state,
and never claims that any mysteries were revealed to
him while in a state of trance.   There is not the slightest
trace of hysterical emotion in Plotinus.

His health, never strong, began to fail some time before
his death, but the details of his infirmities given by
Porphyry do not enable us to specify the disease which
terminated his life.   He was at a country house in
Campania when fatal symptoms appeared.   His friend
and physician Eustochius was sent for from Puteoli, and
arrived just in time to hear the philosopher's last words :
' I was waiting for you, before that which is divine in me
departs to unite itself with the Divine in the universe.'[1]
His other friends were all absent, Amelius in Syria,
Porphyry in Sicily, Castricius at Rome.

[1] There is an interesting parallel in the last words of Descartes,
reported by Cherselier : ' My soul, thou hast long been held captive ;
the hour has now come for thee to quit thy prison, and to leave the
trammels of the body. Suffer then this separation with joy and
courage.'   Compare also the last testament of Labadie : ' I surrender
my soul heartily to my God, giving it back like a drop of water to its
source, and rest confident in him, praying God, my origin and ocean,
that he will take me into himself and engulf me eternally in the divine
abyss of his being.'

LECTURES VI, VII, VIII

THE WORLD OF SENSE

THERE are two fundamental triads in Plotinus. One of these is the Trinity of Divine principles— the Absolute (τὸ ἀγαθὸν, τὸ ἕν, τὸ πρῶτον), Spirit (νοῦς), and Soul (ψυχή); the other is the tripartite division of man into Spirit, Soul, and Body. This triadic schematism was becoming almost obligatory for a Greek philosopher. The number-mysticism of Pythagoras provided a framework for all Hellenic speculation. Even Aristotle denies the possibility of a fourth dimension on the ground that ' all things are three and three is everywhere ; for, as the Pythagoreans say, the all and all things are determined by the number three.'[1] Three is the number of perfection ; it is the first number which has beginning, middle, and end ; all excellence, says Photius, depends on and proceeds from this number. Iamblichus, followed by Proclus, says that the number one is the ' cause ' of identity and unification, two of procession and differentiation, three of the return of all things to their first principle.[2] The continual recurrence of the triad in mental processes, especially in the syllogism, led naturally, in the early days of speculation, to a half-superstitious reverence for this symbol. In Plotinus the triad is important, but it does not dominate the whole of his thought, as it does that of Proclus and Hegel. The classifications of Plotinus, as we shall have to insist again and again, are not intended to be rigorous and exclusive. In his

---

[1] Aristotle, *De Caelo*, I, I.   [2] Proclus, *in Tim*. 206.

philosophy there are no hard boundary-lines drawn across
the field of experience. His map of the world is covered
with contour-lines, which, as in the designs of modern
surveyors, are to be understood to indicate not precipices
but gradual slopes. The continuous spectrum of astrono-
mers provides a still better analogy. Neoplatonism deals
throughout with spiritual, non-quantitative relations,
which cannot be represented by diagrams, or treated as
logical counters. The very difficult Platonic doctrine
of 'participation' (μέθεξις, κοινωνία, παρουσία) is an
attempt to express symbolically the interpenetration of
all spiritual existences in an ordered hierarchy. We shall
see that this is eminently true when we come to consider
the 'three Divine principles'—the Absolute, Spirit, and
Soul; but the recognition of it is not less the key to his
anthropology and cosmology.

In their objective aspect, Body, Soul, and Spirit are,
respectively, the world as perceived by the senses (κόσμος
αἰσθητός); the world interpreted by the mind as a
spatial and temporal order; and the spiritual world
(κόσμος νοητός). The organs which perceive the world
under these three aspects are the bodily senses, discursive
thought (διάνοια), and spiritual perception or intuitive
knowledge (νόησις). Of these, the last alone perceives
the world as it really is, *sub specie æternitatis*. It is only
when we exercise this highest faculty of our nature,
'a power which all possess but few use,'[1] that we are
ourselves completely real and in contact with reality.
This reality is neither an independently existing external
universe, nor a subjective construction thrown off by
the mind. It is constituted by the unity in duality of
the spiritual faculty and the spiritual world which it
'beholds' in exercising its self-consciousness. Spirit
and the spiritual world imply and involve each other;
neither has any existence apart from its correlative. If
we call the spiritual world the self-externalisation of
Spirit, we must add that with equal propriety Spirit may

[1] 1. 6. 8.

be called the self-consciousness of the spiritual world.
This doctrine of Spirit and the spiritual world will be
further elucidated in a later lecture. Here it is only
necessary to say that the spiritual world is the only
fully real world, the reality of Soul and its world being
purely derivative and dependent, and the phenomenal
world being an appearance only, not possessing reality
(οὐσία).[1]

Refutation of Materialism

The relations of the eternal and the temporal, of reality
and appearance, of Spirit and Matter, or, to use the
favourite antithesis of Plotinus, of Yonder (ἐκεῖ) and
Here (ἐνταῦθα), constitute the first and last problem of
philosophy. To the earlier Greek thinkers the greatest
crux was the reconciliation of *change* and *permanence*.
It was not till much later that the debate took the modern
form of a war between idealism and materialism. At first
there were naïve attempts to solve the contradiction by
negating one of its terms. Heracleitus seemed to some
of his critics to ignore or deny the static aspect of reality
altogether;[2] and the Eleatics, according to their critics,
could give no intelligible account of change. The alternatives for these pioneers were to say either ' All things will
die, Nothing will change,' or ' All things will change,
Nothing will die.' But Plato, and perhaps still more
clearly Aristotle, had recognised that each of these is
a thesis which is untrue or unmeaning if divorced from
its antithesis, and that the solution, if it is attainable at
all, must lie in a closer investigation of change and
permanence, which will show them to be not mutually
exclusive. After Aristotle the controversy began to

---

[1] 3. 2. I. ἡ τοῦ νοῦ καὶ τοῦ ὄντος φύσις κόσμος ἐστὶν ὁ ἀληθινός.
5. 9. 5. ἡ τῶν ἄνευ ὕλης ἐπιστήμη ταὐτὸν τῷ πράγματι.

[2] Heracleitus ἠρεμίαν καὶ στάσιν ἐκ τῶν ὅλων ἀνῄρει · ἔστι γὰρ τοῦτο τῶν
νεκρῶν.   Plut., *de Placit. Philos.*, i. 23.   But for Heracleitus, though
phenomena are in flux, movement (force) is eternal. Mr. Cornford
(*From Religion to Philosophy*) has rightly protested against the injustice
done to this great philosopher by his critics.

pass into a new phase. The philosophy of concepts was
partially discredited, and the discouragement of speculation opened the door to naturalism on the one side and
scepticism on the other. Reality was conceived by both
Stoics and Epicureans either as body itself, or as a
quality or relation of body. In opposition to this materialism was ranged scepticism, not the scepticism of Plato's
Sophist, but a refined, disillusioned agnosticism, which,
by its insistence on the relativity of all knowledge,
destroyed Being not less than thought. The sceptical
method of combating dogmatic materialism was absolutely barred to Plotinus, who had no sympathy with the
disintegrating speculation of the Academy. To refute
materialism by scepticism would have been to cast out
devils by Beelzebub. He carries on war upon two fronts—
against materialism and against scepticism. It is always
by the standard of a higher and surer knowledge that he
condemns the premature synthesis of an infra-spiritual
view of the world.

In dealing with the materialists, he sees the issue more
clearly than any previous thinker. Neither Cicero nor
Plutarch ever alludes to the Stoics and Epicureans as
materialists. It is to Plotinus more than to any other
thinker that we owe a definite doctrine of spiritual
existence. His first object is to prove that the Soul is
not corporeal. Life, he says, cannot be generated by
an aggregation of lifeless particles, nor can intelligence
be produced by things without understanding. If it be
suggested that when the molecules are arranged in a
certain *order,* life results, then the principle which produces the order, and not the molecules which are so
arranged, should be called the Soul or vital principle.
Body is produced, through the agency of the seminal
Logoi,[1] by Soul, which gives form to indeterminate
' Matter.' Every body is compounded of Matter and
Form. But the Soul is by definition an uncompounded

[1] For the meaning of λόγος in Plotinus see p. 156. The Stoical
λόγοι σπερματικοί are much the same as the Platonic φύσις.

substance; it cannot then be Body. Nor can it be a simple manner-of-being of Matter; for Matter, being pure indetermination, cannot give itself Form. Without the coherence given by Soul, Matter would have no determinate existence.[1] The Stoics, against whom Plotinus is arguing, admit the existence of an intelligent Spirit (πνεῦμα νοερόν); and yet they assert that all things, even God, are only states of Matter (ὕλη πως ἔχουσα), a *banal* phrase to which they resort when in difficulties.[2] That which πως ἔχουσα adds to Matter is, in fact, the formative power of the Soul.[3] Plotinus goes on to show by other arguments of the same kind that the very conception of Soul includes elements which cannot be explained in terms of Body; while on the other hand Body is explained by Soul, since Body plainly has a 'form' which does not belong to the material part of it. Changes in the Soul, such as the acquisition of new knowledge, are rightly spoken of as an increase of wisdom, but there is no local or material augmentation. The Soul can neither lose nor acquire parts, as the Body can.[4] When we pass from Body to Soul, we have to deal with a different kind of existence, having laws of its own. The quantitative categories do not apply to Soul. It is impossible for the Body to feel or think; these operations cannot be explained materialistically. The perceiving Soul must be an unity everywhere identical with itself. Still less can the Body

---

[1] 4. 7. 3. Bouillet shows how closely Augustine reproduces this argument in *De Immortalitate Animae*, 8.

[2] 2. 4. 1; 4. 7. 4.

[3] For the Stoics, the Soul is a mirror which passively receives the impressions derived from the senses. Plotinus has no difficulty in showing that discursive thought (διάνοια) is not passive, but selects, combines, and distinguishes. Boethius, following Plotinus, brings this out very well (*Consol.*, V, 4, 5). The Stoics also contended, as conscientious materialists, that the Soul is an exhalation or emanation from solids, a theory which evoked great indignation from Longinus and Porphyry.

[4] Cf. Augustine, *De Quantitate Animae*, 19. 'Recte dicitur anima discendo quasi crescere, et contra minui dediscendo, sed translato verbo, ut supra ostendimus. Tamen illud cavendum est, ne quasi spatium loci maius occupare videatur,' etc.

think. How can an extended substance have ideas of
what is not extended, such as abstract conceptions ?[1]
Justice and virtue cannot be stated in terms of extension.
The Stoic doctrine that Soul and Spirit are developed out
of lower faculties is rejected on the ground that the lower
can never generate the higher. In other words, the
explanation of a thing must always be sought in what is
above it in the scales of value and existence, not in what
is below.[2] The higher does not need the lower, but the
lower does need the higher. In the Sixth Ennead he
objects that the Stoic doctrine gives the first place to that
which is only potential ($\delta\upsilon\nu\acute{a}\mu\epsilon\iota$), whereas the possibility
of passing into activity and actuality ($\grave{\epsilon}\nu\acute{\epsilon}\rho\gamma\epsilon\iota\alpha$) is the
only thing that makes Matter respectable. This possi-
bility, however, would not exist if Matter were anterior
to Soul. Matter cannot improve itself ; it can only pass
into activity by the help of what is above and before it.
Matter, in short, has only a contingent existence, and the
contingent cannot be the first principle. If the Stoics had
thought this out, they would have found themselves
obliged to seek for that which has an existence not contingent, and so would have reached the conception of
the Absolute.[3] If they insist that their ' Matter ' *can*
undergo inner development, without being acted upon
by anything from outside, Plotinus answers in effect
that $\H{\upsilon}\lambda\eta$ *means* that which is the subject of action from
without, and that what the Stoics wrongly call ' Matter '
is ' all things.' In modern language, while professing to
be materialists, they slide into pantheism. Their principle that sensation is the only evidence of real existence
compels them to identify absolute being with what has
only a contingent existence, and to assign an inferior
degree of reality to the higher objects of thought which

---

[1] 4. 7. Cf. Whittaker, *The Neoplatonists*, p. 45.
[2] Aristotle's $\H{\eta}$ $\phi\acute{\upsilon}\sigma\iota\varsigma$ $\tau\acute{\epsilon}\lambda o\varsigma$ $\grave{\epsilon}\sigma\tau\iota\nu$ is the classical statement of
this truth. Aristotle, however, also recognised the partial truth of
what may be called the Darwinian method. ' He who considers things
in their first growth and origin, whether a State or anything else, will
obtain the clearest view of them' (*Pol.* I. 2. I).   [3] 6. I. 26.

are not objects of sensation. But this invalidates their
own arguments, for sensation cannot prove a philosophy.

Matter (ὕλη)

What, then, is this ' Matter,' to which Plotinus finds
that the Stoics ascribe qualities which cannot belong to
it? It is most unfortunate that we have to use so mis-
leading a word as the equivalent of ὕλη. In modern
English, Matter means ponderable and extended stuff,
the texture out of which objects perceived by the senses
are woven, the substance which physicists classify as
consisting of this or that ' element.'[1] But ὕλη in Plotinus
has no resemblance to Matter in this sense : it is *not
material*.[2] It is in fact a mere abstraction, a name for
the bare receptacle of Forms ; the subject of energy,
as we would say, viewed by abstraction as separated
from the energy which alone gives it being and reality.
The most modern physics is approximating, it would
seem, to the ancient notion of Matter. The particles of
which the molecule consist have been divided and subdivided into atoms, corpuscles, and electrons, till they
are on the point of vanishing altogether except as the
subjects of electrical energy. Ostwald, in his *Natur-
philosophie* (1902), and most physicists at the present
time, wish to reduce all Matter to energy. All is energy,
and there exists nothing else. Plotinus, I think, would
have refused to take this last step. Energy, he would

---

[1] Maher, *Psychology*, p. 560, has an interesting note on the change
in the meaning of ' Form ' and ' Matter.' ' The original usage is almost
completely inverted.' For the schoolmen, *forma* or *actus* connoted full
actuality, the complete realisation of being ; while *materies* or *potentia*
signified the unrealised, the indeterminate. Now we speak of a merely
formal observance ; while *material* is equivalent to important. ' In
strictly philosophical literature, Kant did most to bring about the
change.'

[2] It is ἀσώματος, 2. 4. 8 and 12 ; 3. 6. 7. The Stoics ascribed size
(μέγεθος) to ὕλη, and called it ἄποιον σῶμα. The Pythagoreans,
Platonists, and Aristotelians agreed that Matter is incorporeal ; but
some of them distinguished two Matters, one the substance of bodies
(the Stoic ὕλη), the other the subject of forms and immaterial essences.

have said, must move something; motion cannot be moved. He would have been better content with the hypothesis of *ether* as the ultimate form of Matter.[1] Ether has been defined as ' undifferentiated, imperceptible, homogeneous plenum.' Plotinus says that Matter is the infinite (ἄπειρον) in the sense of the indeterminate (ἀόριστον). Its nature is to be the recipient of Forms. In itself it is no thing (τὸ μὴ ὄν), though not absolutely nothing (οὐκ ὄν). In the *Timaeus*, ' primary Matter' cannot be distinguished from Space in three dimensions. But for Plotinus Space is ' later ' than Matter and bodies.[2] In discussing Matter, he combines the Aristotelian distinction of δύναμις and ἐνέργεια with the Platonic conception of a world formed by the union of being and not-being, of the same and the different, of the one and the many. Plotinus calls Matter pure δύναμις, i.e. potentiality without any potency.[3] In one of his fullest descriptions of it,[4] he says, ' Matter is incorporeal, because Body only exists after it; Body is a composite of which Matter is an element. . . . Being neither Soul nor Spirit nor life nor form nor reason nor limit (for it is indefiniteness) (ἀπειρία), nor a power (δύναμις);[5] for what does it produce? but falling outside all these things, it cannot rightly be said to have Being, but should rather be called Not-being (μὴ ὄν). . . . It is an image and phantom of extension (εἴδωλον καὶ φάντασμα ὄγκου), an aspiration to exist (ὑποστάσεως ἔφεσις). It is constant only in change (ἑστηκὸς οὐκ ἐν στάσει); it

---

[1] Moore (*Home University Library*—' *Nature and Origin of Life* ') thinks it probable that atoms are generated out of the ether. Mendeléeff, too, has argued that the ether, instead of being some mysterious form of non-matter, is the lightest and simplest of the elements. The atomic weight of the ether he concludes to be nearly one-millionth of that of hydrogen. Duncan, *The New Knowledge*, p. 250.

[2] 2. 4. 12. It is not easy to reconcile this with Plato, *Timaeus*, p. 49.

[3] 2. 5. 5.

[4] 3. 6. 7.

[5] δύναμις in Plotinus means sometimes potency, sometimes potentiality. In the former sense ὕλη is the negation of δύναμις, in the latter it is pure δύναμις. There is the same unfortunate ambiguity about ἐνέργεια, which means sometimes activity, sometimes actuality.

I.—K

is invisible in itself, escaping him who wishes to see it.
When one is not looking at it, it is there ; when one gazes
at it, it is not seen.   It is made up of contradictions ;
it is great and little, less and more, defect and excess.   It
is a phantom which can neither stay nor flee.   Flee it
cannot, for it has received no strength from Spirit, but
is the negation of all being.   In consequence it deceives
in all that it professes to be.   If it is represented as great,
it straightway appears as little ; if as the more, it appears
as the less.   Its being, when one tries to conceive it,
appears as not-being ; it is a fugitive bauble (παίγνιον),
and so are the things that appear to be in it, mere shadows
in a shadow.   As in a mirror the semblance is in one place,
the substance in another, so Matter seems to be full when
it is empty, and contains nothing while seeming to contain all things.   The copies and shadows of real things
which pass in and out of it, come into it as into a formless
shadow.   They are seen in it because it has no form of
its own ; they seem to act upon it, but they produce
nothing ; for they are feeble and weak and have no
power of resistance.   But neither has Matter any such
power ; so they go through it like water without clearing
a passage.'

In this picturesque and half humorous way Plotinus
bids us contemplate his abstraction[1]—that intangible
impalpable all-but-nothing which remains when we sub-
tract from an object of thought all that gives it form,
meaning, and definite existence.[2]   We shall understand

---

[1] It is an abstraction, because it never and nowhere exists without
form: 2. 4. 3.   The comparison with a mirror is not exact, because the
mirror of ὕλη disappears with the reflected images, when they are withdrawn.   That ὕλη and ψυχή can only be separated by abstraction is
made very clear by 4. 3. 9.   οὐκ ἦν ὅτε οὐκ ἐψυχοῦτο τόδε τὸ πᾶν, οὐδὲ
ὕλη ποτὲ ὅτε ἀκόσμητος ἦν, ἀλλ' ἐπινοῆσαι ταῦτα χωρίζοντας αὐτὰ ἀπ'
ἀλλήλων οἷόν τε.   The interesting definition of Matter as *mens moment-
anea* calls attention to the fact that *Time* is ignored in our attempts
to picture Matter.   Plato in the *Timaeus* makes Space the unchanging
receptacle of changing bodies.

[2] Herbert Spencer (*First Principles*, 1, 67) says : ' There is some
thing which alike forms the raw material of definite thought, and
remains after the definiteness which thinking gave to it has been
destroyed.'

his meaning better when we realise that (as will be explained below) Matter is Matter only in relation to that which is next above it, and which gives it form, meaning, and definite existence. Thus the same thing may be form (εἶδος) in relation to what is below it, and Matter in relation to what is above it. A thing is Matter in so far as it is acted upon by a higher principle. It is a purely relative term : every stage in the hierarchy of being, except the highest, is ὕλη, every stage except the lowest is εἶδος. Every εἶδος *makes* its own ὕλη. But ὕλη is generally the name of the lowest rung in the ladder. When the lower Soul turns to itself, wishing to create that which shall be next in order below itself, it makes τὸ μὴ ὄν, which is its own image, indefinite and dark through and through.[1] At this stage we reach the limit of the downward movement.

But Matter is not always spoken of as pure negativity. There are many passages where it is said to exercise a positive influence of a sinister kind. The defects and hindrances to which the Soul is liable are due not to the privation of something which it ought to have, but to the presence of something which ought not to be there. Matter is like a beggar at a feast ;[2] it intrudes where it has no right to be. It obscures the light which shines upon the soul, by mingling its own darkness with it. As the nature (φύσις) which resists Form, Matter is evil. This is so surprising a statement, after all that Plotinus has told us about the helplessness and pure negativity of Matter, that we must consider carefully what he means by it.

The difficulty consists in the inter-relation of the two kinds of judgment—that of existence and that of value.[3] Hitherto, in dealing with Matter, we have been considering exclusively its claim to substantial reality (οὐσία). But the word ' evil ' at once introduces another

---

[1] 3. 9. 2.   [2] 1.8.14; cf. Plato, *Symposium*, 203 B.
[3] I do not mean to imply that this distinction is clearly drawn by Plotinus or any ancient philosopher.

scale—that of value. The problems of physical science have, strictly speaking, nothing to do with comparative values. An 'appearance,' as opposed to 'reality,' is a presentation of reality which needs to be enlarged or harmonised, in order to make it a true presentation. It is false if it claims to be a presentation of a fact in all its relations, whereas in truth it ignores some of those relations. It is an error to mistake appearance for reality ; for example, it is an error to regard the world of sense as an objective self-existing cosmos. This error may be, and probably will be, a cause of moral fault ; but the moral aspect of the mistake begins with the effect upon the will of a mistaken judgment about the nature of reality ; there is nothing immoral about the appearance itself. A shadow has its place in the order of the world, as well as the substance which casts the shadow ; we blame neither the body for casting a shadow, nor the shadow for being a shadow. It is, however, practically impossible to confine ourselves to the purely existential aspect of the world. Even in natural science such words as progress, degeneration, survival of the fittest, are freely used, and those who use them are often unaware that they are introducing qualitative and ethical categories into an investigation which they wish to restrict to measurable quantities. If these value-judgments are rigidly excluded, it will be found that natural science approximates to pure mathematics. Qualitative estimates are based on fact, no less than quantitative. These, however, give us a different standard, and a different arrangement from the other ; and we are threatened with an intractable dualism. For Plotinus it is a matter of faith that the hierarchies of existence and of value must ultimately be found to correspond. His whole philosophy is based on this assumption. It follows that that order of phenomena which has the lowest degree of reality in the existential scale, must have the lowest degree of value in the ethical or spiritual scale. And whereas, in estimating degrees of reality, we regard that as least real which needs most

supplementing and rearranging, in order to make it conform to the two requirements of inner harmony and
universality, so in value-judgments we pronounce that
to be worst which we conceive to be furthest removed
from the thought and will of God, or from our ideal of
what ought to be.

But there is an important difference in the two series.
In the scale of existence there are no *minus* signs.
The lowest rung of the ladder is occupied by that
which is all but non-existent. But in the scale of
values, as in our thermometers, we have to register
temperatures far below freezing-point. There are many
facts, and some characters, on which the moral verdict is
that it would have been better if they had not come into
existence. It is this difference, above all others, which
makes it difficult to bring judgments of value into line
with judgments of existence. The moral standard is
essentially dualistic, and the dualism cannot be transcended without transcending the standpoint of morality.
The existential standard is monistic: all things are
ranked by the degree in which they fall short of inner
harmony and universality. But harmony and universality
are clearly values, and we cannot deny that the purely
existential aspect of things gives us no scale at all. The
attempt to separate existence from value seems in truth
to be an impossible enterprise, though it forms the basis
of the Ritschlian theology. That which has no value has
no existence, and that which has no existence has no
value. But the quarrel between the ethical and scientific
views of the world is a fact ; and various attempts at
reconciliation have been made. The existential scheme
may be forced into correspondence with the ethical by
making ' Matter ' or ' flesh ' a substantial reality with
evil characteristics, in which case we have accepted
metaphysical dualism. Or we may retain the monistic
conception of existence, and force our value-judgments
to conform to it by holding that evil is only a defect of
goodness, its appearance of positive malignity being
valid only within the sphere of the moral struggle. Accord-

ing to this view, the *minus* signs disappear when we contemplate the world under the form of eternity. The latter is the solution to which Plotinus inclines [1] ; but he is too much in earnest about morality, and too conscious of the positive hindrances which impede moral progress, to be at his ease in describing evil as the mere defect of determination by Spirit and Soul. When we come to the consideration of his Psychology and Ethics, we shall find abundant proof of his embarrassment in dealing with the problem of moral evil, an embarrassment which I think is felt by every philosopher whose system is in contact with the facts of life. Here we have to notice traces of the same hesitation in speaking of the properties of Matter, and its place in the ordered scheme of the universe.

There are unquestionably passages in which Plotinus seems to make Matter the principle of evil. Side by side with such expressions as ' absence of good,' ' deprivation,' ' absolute poverty,' we find that Matter is ' the first evil.' [2] In one place [3] he tries to prove that Matter may be at the same time ' without qualities,' and evil by nature. Matter is ' without qualities ' because it has no determination that it does not receive from without ; but it has a ' nature,' which is to be ' without qualities,' and this is to have a bad nature. But this argument does not justify him in investing Matter with powers of resistance to Form, and this is what is required, if it is to represent the principle of evil in the sphere of conduct. Plotinus' Matter is the absence of order, which when isolated by abstract thought becomes the foe of order. In a philosophy which never forgets the partial truth of naturalism, and endeavours to bring all things under one law, the influence of Form upon Matter is regarded as analogous to the moral activities of the Soul. But in the will-world, which is the soul-world, obstacles are not inert. We wrestle against principalities and powers. Thus that dualism, which is the only atmosphere in which

---

[1] There is a clear statement of evil as defect in 5. 9. 10 *ad fin.* ; and in 2. 2. 3, ὁ ἐκ τῶν μερῶν τὸ ὅλον αἰτιώμενος ἄτοπος ἂν εἴη.

[2] 1. 8. 3 ; 2. 4. 16.   [3] 1. 8. 10.

ethics can live, threatens to infect natural science, where
it has no place.   In the polemic against materialism
Matter naturally becomes the principle of *externality*,
the ' muddy vesture of decay ' which impedes our vision
of things invisible to mortal sight.   But he is sometimes
tempted to meet the Stoics on their own ground, and to
use Matter in the Stoical sense rather than in his own.
Instead of being content with showing that the Stoics
are inconsistent materialists, in attributing to Matter
qualities which Matter cannot have, he sometimes
attempts to argue that the principle which they call
Matter—the visible as opposed to the invisible order—is
an obstacle to the higher life.   So a modern idealist might
argue that the God of naturalism, if he existed, would not
be worthy of reverence.   When he attributes a positive
evil nature to Matter, Plotinus is thinking of the materialist's Matter, not of his own doctrine.   Zeller does not seem
to me to be justified in saying that Plotinus follows the
Neopythagoreans and Philo, rather than Plato and
Aristotle, in making Matter the evil principle.[1]   Against
the few polemical passages which might seem to support
this contention, must be set the whole tendency of his
philosophy.   He is careful to point out that though
Matter in itself would be evil, if it could exist by itself,
yet Matter as we know it has the promise of good.   It is
' potentially all things ' ; its being consists in what it
may become.[2]   It is the necessary condition of all good,
in so far as good is a progress from potentiality ($\delta \acute{v} \nu a \mu \iota s$)
to actuality ($\acute{\epsilon} \nu \acute{\epsilon} \rho \gamma \epsilon \iota a$).   There can be no cosmos without
form working on Matter.[3]   Matter is always the inferior
element in that of which it forms a part, but there could
be no greater misunderstanding of Plotinus than to suppose that it constitutes a bad world, set dualistically in
opposition to the good world of Spirit and Soul.   There
is such a thing as ' divine Matter,'[4] which in receiving
its proper form, has a ' definite spiritual life,' i.e. it is
enriched and glorified by the Spirit which is infused

---

[1] There is a very striking passage in 2. 9. 12, in which he carries
up the cause of evil to the Soul ; $\tau \grave{a} \; \kappa a \kappa \grave{a} \; \pi \rho \grave{o} \; \tau o \hat{v} \; \kappa \acute{o} \sigma \mu o v \; \tau o \hat{v} \delta \epsilon$ etc.
[2] 2. 5. 5.   [3] 2. 4. 4.   [4] 2. 4. 5.

into it, and which gives it a place within real Being. It
is only on the lower levels of existence that Matter, even
when it has received its form, remains a 'decked-out
corpse.' On these levels, form and substratum are still
to some extent held apart; 'Yonder,' Matter too is
delivered from the bondage of corruption. And the
reason why 'Here' Matter remains dark and dead,
imperfectly informed by Soul, is that 'Here' even Form
is but an image (εἴδωλον), and so the substratum remains
an image too. But 'Yonder,' where the form is genuine,
the substratum has reality (οὐσία), or rather, Form and
Matter together are one 'illuminated reality' (οὐσία
πεφωτισμένη).[1] The illumination is veritably appro-
priated by 'the Matter which is Yonder,' though always
as a gift from above.

Matter in this sense is an essential factor in every process, since all things endeavour to rise in the scale of
being. Matter is that without which no effort would be
necessary or possible. Can we go further and say that
Matter, thus regarded, is a negation posited in the
Absolute, a necessary 'moment' in reality, without
which the finite could not become actual? Is it the
benign evil which calls the good into activity, the necessary tension without which there could be no process,
no struggle, no victory? Proclus distinctly says that
Matter is not evil but 'a creation of God' (γέννημα θεοῦ),
necessary to the existence of the world. This thought is
not drawn out in Plotinus, and he would shrink from
endowing his own 'Matter' with active powers of
resistance. Moreover, he never regarded reality (οὐσία)
as the result of conflicting elements in the Absolute,[2] nor
would he have admitted that without tension there can
be no life 'Yonder.'[3] Friction and conflict belong only to

---

[1] 2. 4. 5.

[2] In 1. 8. 6, perhaps the most dualistic passage in the Enneads,
he speaks of a false οὐσία resisting the true οὐσία as its opposite; but a
'false reality' has surely no substantial existence.

[3] But he does say in one place (1. 8. 7), 'The All is made up of
contraries.'

the world of time and change ; they are a condition of the actualising of spiritual activity *on that plane;* and in that world, the world projected by Soul, there is a necessity for a material which shall not be entirely ductile and tractable. If this world is to be of such a kind as to be the scene of moral effort, there must be a hierarchy of values, and there must be real tension.   It is also necessary that reality shall be actualised, not only in every manner but in every degree.[1]   The lowest degree, that which is most widely separated from the Absolute, is Matter. Below this there can be nothing, for the next stage below Matter would be absolute non-entity.   The ' must be ' is for Plotinus a form of the ontological argument.   It belongs to the notion of perfection that it should be able to create in the fullest and freest manner ; and we see that this power has been exercised.   Plotinus often appears to cut knots by saying ' it had to be.'   But he really means that we have to accept the results of the dialectic and the data of experience.   No particular explanation of an universal truth should be demanded. The two hierarchies, of value and existence, are so deeply involved in the constitution of the Soul that they cannot be explained and accounted for, as from an outside standpoint.   Rather, they are the foundations on which philosophy has to build.

But now arises an epistemological difficulty.   Reality, as we have said, is not a purely objective realm, existing apart from the mind.   It is a Trinity constituted by the perceiving Spirit, the Spiritual World as its own counterpart, and the Spiritual Perception (νόησις) which unites subject and object in one.   This law of correspondence and mutual dependence of subject and object holds good all down the scale.   *Like alone sees its like.*   This is one of the fundamental doctrines in the philosophy of

[1] 1. 8. 7. The fullest creation is not a reduplication of a perfection which cannot be measured quantitatively—a self-contradictory idea— but the creation of a graduated hierarchy, all linked with its divine original.

Plotinus : it is an integral part of the real-idealism of the
later Platonists. It is found in Plato and Aristotle ; and
in a poetical, rather crude form, in Empedocles,[1] whom
Aristotle quotes as the author of the canon ἡ γνῶσις τοῦ
ὁμοίου τῷ ὁμοίῳ. It has been reaffirmed by many later
writers. For instance, the seventeenth-century mystic
Angelus Silesius writes :—

> Soll ich mein letztes End und ersten Anfang finden,
> So muss ich mich in Gott und Gott in mir ergründen,
> Und werden dass, was Er ; ich muss ein Schein im Schein,
> Ich muss ein Wort im Wort, ein Gott in Gotte sein.

The doctrine has a central position in the nature-philos-
ophy of Wordsworth and Coleridge. They were anticipated by Blake, who says :—

> The sun's light, when he unfolds it,
> Depends on the organ that beholds it.

Lotze denies it ; but no Platonist can do so. It is the
real meaning of Plotinus' famous canon, that 'the
spiritual world is not outside Spirit' (οὐκ ἔξω νοῦ τὰ
νοητά). Thought and thing depend upon and correspond
to each other. This does not imply that Spirit has no
knowledge of Soul, or Soul of Matter.[2] It is no declen-
sion in Soul to know Matter to be what Soul in fact has
made it. But Matter standing alone is only thinkable
if it is invested with a spurious substantiality. We do,
in fact, frequently so think of it ; and the existence of
such false opinions (ψευδεῖς δόξαι) requires explanation.
The senses regard the objects of perception as real ; this
judgment seems to be an activity of the Soul ; and yet
sensation is not the proper activity of the Soul, nor are
its objects real for the Soul. There must be, Plotinus
says, an element of *indeterminateness* in the Soul ; and
it is this part of the Soul which apprehends the indeter-

---

[1] γαίῃ μὲν γὰρ γαῖαν ὀπώπαμεν, ὕδατι δ' ὕδωρ,
αἰθέρι δ' αἰθέρα δῖον, ἀτάρ πυρὶ πῦρ ἀΐδηλον,
στοργῇ δὲ στοργήν, νεῖκος δέ τε νείκεϊ λυγρῷ.

[2] Though, strictly, what the soul perceives are ἤδη νοητά.

minate, Matter. Νοῦς has to reduce itself to ἄνοια ;
it perceives Matter by an illegitimate kind of thought
(νόθῳ λογισμῷ).[1] The apprehension is dim, dark, and
formless, like its object. Nor can such an experience
bring satisfaction. The half-blinded spiritual faculty,
the clouded perception, and the shapeless indeterminate
object all ' desire ' to rise together into a clearer light,
where all three will be transformed. From this it might
be inferred that Matter, as an object of thought, is nothing
more than a delusive appearance, which vanishes, as such,
when the Soul is ' awake.' Plotinus would accept this
statement ; Matter has no reality (οὐσία) ; but the
activity of the irrational Soul which produces these
phantasms is none the less a fact. In denying reality to
Matter, we do not affirm that it is absolutely non-existent.

Matter in the Spiritual World

When the Soul is awake, and exercising its proper
activities, it begins to contemplate a yet higher flight
than the knowledge of its own states. It aspires to the
life of Spirit ; and forthwith that which on a lower plane
was Form, becomes now Matter. ' Soul may in a sense
be called the Matter of Spirit.' Those who wish to find
in Plotinus a dualistic conception of the world will be
puzzled by learning that the same thing may be Form
in relation to that which is below it, and Matter in relation to that which is above it. And they will ask why we
have so many warnings against ' Matter,' if the word
means only the indispensable lower end of each upward
progress, the outside of every inside. Why should we
kick away the ladder by which we have mounted ? The
answer to this question will help us to understand several
difficulties in Plotinus. The Soul, as we shall see in a
later chapter, is a wanderer through all the fields of

---

[1] Borrowed from Plato, *Timaeus*, 52. Matter, strictly, cannot
be known, for if we know it, it is no longer Matter that we know.
Cf. Aristotle, *Metaph.* 10, 1036 a 8.

existence. It has its affinities to all the grades of reality
But it has its own proper sphere, just within the confines
of the real or spiritual.[1] Spirit also, though it may divest
itself of its proper attributes in order to contemplate
Matter, has its own exalted sphere, where it is at home.
So too has Matter its own place at the bottom of the
scale. When Plotinus speaks of Matter, he generally
means that phantasmal abstraction which we have been
discussing, the indefinite and nebulous substratum on
which the Soul in the exercise of its lowest and least
spiritual activities impresses a vague and fugitive form.
But the word is also used of that which, in any stage,
occupies the same position in relation to that which is
next above it, that Matter, in the world of appearance,
occupies in relation to Form. Plotinus speaks of ' what
we incorrectly call reality in the world of sense ' (ἡ ἐνταῦθα
ὁμώνυμος οὐσία). He might (though he does not) speak
of ἡ ἐκεῖ ὁμώνυμος ὕλη. The word Matter is thus used
in more than one sense, and care is needed to consider
the context of passages where it occurs. But if Plotinus
had held the dualistic view about material things which
has been often laid to his charge, he could not have
brought ' divine Matter ' into the world of Spirit.

Plotinus probably got his conception of ' divine
Matter ' from Aristotle, who also speaks of νοητὴ ὕλη.
But Aristotle's doctrine is different, since he does not
conceive ' intelligible Matter ' as entering into the objects
of pure intuitive reason. His conception resembles Kant's
doctrine as to the forms of sense. Perceptions, Aristotle
says, are not passive impressions ; sense is an activity
which apprehends ' sensible Forms,' not ' sensible Matter.'
These sensible Forms have an ' intelligible Matter '
attaching to them, as being images of spatial and temporal objects, not objects of pure thought.[2] Plotinus,
on the other hand, teaches that Matter proceeds from

[1] 4. 4. 2. τῆς ψυχῆς ἐν οἷον ἐσχάτοις τοῦ νοητοῦ κειμένης.
[2] Cf. E. Caird, *Evolution of Theology in the Greek Philosophers*,
Vol. I. p. 336.

the Absolute. 'The infinite' (=Matter), he says, 'is
generated from the infinity or powers or eternity of the
One; not that there is infinity in the One, but that it is
created by the One.'[1] The 'Matter' which is created
directly by the Absolute is the substratum of Spirit, the
recipient of its illumination; and this is hard to distinguish from the Universal Soul. Lower kinds of Matter
are created mediately by the Absolute.[2] 'We must not
everywhere despise the indeterminate and formless, if it
gives itself as the subject of higher things; the Soul is
indeterminate with respect to Spirit, which gives it a
better form than its own.'[3] 'Divine Matter' shares in
the properties of spiritual life. The Matter of sensible
things is dead, while that of spiritual things, in receiving
the Form which determines it, possesses a spiritual and
determined life. 'The Form of sensible things being only
an image (εἴδωλον), their Matter is so too. Since the form
of the νοητὰ is real, so is their Matter.' In another
place[4] he makes Soul the Matter, or the potentiality
(δύναμις) of spiritual things (νοητά). He asks whether,
if there is Matter 'Yonder,' we can say that all things
there are ἐνεργείᾳ, and not δυνάμει. This question leads to
an interesting discussion, in which Plotinus shows that he
is conscious of the difficulty. Even if Matter 'Yonder'
is different from Matter 'Here below,' it must (we shall
be told) have the essential nature of Matter. Must we
then admit into the spiritual world the terrestrial triad
of Matter, Form, and the compound of them? To this
Plotinus answers that Matter 'Yonder' is itself Form,
being in fact Soul. Is it then Form in one aspect and
Matter in another? For our thinking it is so; but there
is no real distinction between the Form and the Matter
of a spiritual being; 'the two are one nature.' But, says

---

[1] 2. 4. 15.
[2] 4. 8. 5. καὶ γὰρ ἀφ' ἧς ἀρχῆς ἕκαστα, εἰ καὶ τὰ μεταξὺ πολλά, καὶ τὰ
ἔσχατα εἰς αὐτὴν ἀναφέρεται. Proclus, however, makes the One act
directly upon Matter. His doctrine is that the higher the principle,
the further down does its power extend.
[3] 2. 3. 3–5.   [4] 2. 5. 3.

the objector, the Soul is capable of growth; it acquires powers which it had not always; if the Soul, then, is a spiritual being, must we not admit that there is potentiality (τὸ δυνάμει) in the spiritual world? Not precisely, because Soul itself is their potency (δύναμις). Every spiritual being is a Form and perfect in itself. That which is only potential requires some force from outside to bring it into actuality; that which is eternal and self-sufficing is actual (ἐνεργείᾳ).[1] The Soul in the spiritual world is in this state; and even in Matter the Soul is actually (ἐνεργείᾳ) what it is. The Soul therefore is δύναμις rather than δυνάμει; and it is always ἐνεργείᾳ. Can we then say that spiritual things are at once ἐνέργεια and ἐνεργείᾳ? We must say so, because in the spiritual world all is awake, and all is life. 'The place of spiritual realities is the place of life, and the principle and source of the true Soul and Spirit.' The category of *life* seems to Plotinus to offer the best solution of the difficulty. There is no real distinction between Form and Matter 'Yonder'; but whereas the Soul is capable of real development, through its own nature, we must, if we wish to analyse its activities, postulate something in it which is analogous to Matter in the world of sense.

In the fourth book he says 'the activity of man is directed towards the spiritual world, and he *becomes* νοητόν, giving himself as Matter for Spirit and Form, and taking its Form in accordance with what he sees; and henceforth he is only δυνάμει himself.'[2] The Soul which constitutes our personality may become the Matter of Spirit. In doing so, Soul, which is essentially true being or reality (οὐσία), becomes illuminated reality (πεφωτισμένη οὐσία), in presenting itself passively to receive what Spirit has to give; and renouncing its own

[1] τὸ δυνάμει may be acted upon by alien forces, by its own inner nature, or by its desire to rise. 2. 5. 1. Matter never becomes ἐνέργεια; but that which was (e.g.) a statue δυνάμει may become a statue ἐνεργείᾳ. The fullest discussion is in 2. 5.
[2] 4. 4. 2.

activity, it is exalted. Every grade of being performs its highest act in becoming the Matter of the grade above it. Thus the all-but non-existent Matter at the bottom of the scale is redeemed in giving itself as the recipient of Form. In so doing, it is an image of the great self-surrender whereby the World-Soul receives illumination from Spirit, and of the ineffable self-surrender by which Spirit itself awaits the visitation of the Absolute Godhead.[1]

Creation of Matter

The following passage from the *Timaeus* of Plato may be taken as the foundation of the Neoplatonic doctrine about the creation of the visible world. ' Let me tell you why nature and this universe of things was framed by him who framed it. God is good ; and in a perfectly good being no envy or jealousy could ever arise. Being therefore far removed from any such feeling, he desired that all things should resemble himself as far as possible. This is the prime cause of the existence of the world of change, which we shall do well to believe on the testimony of the wise men of old. God desired that everything should be good and nothing evil, so far as this could be. Therefore, finding the visible world not at rest but moving in a disorderly manner, he brought order out of disorder, thinking this in every way an improvement. Now it is impossible that the best of beings should produce any but the most beautiful of works. The Creator therefore took thought and discerned that out of the things that are by nature visible no work destitute of reason could be made so fair as that which possessed reason. He also saw that reason could not dwell in anything devoid of Soul. This being his thought he put Spirit in Soul and Soul in Body, that he might be the maker of the fairest and best of works. Hence we shall probably

[1] On the subject of $\dot{\eta}$ ἐκεῖ ὕλη it is interesting to note that Kant speaks of ' *Die transcendentale Materie aller Gegenstände, als Ding an Sich.*' Compare too the Pauline doctrine of a ' spiritual body.'

be safe in affirming that the universe is a living creature endowed with Soul and Spirit by the providence of God.[1]

Plotinus holds that Matter was created, though not in time.[2] It was created 'of necessity,' a phrase which Zeller and others take as excluding any voluntary action on the part of the Creator.[3] But Proclus is not deserting his master when he says that 'with God necessity and will always correspond.'[4] Matter was created in order that the will-activities of Soul and Spirit might become actualities. Was creation 'out of nothing,' as Christianity teaches? The question has a meaning if creation took place at a point of time; but this is not the doctrine of Plotinus. Eternal creation—creation which had no date—seems to be only another way of saying that the world is lower than God and always dependent on Him. The creation of finite things is going on perpetually; there was never a time when God was not creating. Plato, as we have seen, thinks of God as intervening first to reduce 'irregular and disorderly motion' to harmony. But motion must be motion of something. Eckhart is in the same difficulty as Plato. He says that there was no Matter before creation; but there was 'indetermination' (*Unbestimmtheit*). Chaos, then, was not created by God. This seems to be Plato's opinion; and it may, of course, suggest the hypothesis of some other creative agent, blind or malevolent. Plato's disciples differed as whether their master believed in the eternity of the world; Plutarch and Atticus held that he did not, probably wrongly.[5] Nor was the school agreed whether

---

[1] Plato, *Timaeus*, 29, 30.   [2] 3. 2. 1.

[3] Plato (*Timaeus*, 68) assigns two causes, one 'necessary,' the other 'divine.' Here 'necessity,' as Professor Taylor has pointed out to me, 'is not the mechanical cause, but rather πλανωμένη αἰτία, what James Ward calls 'contingency in the heart of things.' I do not find this distinction in Plotinus, and it is repudiated by Proclus.

[4] Proclus *in Tim.* 49. ἡ θεία ἀνάγκη συντρέχει τῇ θείᾳ βουλήσει. Origen, arguing against dualism, asks how Matter could have been exactly suited to receive all the forms which God wished it to take, if it had not been created for the purpose by God Himself (Eusebius, *Praep. Evang.* 7, 20).

[5] Xenocrates and other early Platonists held that the world was represented as having a beginning in time only for the purpose of exposition (διδασκαλίας χάριν). Burnet, *Greek Philosophers*, p. 340. Here, as in the problem of evil, Platonism seems to have suffered by not being quite honest with the outside public.

the Soul of chaos, or what took the place of a Soul (some σύμφυτος ἐπιθυμία) was a passive resister or actively obstructive. The more dualistic view gained ground till Plotinus, who rejects it. He repudiates the idea of a spatial chaos into which the higher principle descends with its Forms.[1] But he seems to me to have been almost afraid to clarify what Plato had left obscure. In one place he says that Soul could not have ' come,' if Matter had not been there already.[2] Chaignet finds that Plotinus contradicts himself here ; and there would be a contradiction if the language about Time was meant to be taken literally. But it is not, either here or in the opposite statement that ' efficient cause must precede Matter.'[3] The higher principle is ' before ' the lower ; but on the other hand the higher principle cannot begin to mould the lower unless it finds something to work upon. The doctrine of an eternal creation is certainly not free from difficulties.

The traditional Christian doctrine, developed into a dogma after the dispute with the Gnostics, was that the world was created out of nothing by an act of the Divine will, and in time. Creation out of nothing has been ignorantly ridiculed, as if it meant that God took some ' nothing ' and made a world out of it. Augustine says that God made the world because He wished to make it (quia voluit fecit). He adds, ' When we say that He made it out of nothing, we mean that there was no pre-existent Matter, unmade by Himself, without which He could not have made the world.'[4] Aquinas explains the orthodox doctrine of creation as follows. ' Creation is a production of a thing according to its whole substance, nothing being presupposed, whether created or uncreated.'[5] Christian orthodoxy denies (1) the pantheistic theory that the world is God ; (2) the theory that Matter

---

[1] 6. 8. 11. [2] 1. 8. 14. [3] 2. 4. 8.

[4] Augustine, *Ad Orosium*, 1-2. *De Div. Quaest.* 83. The statement of the Epistle to the Hebrews that ' things which are seen were not made of things which do appear,' is supported by modern science. The final analysis of the physicist leaves us with an invisible, all-pervading energy, and an invisible, impalpable medium of expression.

[5] *Summa*, 1. 65. 3.

I.—L

is uncreated, and that creation consists in shaping it. The assertion that the creation took place by a free act of God's will denies the Hegelian doctrine that the world is a necessary self-evolution of God. The third statement, that the world was created in Time, was a stumbling-block from the first. Origen could not be satisfied with the beginning of the world in Time, and taught instead that there is a series of worlds succeeding each other without beginning and without end. Augustine held that the world was created not in Time, but with Time; [1] and Aquinas almost implies that he accepts the orthodox doctrine of creation in Time solely on the authority of the Church. Scotus Erigena makes creation co-eternal with God, who is prior to the world only as its cause. ' When we hear it said that God makes all things, we ought to understand simply that God is in all things ; that is, that He subsists as the Being of all things.' Action and Being are in God the same thing. The world was not made out of nothing, for it was made out of God. The world is the thinking out of God's thoughts. God is the First Cause— He is Being, Wisdom, and Life. He is the immediate Creator of the Ideas, which in their turn create the phenomenal world. But through these the Creator himself descends to the lowest created things, which all manifest His eternal power and Godhead. This is very much like Plotinus ; but the Irish philosopher is less careful than the Neoplatonist to keep the Being of God unentangled with the world of change. Eckhart teaches that the Word of God, to whom he gives the attributes of the Platonic Nous, is the creative principle of the world, and that He creates from all eternity and constantly.[2] ' We must not suppose that God stood waiting till the

---

[1] See the passage in *Confessions*, 11. 30, ending : ' Videant itaque nullum tempus esse posse sine creatura et desinant istam vanitatem loqui,' in answer to the question, ' What was God doing before He made the world ? '

[2] Eckhart, 553. 6. ' Principium in quo Deus creavit caelum et terram est Nunc simplex aeternitatis, ipsum inquam illud Nunc penitus in quo Deus est ab aeterno, in quo etiam est, fuit, et erit aeternaliter personarum divinarum emanatio.'

time came for Him to create the world. He created the
world as soon as He was God, as soon as He begat His
co-eternal Son.' The *Theologia Germanica* argues that
God can never have been idle, and that therefore there
can never have been a time when there was no world.
Leibnitz says that God was obliged to create the world,
but that the necessity was a moral one. Hegel, on the
contrary, teaches that it belongs to the *essence* of God to
create ; He would be imperfect without His world. This
is not the view of Plotinus, who is entirely free from a
doctrine which would in a sense subordinate God to the
category of Time. He says indeed that the world was
necessary for the *manifestation* of the Divine thought and
will ; but the necessity proceeds from God's eternal perfection, not from His supposed temporal imperfection.

Proclus is more emphatic in rejecting the dualistic
interpretation of the nature of Matter. Matter, he says,
cannot struggle against the Good, since it cannot act in
any way. It is not disordered movement ; for movement implies force, and Matter has none. It is not the
evil principle, since it is an essential part of the composition of the world, and is derived from the One. It
is not ' necessity,' though it is necessary. What then is
it ? Take away order from everything that is orderly,
and what remains is Matter. It is that which, if it had
any active power, which it has not, would produce
disintegration in that which is integrated, disconnexion
in that which is connected. It is in a word that which is
no thing, though not absolutely nothing ; it is a ' true
lie.' [1]

Value of Plotinus' doctrine of Matter

When Plotinus shows that to strip an object of its
qualities, its values, its meaning in a moral and spiritual
scheme, and its æsthetic properties, is the way to reduce it
to all-but nothing, he gives us a refutation of materialism,

[1] Proclus, *Comm. in Alcib.* 2. 219, 251.   Bouillet, Vol. I. p. 485

which is still valuable. He reminds us that the universe as conceived by naturalism owes far more to the mind of the observer than the naturalist is willing to admit. The naturalist is not, as he supposes, describing what he sees ; he is interpreting it. He is translating sensuous impressions into the language of human thought. Without this labour of the mind there would no doubt be something left, but certainly not a world. The world as known to science is an abstract view of the real or spiritual world. It is a synthesis based on the ' laws of nature,' externalised by the imagination as if they existed independently of the mind. In constructing this world, the mind deliberately inhibits all qualitative judgments, and treats reality as something measurable and ponderable. Even so, it imports a great deal which does not belong to Matter, and which is certainly not perceived by the senses. Materialism would have to commit suicide as a theory long before it came down to the atoms or electrons in motion with which it professes to deal. We shall see later that this argument by no means carries with it a distrust of the truths which natural science can teach us.

But we are still unsatisfied. The Platonic schools were not thoroughly honest in dealing with the problem of evil. Origen accuses Celsus of giving an explanation which he knows to be unsatisfactory. ' Celsus in the next place, as if he were able to tell certain secrets concerning the origin of evil, but chose rather to keep silence and say only what was suitable for the multitude, continues as follows : " It is sufficient to say to the multitude that evil does not proceed from God but cleaves to Matter and dwells among mortal things." It is true that evils do not proceed from God ; but to maintain that Matter, dwelling among mortal things, is the cause of evil is in our opinion untrue. For it is the mind of each individual which is the cause of the evil which arises in him, and this is Evil ($\tau\grave{o}$ $\kappa\alpha\kappa\acute{o}\nu$) ; the actions which proceed from it are wicked ; and strictly speaking there

is nothing else, in our view, which is evil.'[1] Origen is
not alone in bringing this charge against the Platonists
and Pythagoreans. Simplicius quotes from Eudorus :
' according to their highest teaching, we must say that
the Pythagoreans hold the One to be the principle of all
things ; according to a secondary teaching (δεύτερος
λόγος) they hold that there are two principles of created
things, the One and the nature opposed to it.'[2] After
such testimony we can hardly doubt that some at least
of the Platonists and Pythagoreans taught, as a popular
doctrine, a metaphysical dualism which they did not
believe themselves. They have paid dearly for it. I am,
however, disposed to think that this ' secondary doctrine '
was retained in popular lecturing, not so much from
want of candour (for what had they to gain by it ?) but
from reverence for Plato, who in some of his most eloquent
passages had described the heavy weight which lies
upon the Soul while it is enclosed in this muddy vesture
of decay. Philo and Plutarch are quoted as exponents
of the ' secondary doctrine.' But Philo makes it clear
that if Matter is associated with evil, it is not because it
is corporeal, but because it is a state of flux and change.[3]
This is a most important doctrine, which is the key to
much that is hard to understand in Platonism. For a
Greek, the nature of God means, specifically, immortality.
The gods are deathless and changeless ; the greatest of
evils in this world is that all things change, decay, and
die. Therefore, says Philo, it is not possible, while
dwelling in the mortal body, to have communion with
God.[4] This is why philosophers seek to die to the flesh
while they are yet alive ; their object is ' to participate
in the incorporeal and incorruptible life with him who
is unbegotten and incorruptible.'[5] The body is a dead
weight, not because it is material, but because it is perish-
able. Philo in other places teaches that the mind alone

---

[1] Origen against Celsus, Bk. 4. 66.
[2] Simplicius, *Phys.* 181.
[3] Drummond, *Philo Judaeus*, Vol. 2, p. 296 sq.
[4] Philo, *Leg. All.* 3. 14.   [5] *Gigant.* 3.

is the abode of virtue and vice ; the principle of moral evil is in the false relation which the Soul assumes to the body. False opinions (avarice, ambition, etc.) are further from Soul than the body is. The body, after all, was made by God, to manifest His glory. He also speaks of psychical but irrational Powers, which lead men to ruin. Vice is a kind of higher ignorance, the penalty of a misdirected will. Plutarch also does not really make Matter the principle of evil. ' We must conceive of Matter as having a share of the primal God, and as united to Him by love of the goodness and beauty which surround Him. Matter desires God, and is ever in His presence, and is filled with the most powerful and purest parts of Him.'[1] For him the principle of evil is not Matter, but the evil World-Soul.

These writers seem to have grasped, perhaps more closely than Plotinus himself, the truth that the Soul can fight its battles only on its own ground. Its enemies must themselves be psychic ; corporeity, as such, cannot be a real obstacle to the flight of the Soul towards God. When he says that evil is an essential property of the corporeal, and only an accidental property of the psychical,[2] he is at least liable to misinterpretation. The radical optimism of his philosophy makes him reluctant to give evil any footing within the world of reality, which is eternal ; in the flux of Matter he found a kind of symbol of reality in a state of complete disintegration. It is the symbol of the indeterminate and dark, and these qualities are evil. Whatever is material (or rather, transient and changeable), is not yet what it ought to be. It embodies the subordinate pessimism which results from a radical optimism, since each concrete fact or phenomenon is condemned by reference to a standard of perfection. We may contrast with this philosophy the attitude of writers like Robert Browning, who, being intellectually a pessimist, will not allow us to disparage the world of will and striving.

[1] Plutarch, *De Isid. et Osir*, 58.   [2] I. 8. 3.

The World of Appearance (κόσμος αἰσθητός)

'Natural phenomena,' says Berkeley in the *Siris*, an essay which illustrates several points in Plotinus, 'are only natural appearances. They are such as we perceive them—passive, fluent, changing. The mind takes her first flight and spring by resting on these objects ; and therefore they are not only first considered by all men, but most considered by most men. They and the phantoms that result from these appearances—the children of imagination grafted upon sense—are thought by many the very first in existence and reality.' When Berkeley tells us that natural phenomena *are* such as we perceive them, he means no more than Mr. Bosanquet,[1] when he says, 'Everything is real, so long as you do not take it for more than it is.' The world of appearance may be regarded *either* as the real, the spiritual world, dimly seen by an imperfect instrument and through a distorting medium, *or* as an actual but imperfect copy of the perfect archetype. The real-idealism of Plotinus holds these two views together. An imperfect world and an imperfect vision of the world reciprocally imply each other. 'A feeble contemplation makes a feeble object of contemplation.'[2] The world of appearance differs from its archetype in presenting us with a diversity which exists by the side of unity, unreconciled by it (ἓν καὶ πολλά), instead of the complex or concrete unity (πλῆθος ἕν) of Spirit ; with mutual exclusion as the mark of differentiation, instead of the mutual inclusion or compenetration which exists in the spiritual world ; with strife and opposition in the place of harmony ;[3] with time in the place of eternity ; with perpetual flux and change in the place of the unchanging activity of Spirit.

---

[1] Bosanquet, *Principle of Individuality and Value*, p. 240.
[2] 3. 8. 4.
[3] 3. 2. 3 ; and especially 6. 3. 2, where the contrast between real being and ἡ ἐνταῦθα ὁμώνυμος οὐσία is drawn out in detail.

Although reality is not, as Aristotle thought, a mixture
of Form and Matter, these ingredients may be said to
constitute what we erroneously call the reality (ἡ ὁμώνυμος
οὐσία) of the world of appearance. 'Quality' is the
manner in which reality plays upon the surface of things.[1]
It is that which affirms itself as the attribute of a subject
other than itself. It is only an appearance of reality,
which is itself independent and non-contingent. Thus
Plotinus seeks to overcome not only Stoic and Epicurean
naturalism, but Aristotelian pluralism. The Form (εἶδος)
in 'sensible reality' (αἰσθητὴ οὐσία) is without activity
and therefore unreal; and its Matter too is unreal.
'Sensible reality' is at best only a sharer in true reality.[2]
The sensible world is a reflexion of the spiritual world in
the mirror of Matter.[3]

The knowledge which we have of this half-real world
is a kind of half-knowledge. Plotinus calls it opinion
(δόξα), following Plato. Opinion is abstract or unsystematised knowledge of the sensible world. As Aristotle
says, it accompanies sensation or comes from sensation.[4]

Modern science is well aware that the world with
which it deals is a mental construction from very imperfect knowledge. The visible spectrum occupies only $\frac{1}{27}$
of the known range of ethereal vibrations. We only see
that small fraction of the colours which eyes differently
constructed might see. The same is true of sound. We
hear over a range of about eleven octaves, but physicists
assure us that there must be thousands of octaves.[5] Our
mental picture of the world is like that which would be
conveyed to an audience by a musician who played on
a piano, of which all but half a dozen notes were dumb.
If that audience got any notion of a tune, the tune would
be largely the work of their own imagination, and would

[1] 2. 6. 1–3.   [2] 6. 3. ; 6. 8.
[3] Outward perception (ἡ αἴσθησις ἡ ἔξω) is only an image of the
perception proper to the Soul. The Soul does not perceive τὰ αἰσθητά,
but their forms, which are ἤδη νοητά. In contemplating these forms,
the Soul exercises διανοίαι, δόξαι, νοήσεις, ἔνθα δὴ ἡμεῖς μάλιστα.
[4] Aristotle, De Anima, 3. 3.
[5] Simpson, The Spiritual Interpretation of Nature, p. 17.

be very unlike the tune composed by Mozart or Beethoven. In these circumstances, science aims at consistency rather than completeness.

Nature (φύσις)

The conception of Nature which has come down to us from Greek philosophy has had such an important influence upon human thought down to the present time that a few preliminary remarks upon the use of the term before Plotinus will not be out of place. The early cosmologists made ' Nature ' the object of their speculations, and by Nature they meant the primary substance—that which Aristotle called ἀρχή. If we ask how they came to apply a word which means ' growth '[1] to the first principle of the universe, the answer is not easy to find. They all, including Thales, held that in some sense ' the All has Soul.' The gods were the departmental powers who were in charge of the elements. According to Herodotus,[2] they only acquired names and personal attributes by degrees. Behind the gods was Moira—impersonal and unalterable Law. The philosophers tended to exalt Moira and to disregard the personal gods—in other words they favoured naturalism against supernaturalism. But they were far from regarding the Law of Nature as non-moral. In all early societies the customary *is* the moral. There was, for these early thinkers, a complete solidarity between the sacred traditions of human society and the order of the world generally. The ' Nature ' which is the sanction of both alike is a metaphysical entity, a substance which is also Soul and God. The Milesians no doubt tended to think of this living substance as a subtle and attenuated Matter—a kind of

---

[1] We must remember that the Atomists called the atoms φύσις ; the word does not seem to have suggested to them the idea of ' growth.' Burnet, *Greek Philosophy*, p. 27.

[2] Herodotus, 2. 52.

materialism which has proved very hard to kill. But Aristotle seems to have overemphasised this side of Ionian thought. Nature, we must remember, was 'alive' and 'full of gods.' The Ionians regarded Nature as Soul-substance even when they identified it with one or other of the 'four elements.'

But as soon as the Greeks began to treat natural science as a special study,[1] the old hylozoism fell to pieces. The religious and metaphysical elements[2] in the idea of Nature were allowed to fade, and a picture of the world was constructed which showed only Space filled by Matter, or, as Leucippus was the first to teach, Matter and a Vacuum. The only divine attribute which was left to Nature was unchangeableness; the only vital attribute was motion in Space. Thus arose the philosophy of the Atomists. Empedocles has not reached the Atomist position. He denies that there is such a principle as Nature ($\phi\acute{v}\sigma\iota\varsigma$); there is, he says, only a continual aggregation and dissolution of compounds, and this is what men call Nature. But though he thus strips Nature of creative activity, he ascribes a kind of vital force to his two principles of Love and Strife, which 'make the world go round' by their interplay of attraction and repulsion. Anaxagoras is still more emphatic in denying that there is any *évolution créatrice* at work in the world. With Leucippus and Democritus we come to real Atomism, and Nature as an intelligent principle disappears. Thus the scientific and the spiritualistic tendencies in Greek thought fell completely apart. The mystics emphasised the community of life in all Nature, and sometimes, like the Indians, condemned the taking of animal life for food, on this ground. Heracleitus identifies Nature with justice, law, and reason, and bids

[1] Burnet has shown that the Ionian $\phi\nu\sigma\iota\kappa\acute{o}\iota$ were real men of science, and that their errors were due rather to scantiness of data than to false method.

[2] We must however remember, in the case of the early philosophers whose works are lost, that the Greeks had an inveterate tendency to read later ideas into writings of the 'blessed ancients.'

us remember that it admits of no 'private interpretation,' but is the source of true wisdom for all alike.   But it is not till later that we find the fruitful conception that the life of Nature is essentially an *aspiration* towards higher forms of activity, an upward striving, a doctrine which dominates all the thought of Plotinus on this subject.

In the Enneads the sensible world is the creation of the Universal Soul, through the medium of Nature which is its moving power.   Nature is the active faculty of the World-Soul, its outer life, the expansion of its energy, that without which it would be shut up in itself, mute and inactive.   On the other hand Nature is the activity of Matter ; it is that which, added to Matter, gives it its substantiality, and without which Matter is a mere abstraction or nonentity.   Nature is ' a sleeping Spirit ' (*ein schlafender Geist*), as Schelling says.   It is the lowest of the spiritual existences.[1]   All its activity comes from Soul ; it is itself unconscious, but casts upon Matter a reflexion of the forms which it has received from above. Thus Plotinus concedes reality or spiritual existence to ' Nature,' though not to the material bodies which receive, through Nature, the impressions of the World-Soul.   ' All that is below Nature is but a copy of reality.' The four elements are said to be the direct product of Nature.   The thoughts of the Soul are not ideas but creative powers (λόγοι).   These λόγοι, however, are traced back directly to Spirit.   ' Spirit,' he says,[2] ' giving part of itself to Matter, made all things, remaining itself in peace and at rest ; this is the creative power that flows out of Spirit.   That which flows out of Spirit is creative power, and it flows continually, as long as Spirit is present in real existences ' (i.e. until we reach the limit which divides real existence from appearance).   This λόγος is elsewhere defined as ' neither spiritual percep-

---

[1] 4. 4. 13. Nature is θεωρία, θεώρημα, and λόγος ; and its εἶναι is ποιεῖν. It is a ψυχή, γέννημα ψυχῆς προτέρας δυνατώτερον ζώσης . . . ἡσυχῇ ἐν ἑαυτῇ θεωρίαν ἔχουσα οὐ πρὸς τὸ ἄνω οὐδ' αὖ πρὸς τὸ κάτω. 3. 8. 4.
[2] 3. 2. 2,

tion nor vision, but a power that acts upon Matter, not knowing but only doing.'[1] It is very difficult to find an English equivalent for λόγος. Sometimes ' creative power ' conveys the sense, sometimes one is tempted to translate it by ' reason ' or ' meaning.' It is that which, proceeding from Spirit, either directly or through the medium of the World-Soul, and identical in its nature with Soul,[2] conveys the energy of Spirit and Soul into Matter. And that which proceeds from Soul to irradiate Matter is Nature.[3]

But the most illuminating passage on Nature is in the eighth book of the Third Ennead, which is one of the finest and most characteristic parts of the whole work. I give it *in extenso*.

' If, before embarking on the serious discussion of Nature, we were to say, speaking lightly, that all living beings, not only rational but irrational, and all vegetables and the earth which produces them, aspire to contemplation and look to this end, and attain to it as far as in them lies; and that some of them arrive truly at contemplation, while others achieve only a reflexion and image of it, would anyone accept so parodoxical a statement ? But now that we are discussing the matter among ourselves,[4] there is no objection to our maintaining this paradox in play. Are not we ourselves contemplating while thus playing ? And not ourselves only, but all who play, are not they doing the same and aspiring to contemplation ? One might say that the child at play, as well as the man in earnest, has the same end, to arrive at contemplation ;[5] and that all action earnestly aims

---

[1] 2. 3. 17. Cf. too ἀρχὴ οὖν λόγος καὶ παντα λόγος. 3. 2. 15; and even ὁ τοῦ παντὸς νόμος. 3. 2. 4.

[2] οἱ λόγοι πάντες ψυχαί. 3. 2. 18.

[3] 2. 3. 17.

[4] This passage shows that we have Plotinus' lecture-notes rather than a work written for publication.

[5] Compare Findlay, *The School*, p. 85. ' To play is to image an activity and act out the image, instead of merely displaying immediate impulse in response to stimulus. . . . All the child's actions are directed to the learning of facts, to a better estimate of values, and play is the process by which he attempts to relate these to himself.'

at contemplation. Necessary action turns contemplation chiefly towards external things; that which is called free does this less, but itself too exists through desire of contemplation. But we will deal with this subject later. Let us begin by explaining what kind of contemplation may be attributed to the earth, to trees and plants, and how we can ascribe the products and progeny of the earth to the activity of contemplation; how, in a word, Nature, which is regarded as void of reason and imagination, has a power of contemplation in itself and produces all its works in virtue of a power of contemplation which, strictly speaking, it does not possess.

'Nature evidently has neither feet nor hands, nor any artificial or natural instrument. It only needs Matter, on which it works, and to which it gives a Form. The works of Nature are not produced by any mechanical operation. It is not by impulsion, nor by levers and machines that it produces the various colours and forms of objects. Even workers in wax, whose mode of working is often compared with that of Nature, can only give to the objects which they make colours which they bring from elsewhere. We must also remark that these craftsmen have in them a power which remains unmoved, in virtue of which alone they manufacture their works. In the same way there is in Nature a power which remains unmoved, but needs no assistance of hands. This power remains entirely unmoved; it does not need some parts which move and others which do not move. Matter alone is moved; the formative power does not move at all. If the formative power were moved, it would not be the first mover; the first mover would then not be Nature, but that which would be immovable in the whole. No doubt, it may be said, the seminal Reason[1] is immovable; but Nature is distinct from Reason, and does move. But if we speak of Nature in its entirety, we include Reason.

[1] λόγοι σπερματικοί. This famous Stoical term is defined by Marcus Aurelius (9. 1) as 'certain germs of future existences, endowed with productive capacities of realisation, change, and phenomenal succession.' See Davidson, *The Stoic Creed*, p. 88.

If any part of it is immovable, that part will be Reason. Nature must be a form, not a composite of matter and form. . . . In animals and plants, it is the Reasons which produce; Nature is a Reason which produces another Reason, which is its offspring and that on which it works, while remaining itself. The Reason which consists in the visible form holds the last rank; it is dead and cannot produce yet another Reason. The living Reason, being brother of the Reason which produced the visible form, and possessing the same form as that Reason, produces alone in the created being.

' How then can Nature produce, and, so producing, to what contemplation can it attain ? Since it produces while remaining immovable in itself, and is a Reason, it must itself be a contemplation. Every action is produced according to a Reason, and in consequence differs from it. Reason assists and presides over action, and in consequence is not itself action. Since then it is not action, it must be contemplation. In every chain of reasoning, the last link proceeds from contemplation, and is contemplation in the sense that it has been contemplated. As for the previous link, this may be not Nature but Soul, or again it may be in Nature and be Nature.

' Does Reason considered as Nature proceed from contemplation ? Certainly ; but has it not also contemplated itself ? For it is the product of contemplation and of a contemplator. How does it contemplate itself ? It has not that kind of contemplation which comes from discursive consideration of what one has. How comes it that being a living Reason, a productive power, it does not consider what it has in itself ? It is that one only so considers what one has not got yet. Now, as Nature does possess, it produces because it possesses. To be what it is and to produce what it produces are for Nature the same thing. It is contemplation and the object contemplated because it is Reason. Being contemplation, the object contemplated, and Reason, it produces in virtue of being these things. Production then has been proved to be contemplation ; for it is the result of the contemplation, which remains unmovable, which does nothing but contemplate, and which produces in virtue of being contemplation.

' If anyone were to demand of Nature why it produces, it would answer, if it were willing to listen and speak : " You should not ask questions, but understand, keeping silence as I keep silence ; for I am not in the habit of talking.[1] What ought you to understand ? In the first place, that which is produced is the work of my silent contemplation, a contemplation produced by my nature ; for being born myself of contemplation, I am naturally contemplative ; and that which contemplates in me produces an object of contemplation, as geometers describe figures while contemplating. I, however, do not describe figures, but while I contemplate I let fall, as it were, the lines which mark the forms of bodies. I preserve the disposition of my mother and of the principles which produced me.[2] These too were born of contemplation ; and I was born in the same way. They produced me without acting, by virtue of being more potent reasons and contemplating themselves." What do these words mean ? That Nature is a Soul engendered by a superior Soul which possesses a more powerful life, and that its silent contemplation is contained in itself, without inclining either to what is above or to what is beneath itself. Remaining in its essence, in its own stability and self-consciousness, it beheld, by this understanding and self-consciousness, that which is below itself, so far as this is possible, and without seeking further produced a brilliant and pleasing object of contemplation. And if anyone wishes to attribute to Nature a kind of understanding or sensation, these will only resemble the knowledge and sensation which we attribute to other things

---

[1] So Walt Whitman says, ' The elemental laws never apologise.' George Meredith frequently inculcates the same lesson in his poems. And compare the fine line :

ἄπαντα σιγῶν ὁ θεὸς ἐξεργάζεται.

[2] These are the Universal Soul and the creative Logoi

as those of a man asleep resemble those of a man awake.[1]
For Nature contemplates its object peaceably, an object
born of itself from the fact of its abiding in and with itself,
and of its being itself an object of contemplation—a contemplation silent, but feeble. For there is another power
which contemplates more clearly ; Nature is only the
image of a higher contemplation. For this reason that
which it produces is altogether weak, because a weak
contemplation engenders a weak object. So there are
men who are too feeble for contemplation, and who find
in action a shadow of contemplation and Reason. Being
unable to raise themselves to contemplation, from the
weakness of their Soul, unable to behold spiritual reality
and fill themselves with it, but desiring to see it. they are
driven to action, that they may see that which they could
not see with the spiritual eye.[2] Thus, when men act,
they wish to see reality themselves, and they wish others
also to contemplate and perceive it, when their object is,
as far as possible, expressed in action. We shall everywhere find production and action to be either a weakness
of contemplation or an accompaniment of it ; a weakness, if, after having acted, we have nothing further ;
an accompaniment, if after the action we can contemplate
something better than what we have produced.[3] Who that
is able to contemplate the reality would prefer to go to the
image of the real ? A proof is afforded by the fact that
the less intelligent children, who are incapable of theoretic
knowledge, turn to the practice of manual crafts.'[4]

[1] ' Sensation,' he says elsewhere (3. 6. 6), ' is the dream of the soul.'
When the soul awakes, it separates itself from the body.
[2] For the majority of mankind the way to spiritual vision lies
through outward activity, undertaken without any clear perception
of the spiritual principles which are implied by it. The spiritually
enlightened man is not less active, but his activity flows almost
unconsciously from his ' contemplation.' Cf. 1. 5. 10.
[3] This seems to be quite true. A product of human labour, in
which the spirit and intellect have no share, is a pale copy of reality ;
while a work of genius appears to be thrown off from the mental and
spiritual life of its author, rather than to be the direct object of his
deliberate activity.
[4] This disparagement of skilled handicraft is a well-known weakness
not only of Platonism, but of Greek thought generally.

Plotinus proceeds to show how contemplation is the source of life in the higher regions of Soul and Spirit. 'All life,' he says, 'is a kind of spiritual vision.'[1] He affects to speak in jest about the contemplative aspirations of the lower kinds of life ; but he is really in earnest. Aristotle (more definitely than Plato) had expressed the same opinion. Every natural thing, he holds, in its own way longs for the Divine and desires to share in the Divine life as far as it can.[2] ' The Good moves the whole world because it is loved.' This is to admit a principle of movement and progress in Nature.[3] Wordsworth too cherished the ' faith that every flower enjoys the air it breathes.' There is an unbroken chain from the highest order of creation to the lowest. Soul, in the very act of turning towards the source of its own life, creates a fainter image of that life—a grade inferior to its own, but a true if indistinct copy of the radiant existences in which God beholds His own glory. Thus the natural world, which we see with our eyes, is spiritual throughout and instinct with life, though its life may seem to sleep, and though its spiritual characters are faint and hard to trace. In looking for them, we make as well as find them.[4] The Soul that understands Nature is continuous and homogeneous with the Soul that creates it. And we understand Nature best by looking above what is merely presented to our senses. We are to do what, in fact, both men of science and poets do, in their different ways. We are to seek for the vital laws, the λόγοι, which give a meaning to phenomena. These laws may be scientific, or æsthetic, or moral. In each case it is by studying them that we understand the place which particular phenomena hold in the whole economy. The downward look which Plotinus deprecates is not the

[1] 3. 8. 8.   [2] De Anima, 2. 4. 415 ; Metaph. 10.
[3] Cf. Miss Stawell's Essay in Marvin, Progress and History, p. 58.
[4] Professor A. E. Taylor (Elements of Metaphysics, p. 242) argues cogently that the Kantian distinction between what is ' given ' and ' the work of the mind,' is untenable. No such dualism is to be found in Plotinus.

I.—M

reverent and intelligent scrutiny of the scientist, the
artist, or the poet ; but interest in sensuous particulars
for their own sake, as vehicles of voluptuous sensation
or animal gratification.

Nature is the rational and therefore unvarying expression of a perfect intelligence.[1] Footprints (ἴχνη) of the
Universal Soul can be traced in bodies.[2] It follows that
the scientific view of the world is reality, not merely
appearance. Only we must not make the mistake of
supposing that the phenomenal world is real apart from
the Soul that perceives it, or that the Soul registers
passively a kingdom of facts external to itself. The
world of the scientist is demonstrably spiritual, not
material. What is real in it is not the aggregation of
ponderable matter, but the laws which Soul both makes
and finds there.

Natural science limits itself to the relations of visible
and ponderable things, interpreted by Soul. It endeavours
to understand the ' order and limitation ' (τάξις and
πέρας) which the World-Soul has impressed on the
spatial and temporal world. But for Plotinus it is inconceivable that the laws of Nature should be alien or
contrary to the laws of Spirit. They ' imitate ' them, and
express them in their own way. As Malebranche says :
' Il n'y a pas d'autre nature, je veux dire d'autres lois
naturelles, que les volontés efficaces du tout-puissant.'[3]

Extension

The ground-form of all appearance is Extension (τόπος).
Extension is the necessary form which results from the
inability of Matter to receive all forms without dividing
and separating them.[4] Mutual externality is the condition of things in the world of sense, as mutual inclusion
on compenetration is the character of the spiritual world.

[1] Whittaker, *The Neoplatonists*, p. 91.   [2] 2. 3. 9.
[3] Quoted by Ward, *The Realm of Ends*, p. 251.
[4] 3. 6. 18 ; 4. 2. 1.

Space implies limit (πέρας) ; the purely indeterminate and infinite (ἄπειρον) is spaceless ; extension is given to it by Soul.

There is no such thing as empty space. This is also the doctrine of Leibnitz, who says, ' If there were no creatures, there would be neither time nor place, and in consequence no actual space.'[1] We must remember that empty space is not the same as physical vacuum. What physicists call a vacuum is simply a space in which there is no matter of the kind with which they are dealing. Strictly, I suppose, there is no such thing as a real vacuum in nature ; the hypothetical ether, whatever properties it may possess or lack, must in some sort fill space. But ' empty space,' regarded as a blank sheet on which forms may be subsequently drawn, seems to be an illusion arising from the abstract conception of objects as differentiated only by local position [2]

If Space were real, externality would be an ultimate fact, for space is the form of externality.[3] Also, objects in a real space would be unrelated to each other, for they could not affect each other internally without overlapping. Two parts of one space cannot penetrate each other.[4] But in reality there are no merely external relations. ' The merely external is our ignorance set up as reality.'[5] In the spiritual world, which is the fully real world, there are no spatial partitions, and no obstacles to the free intermingling of existences which are inwardly in harmony with each other.

The space which we think of as containing the physical order is conceptual, not perceptual ; and so are all divisions of space, which, as Plotinus would say, are ' limits ' imposed on matter by Soul. Perceptual space is continuous. Even percepts of space are never merely quanti-

[1] *Letters to Clarke*, III.
[2] Taylor, *Elements of Metaphysics*, p. 249.
[3] 4. 2. 1.
[4] On this difficult point, cf. Bradley, *Appearance and Reality*, pp. 288–9.
[5] Bradley, p. 577.

tative, since they involve form, which is qualitative. And it is probable that our perceptions of space are always determined by reference to our own spatial position. The above statements apply also, *mutatis mutandis*, to time. That neither can be more than an appearance of reality is argued with great force by Professor Taylor, in the following paragraph.[1]

' An all-comprehensive experience cannot apprehend the detail of existence under the forms of space and time for the following reason. Such an experience could be neither of space and time as we perceive them, nor of space and time as we conceptually reconstruct them. It would not be of perceptual space and time, because the whole character of our perceptual space and time depends upon the very imperfections and limitations which make our experience fragmentary and imperfect. Perceptual space and time are for me what they are, because I see them, so to say, in perspective from the special standpoint of my own particular *here* and *now*. If that standpoint were altered, my whole outlook on the space and time order would suffer change. But the Absolute cannot look at the space and time order from the standpoint of my *here* and *now*. For it is the finitude of my interests and purposes which confine me in my outlook to this *here* and *now*. If my interests . . . were coextensive with the life of the whole, every place and every time would be my *here* and *now*. . . . Hence the absolute experience, being free from the limitations of interest which condition the finite experiences, cannot see the order of existence from the special standpoint of any of them, and therefore cannot apprehend it under the guise of the perceptual space and time system.

' Again, it cannot apprehend existence under the forms of space and time as we conceptually reconstruct them. For reality, for the absolute experience, must

---

[1] *Elements of Metaphysics*, p. 254–5. I am not sure that the distinction between perceptual and conceptual Space is not over-emphasised in the passage quoted.

be a complete individual whole, with the ground of all
its differentiations within itself. But conceptual space
and time are constructed by deliberate abstraction from
the relation to immediate experience implied in all
individuality, and consequently they contain no real
principle of internal distinction, their constituent terms
being all exactly alike and indistinguishable. In short,
if the perceptual time and place systems of our concrete
experience represent individual but imperfect and finite
points of view, the conceptual space and time of our
scientific construction represents the mere abstract
possibility of a finite point of view ; neither gives a
point of view both individual and infinite, and neither
therefore can be the point of view of an infinite experience.
An absolute experience must be out of time and out
of space, in the sense that its contents are not apprehended in the form of the spatial and temporal series,
but in some other way. Space and time then must be
the phenomenal appearance of a higher reality which is
spaceless and timeless.'

This argument, which could not be shortened, belongs
to a maturer stage of metaphysical analysis than the
Enneads of Plotinus. But the conclusion at any rate is
the same. Space is only appearance. But of *what* is it
the appearance ? Kant, as is well known, taught that
Space is only a form of perception, and added that
there can be no comparison between the space-world
and the world of real existence. The latter statement
does not follow from the former, and Plotinus would not
have accepted it. Forms must be suitable to that which
they represent. It is reasonable to suppose that there
are real relations between things, which are reflected in
corresponding forms of spatial relation. The belief that
' the invisible things of God are clearly seen, being understood by the things that are made,' is fundamental for
Platonism. What then are the ideas which we learn from
our experience of Space ? Leibnitz was no doubt right
in calling it ' an order of coexistence.' But this does

not exhaust the idea of Space. It is also the form by which we recognise the relations of whole and part, and of near and far. The former of these, which shows us ' wheels within wheels,' is as important as coexistence, and without Space we could not conceive of this relation. Further, the incompenetrability of objects in space must stand for something in the real world, though it does not hold good for spiritual existences. It is mainly Space, perhaps, which assures us of our individuality. Again, we can hardly draw comparisons without using spatial images. All plurality must be distributed in Space, all unity must be fenced off by boundary-lines, if we wish to make unity and plurality clear to the mind. Words like ' content,' and many others, show how little we can dispense with spatial images, which, as Bergson has shown, unconsciously mould our thought about Time also.

The external world, as viewed spatially, has much to teach us about ultimate truth. Plotinus insists especially on the attributes of order and limitation ($\tau \acute{\alpha} \xi \iota s$ and $\pi \acute{\epsilon} \rho \alpha s$) which the observation of Nature proves to be products of the Divine mind. Modern science has added the wondrous contrast of the immeasurably great and the immeasurably small, and by proving the immense prodigality of nature in achieving her ends has perhaps given an indication which may help us in dealing with the problem of evil—namely, that the Creator, having all infinity and all eternity to work in, may be as prodigal of values as He is of existences. Plotinus is also too good a Platonist to disparage the reflexions of the Divine beauty which we find in the visible world. His quarrel with the Gnostics is mainly on this ground. They see no value in the beautiful world, forgetting that the Soul beholds genuine reflexions of Spirit in Nature. The world which they ignorantly despise is created by Soul after the pattern of Spirit ; in the mirror of Matter it reflects the realities of the eternal world. ' All things that are Yonder are also Here.'

Spatial ideas, as Höffding says,[1] are our clearest ideas. But they are also our poorest ideas. The narrow frame in which primitive religious thought sets the world-picture ensures clearness and definiteness. But with the advance of culture there is a growing dislike to give the Deity a local habitation. 'However short the distance between heaven and earth is conceived to be, it is all too wide for religious needs. The Deity must stand in a far closer relation to man than is consistent with localisation in a particular place.'[2] When once the idea of the omnipresence of God has begun to occupy men's thoughts, it becomes apparent that expressions like 'higher' and 'lower,' 'here' and 'yonder' have only a metaphorical meaning. Plato clearly sees that we are no nearer heaven by gazing at the sky. 'Those who elevate astronomy into philosophy,' Socrates says, 'appear to me to make us look downwards rather than upwards. In my opinion, that knowledge only which is of Being and the unseen can make a soul look upwards, and whether a man gapes at the heavens or blinks on the ground, seeking to learn some particular of sense, I would deny that he can learn, since nothing of that kind is matter of science ; his soul is looking downwards, not upwards, whether his way to knowledge is by water or by land, whether he floats or lies on his back.'[3] Thus philosophy in the fourth century before Christ had already condemned the popular religious picture of the world as a building in three storeys. But the clearness and definiteness of the old picture

---

[1] Höffding, *Philosophy of Religion*, p. 42 sq. I should rather say that they provide our clearest images.

[2] *Id.*, p. 44.

[3] Plato, *Republic*, Bk. VII. p. 529. There is a good parallel in the charming little book called *The Cloud of Unknowing*, a medieval mystical treatise (pp. 265, 268). 'Time, place, and body—these three should be forgotten in all ghostly working. And therefore be wary in this work, that thou take none ensample at the bodily ascension of Christ for to strain thine imagination in the time of thy prayer bodily upwards as thou wouldest climb above the moon. For it should on nowise be so, ghostly. . . . For heaven ghostly is as nigh down as up, and up as down, behind as before, before as behind, on one side as another. Inasmuch that whoso had a true desire to be in heaven, then that same time he were in heaven ghostly.'

gave it a high religious value, and in the early Church there was a reaction towards the idea of a spatial heaven, the residence of God. How far the popular Christian theology is still shaped by this picture, is obvious to all. Augustine regarded it as a happy discovery (which he learned from the Platonists) that he could be a Christian without believing in a local heaven and a material God. The Christian God, he had now learned, is *ubique totus, et nusquam locorum.* The scholastic mystics taught that the Deity has his centre everywhere, and his circumference nowhere. We may say that for Christian philosophy, Space was excluded from the spiritual world long before the downfall of the geocentric cosmology.[1] But popular religion is still almost as naïvely realistic as it was in antiquity, and spatial pictures, as the clearest of our images, hold their own against both philosophy and science, especially in the domain of eschatology. For Plotinus, they have comparatively small value. ' Space,' he says, ' is *after* everything else '[2]—the lowest rung of the ladder. It is inferior to Time; for while Space furnishes the stage and scenery of the world-drama, Time gives us the play itself.[3]

[1] Lossky, a modern Neoplatonist, does not exclude the idea of a νοητὸς τόπος, but says, ' the space which is characteristic of the Kingdom of the Spirit has an infinite number of dimensions (*The World as an Organic Whole*, p. 92). Plotinus (5. 9. 10) says, ὁ δὲ τόπος ἐκεῖ νοερῶς τὸ ἄλλο ἐν ἄλλῳ. Space ἐκεῖ interposes no barriers to compenetration.   [2] 6. 8. 11.

[3] Before leaving the Neoplatonic doctrine of Space, it is necessary to say something about a characteristic theory of Malebranche, who in all his speculation shows a strong sympathy with the philosophy of Plotinus. In his earlier writings, Malebranche speaks of the Ideas as existing in the mind of God, but he develops the theory of *intelligible extension* (étendue intelligible). ' God sees in himself the intelligible extension, the archetype of matter out of which the world is formed and in which our bodies dwell ' (*Entretiens*, 1). Intelligible extension contains in itself potentially all intelligible figures, thus rendering (e.g.) geometry possible. It does not move, but gives us the idea of movement. Malebranche's doctrine of creation (as the result of the will or character of God, not as part of his essence) is very similar to that of Plotinus, and so is his doctrine of the relation of our world to the real or spiritual world. Material extension is to the immensity of God as time to eternity. But intelligible extension is not the same as immensity; it is rather the idea or archetype of distinct and locally separate forms. But Malebranche appears to me to err in making the

Time

Plotinus is well aware that the problem of Time is one of the hardest in metaphysics. In the long chapter [1] devoted to it he approaches it with diffidence, and does not claim to throw any new light upon it. ' Some of the blessed ancients must have found the truth. It is enough for us to select the wisest of their opinions and try to understand it.' We have, no doubt, an instinctive notion of Time, but when we analyse it more closely, we are in difficulties. [2]

Time is, as Plato [3] says, the moving image of Eternity, which it resembles as much as it can. Eternity is the sphere of Spirit, and Time is the sphere of Soul. But we must not, with some of the Pythagoreans, identify Eternity with the spiritual world, and Time with the phenomenal world. For the spiritual world contains particular things as parts of itself, while Eternity contains them as an unified whole—it contains them as they are *sub specie aeternitatis*. Eternity is the atmosphere in which spiritual existences live. As for the phenomenal world, ' things that are born are nothing without their future.' [4] It is their nature and the condition of their existence to be always ' making acquisitions.' Each individual life in this world would be truncated and shorn of its meaning if taken, by abstraction, out of the temporal sequence in which it lives. To talk of ' living in

Idea of extension itself extended ; at least he gave his opponent Arnauld a handle for accusing him of making God corporeal. Malebranche was, in intention at least, far removed from Spinoza; but his critics here accuse him of Spinozism. There can in reality be no spiritual extension any more than spiritual time. Plotinus discusses this question in the sixth book of the Third Ennead. The ' appearance of greatness ' in visible things is a reflexion of real greatness ; but the word ' great ' is used in two senses, since there is no extension in the world of Spirit. I am not sure that Malebranche would have denied this ; he has been much misunderstood by writers who have not read Plotinus.   [1] 3. 7.

[2] So Augustine, *Confessions*, xi. 14, says : ' Quid est tempus ? Si nemo a me quærat, scio ; si quærenti explicare velim, nescio.'

[3] *Timaeus*, 37.

[4] 3. 7. 4.

the present' is, on the plane of ordinary experience, an absurdity. The present is an unextended point, and therefore reality, on this theory, consists of two parts, the past and the future, neither of which is real. Things that are born yearn to continue in existence, because perpetuity is the symbol and copy of the permanence of Eternity, and the effort to make perpetual progress is the symbol and copy of the perfection of Eternity.[1] In the eternal world, on the contrary, there is no future or past. Activity there is ; but if it were possible to take a section of eternal life, as we attempt to do for this life when we separate 'the present' from the past and the future, the section would exhibit all the perfection of the whole. The form of existence in the world of Time is succession (τὸ ἄλλο μετ' ἄλλο) ; the stages follow each other. But in Eternity the whole is in each part ; all is present together in its realised meaning and achieved perfection. Will is not destroyed, nor activity paralysed ; but will and satisfaction, activity and rest, are taken up into a higher unity.

The views of the Stoics and other schools about the nature of Time are found to be erroneous. The Stoics identified Time with motion (κίνησις). But motion is *in* Time.[2] Besides, motion can stop or be arrested, while the process of Time is constant. Lastly, there is no uniform speed of motion. If Time and motion were identical, there should be many times.

A second theory, that Time is 'that which is moved' (τὸ κινούμενον), a view attributed to Eratosthenes and Hestiæus of Perinthus, is dismissed without comment.

Is Time then one kind of motion ? It is not 'the interval of motion' (κινήσεως διάστημα, Zeno), for there is no uniformity in the 'intervals.' As before, this theory would produce 'many times.' Besides, 'interval' is a

---

[1] This does not mean that each period of Time is better, as containing higher values, than the preceding ; but only that upward striving (ἔφεσις) is a constant character of existence in Time.

[2] Cf. Augustine, *Confessions*, xi. 24.

spatial, not a temporal expression. It may be said that motion has a certain 'interval' (between the first and last stages of its subject), because it is continuous. But this only gives us, as it were, the dimensions of the motion, a quantity produced in Time itself. Movements, and their 'intervals,' are in Time; they are not to be identified with Time.

Plotinus then considers the Aristotelian definition,[1] that Time is 'the number and measure of motion.' The difficulty caused by the irregularity of motion here comes up again. If an uniform measure of Time (what Bergson calls clock-time) is used to compare swift and slow movements, we have certainly a standard of measurement, but we are no nearer to knowing what Time is in itself. Time is something else than 'the number which measures motion according to anteriority and posteriority.' Unless these last words are used in a spatial sense, which would be 'to confound Time with Space,' they only repeat the notion of Time which they were intended to explain. Moreover, Time existed before it was used to measure with; it is not merely subjective. That Time was created by the Soul is true; but not in the sense in which the words might be used by a subjective idealist. Plotinus suggests that the Aristotelians ought to have said, and probably meant, that Time is *measured by motion*; Time is the measure of motion only accidentally.[2] While addressing their own school, they have not made it clear to outsiders what they consider Time to be in itself.

Lastly, the Epicurean theory that Time is an accident (σύμπτωμα) or consequence of motion is no explanation at all.

Plotinus now comes to the constructive part of his discussion. Time is natural (φύσει); it had to be. We have already encountered this statement in our author. He wishes us to understand that there are some things

---

[1] Aristotle, *Physics*, 4, 12.
[2] κατὰ συμβεβηκός, 3. 7. 12.

in philosophy which we have to accept as given facts of experience. The intellectual speculations of the meta-physician belong to the life of Soul, not of Spirit. Things that are real to Soul are part of the atmosphere which the discursive intellect breathes. It is bound to accept them; though the contradictions which become apparent when the intellect treats them as ultimate realities are one of the means by which the Soul is forced upward to the intuitive perceptions of the spiritual life. In nothing is this more evident than in speculations about Time. The Spirit and even the Soul transcend it;[1] but we are still so much involved in it that we cannot think it away or put ourselves outside it. It is for us a necessary form of thought. Any explanation of Time in terms of dis-cursive thought must necessarily be inadequate; but the contradictions which modern thinkers have found to inhere in the notion of Time are not of a kind to condemn it as 'contrary to nature.'

Plotinus is so little troubled about the origin of Time, that he half banteringly suggests a mythological explana-tion. 'Shall we refer to the Muses?' Then he gives his own view, that 'Time, still non-existent, reposed in the bosom of Reality (ἐν τῷ ὄντι ἀνεπαύετο οὐκ ὤν), until Nature, wishing to become its own mistress and to enter into possession of itself, and to enlarge the sphere of its activities, put itself, and Time together with itself, into motion.' Thus Time, the image of Eternity, arose through the desire of the Soul of the World to exert its active powers. 'For,' says Plotinus, 'the nature of the Soul is restless; it desires always to translate what it sees in the eternal world into another form.' With this motive the Soul of the World took upon her the form of a servant and the likeness of a creature of Time, and made the creation also subject to Time in all things.[2]

---

[1] πρῶτον μὲν ἑαυτὴν ἐχρόνωσεν ἀντὶ τοῦ αἰῶνος τοῦτον ποιήσασα. ἔπειτα δὲ καὶ τῷ γενομένῳ ἔδωκε δουλεύειν χρόνῳ.   3. 7. 11.

[2] οὐδὲ αἱ ψυχαὶ ἐν χρόνῳ ἀλλὰ τὰ πάθη αὐτῶν καὶ τὰ ποιήματα. 4. 4. 15.

Time is the form which the Soul creates for itself when it desires to reproduce the eternal ideas as living and creative activities. It is ' the life of the Soul as it moves from one manifestation of life to another.'[1] Our measurements of Time had their origin in the observed sequence of day and night, which gave mankind a fixed standard by which to measure duration, and in the seasons of the year. The ' movement ' which takes place in Time is a ' copy ' of the ' first movement ' of Spirit, a transcendental form of activity without change which belongs to the eternal world. We are of course not meant to take literally the statement that there was a time when Time was not. In the vulgar sense of ' eternity,' the time-series, having no beginning and no end, is itself eternal. ' Time is the activity of an eternal Soul, not turned towards itself nor within itself, but exercised in creation and generation.'[2] It is ' the span of the life proper to the Soul; its course is composed of equal, uniform, imperceptibly progressing movements, with a continuous activity.' Thus the external life of the Universal Soul carries with it, not ' outside itself,' but as its inseparable attendant, what we may call real Time. This is uniform and steady, in correspondence with the unbroken activity of its creator. More limited activities, representing particular ideas in the Spiritual World, are spread out, in the world of Soul, over as much Time as is required for their completion. If they were not subordinate to the one all-embracing life of the Universal Soul, we might have to admit the possibility of many time-systems, determined by particular activities.

This theory of Time is interesting in itself, and has obvious points of similarity to Bergson's doctrine of *durée*, which has aroused so much interest among philosophers in our own day. Bergson's enemy is that ' false

---

[1] 3. 7. 11.
[2] 3. 7. 12. In 4. 4. 1 he says that all spiritual perception is timeless—ἄχρονος πᾶσα ἡ νόησις.

intellectualism which immobilises moving ideas into solidified concepts to play with them as counters.' By exposing the fallacy which underlies this method of thinking, he hopes that he has restored the independence of the individual and removed from the freely aspiring human will the cold hand of determinism. He proves that the mechanical theory, which is applicable to inorganic matter and its motions, does not account for the phenomena of life, still less for those of spiritual and purposive life. Psychical facts are not measurable in terms of one another. The methods of mathematics (for these are the methods of mechanical science) are not applicable to living beings. We may describe the course of organic evolution, but not explain or predict it. Bergson even denies teleology, as being 'mechanism in the reverse order'; he insists on real spontaneity and *newness* in the movements of organic life. But at this point some even of his disciples part company with him. If there is no invariable sequence and no inner teleology, what is left but chance? And what is chance but external impulsion by an unknown agent? The 'freedom' which he has vindicated turns out to be mere lawlessness. Science is reduced to playing with appearances which are not even appearances of reality. Reality seems to be wild movement, with nothing to move.

For Bergson, according to his ablest English interpreter, Mr. Wildon Carr, there is no unique sense in which events at different places are simultaneous. This seems to me to be destructive of the idea of Time. Nor can I agree, any more than Plotinus would have agreed, that 'we are within a movement.' If we were, we could not know that we were moving, and for all practical purposes we should not be moving, just as for almost all practical purposes we may think of the earth as stationary. Bergson is also determined to make Time a spiritual reality, while spatial dimension is only 'material.' The body, says Mr. Carr in a striking sentence, is continuous with an infinite present, the mind with an infinite past. But the truth surely is that Time should be regarded as one of the ' dimensions ' in which the Soul pursues its activities.[1] I can see no warrant for degrading one and exalting the other. Nor can I see why the mind is continuous with an infinite past, but apparently not with an infinite future. The future appears to be non-existent for Bergson, though the past exists. He seems to give us an infinite snipped off at one end.

Bergson's most original contribution to philosophy lies in his attempt to connect mechanical and psychical laws with our notions of Space and Time respectively. Our experience of Time he calls *la durée*, a word which has no exact equivalent in English. The characteristic of this experience is that there is no bare repetition, and no summation of discrete moments ; but the past flows on into the present, and modifies it. This interpenetration is one-sided ; the future does not affect the present ; therefore, he says, the process is irreversible, and Time, or *la durée*, must be real. In biology, on the other hand, and in the inorganic sciences, where all so-called changes are explicable in purely quantitative terms, every series is theoretically reversible, since the later stages contain nothing which was not implicit in the earlier. If this were the true character of all changes in the universe, Time would be of no more account in philosophy than it is in mathematics, a science in which duration is wholly

---

[1] So Münsterberg says : ' Things have their space-shape, but are not parts of one space ; they have their time-shape, but do not lie in time.' The idea of Time as a dimension is ingeniously worked out by H. G. Wells in his *Time-Machine*. As to the relations of Time and Space to each other, Schopenhauer says that it is the *union* of Time and Space which constitutes the essence of Matter, which is *action*. Space and Time reciprocally limit each other. Coexistence requires both. Matter, for Schopenhauer, is the possibility of coexistence. The conception of Time as a dimension enters deeply into the mathematical discoveries of Einstein. I much regret that I am incompetent to give an intelligent summary of this most difficult theory, which may or may not prove to have a metaphysical as well as a physical significance. So far as I understand it, it does not seem necessarily to clash with the view of Time held by Plotinus.

disregarded. 'Scientific thinking,' in Bergson's sense,
also eliminates all qualitative estimates and all valuation.
The misapplication of ' scientific thinking ' in this limited
sense (it would be better to call it the mechanical theory)
to psychical experience is largely due, Bergson thinks, to
that ' confusion of Space with Time ' of which we have
found Plotinus complaining. The characteristic of Space
is that it can be subdivided indefinitely, while Time, as
we experience it (though not as we measure it) cannot be
counted or split up. It is like a tune, which loses its
existence as a tune if the notes are taken out and considered separately.[1] Space, for Bergson, is the mere form
of homogeneity, and he differs from Plotinus in making
Space prior to the objects which it contains. This notion
of Space is connected with what we may venture to think
a very vulnerable spot in Bergson's philosophy. He sets
Space and Time too dualistically over against each other,
and forgets that there can be no perception of the purely
homogeneous. Qualitative difference is perceived in any
spatial perception ; and *par revanche*, there can be no
experience of pure heterogeneity ; the changing is only
known, as changing, in relation to an assumed permanent
substance. Bergson, like Leibnitz, impoverishes the content of spatial experience too much. Space is not merely
the form of coexistence, which indeed can be conceived,
though not pictured, non-spatially. Time teaches the
same lesson under a different form. Space and Time for-
bid us to shut ourselves up within ourselves. We know,
if the witness of our consciousness is worth anything,
that they are not the work of our own minds. They are
real over against the psychical consciousness ; real,
Plotinus would say, for the individual Soul exercising its
normal activities. To the Universal Soul they are a
kind of ' Matter,' the field of its external activity, and
they represent orderly arrangements within a whole ;
for Space and Time are uniform throughout, and though
they may stretch out to infinity, they are essentially

---

[1] Lindsay, *The Philosophy of Bergson*, p. 124.

measurable, and therefore constituents of a whole. The
Soul can transcend them, because the true home of the
Soul is in the eternal world. The Soul is not really in
Space and Time, though these are the field of its activi-
ties ; they are rather in the Soul.

As for *la durée*, I offer the following suggestion. In
Time, considered as physical, there is no trace of *intensity*.
But duration, which is perhaps the Soul's apprehension of
Time, is to a large extent an intensive magnitude. In
other words, we are now passing over into the kingdom
of *values*. Plotinus, I think, means something like this
when he says[1] that the Soul recognises anteriority and
posteriority, not in Time, but in *order*. In other words,
the Soul's apprehension of Time is a valuation.[2]

Time, Change, and Causality

It is, or should be, a commonplace of philosophy, that
only the permanent can change, change being a succession
of states within an unity. These states together form
a system, which may be called the consequence of the
nature or ground in which the unity of the system consists. When these states follow each other in time, we
may speak of change within the system. Where the
sequence is only logical, neither time nor change comes
in. The ordinary—and the scientific—notion of efficient
cause resembles that of logical ' ground ' only when time
and change are involved ; but it generally regards events
as being determined, not by the whole nature of the
system to which they belong, but by the events which
precede them in time. But to assert efficient causation
means to distinguish activity and passivity in things,
which in physical science seems to be an illegitimate
anthropomorphism. Physical science, when it refuses
to admit Soul, ought to admit no individual things or

[1] 4. 4. 1.
[2] Mr. Wildon Carr (*Proceedings of the Aristotelian Society*, 1914)
says that psychical Time is ' pure quality.' But is not this to transcend
the category of Time altogether ?

I.—N

individual acts. For it the whole is one thing and Nature one process. Natural science is an abstract monistic philosophy. If it could overcome its prejudice against teleology, as some naturalists, such as Lamarck, have done, it would be, in Plotinian language, the psychic reflexion of the spiritual world, polarised as a world of constant purpose. While it chooses to eliminate Soul, which is the only cause of change, it must consistently eliminate efficient causation. Strictly, there is no activity or passivity in things. Ordinary thought would reject as absurd the notion of an event being determined by the future ; but if the whole series is one system, there is no reason why the earlier members of the series should have more efficient power than the later. Indeed the notion of efficient causality is profoundly unsatisfactory. It ascribes activity to mere links in the chain of events, which cannot possess it, and denies activity to the system as a whole, which may possess it. Things are not vehicles of causation. Some scientific writers are aware of this ; but they cling to what they call causation as a way of denying the intervention of any new factor in evolution. Each stage, they say, is wholly conditioned by its temporal antecedents. Thus when they assert causality they mean to deny that there is any such thing. They assert *continuity*, which, as Bradley has argued, seems to be a self-contradictory notion if it is intended to reconcile change and permanence. Accordingly, some have given up the philosophical problem, and limit the province of science to the discovery of the manner in which Nature usually behaves. They are thus well rid of causality altogether. This is the more welcome to them, as it is plain that if all events are caused by preceding events, there can be no beginning to the series, which stretches back to infinity. But to say that natural science is ' merely descriptive ' is to confess that it is an abstract study, which can give us no view of reality as a whole. For description is only incomplete interpretation.

For Plotinus, things certainly cannot be causes. The

ground of each system is some Idea in the world of Spirit, which has been transmuted by Soul into vital law. The only real causes are final causes. So-called efficient causes are parts of the machinery which Soul uses. They belong to ' Nature.'

Bergson thinks that by insisting on the ' individuality ' of conscious life (by individuality he means that inter-penetration of present by past states which he finds to be characteristic of psychical experience) he has vindi-cated the freedom of the will against determinism. In ordinary ' scientific thinking,' duration is eliminated, as is proved by the fact that if the movement of the whole time-process were greatly accelerated it would make no difference to the calculations. Science therefore, he urges, commits us to the absurdity of change without Time. But in truth the mechanical theory denies real change, if, with Bergson, we hold that there is no real change without the intervention of some causative factor. Alternate evolution and involution have been the pre-destined and predictable lot of material things from the first.[1] But this alternation introduces no new element into things, which therefore remain essentially un-changed. To this it may be answered that Time may measure the periods of each process of evolution and involution, each of which may be a teleological series. If Bergson had said that the *causation* of one thing by another is excluded by the mechanical hypothesis, he would have been right ; and no doubt many scientists who adopt the mechanical theory are open to the charge of talking about causation when they mean only invari-able sequence. Others have confused logical consequence with causality. Causation implies creative action; it is a teleological category, and belongs to the processes of

---

[1] So Empedocles taught long ago.

φύσις οὐδένος ἐστὶν ἁπάντων
θνητῶν, οὐδέ τις οὐλομένου θανάτοιο τελευτή,
ἀλλὰ μόνον μῖξίς τε διάλλαξίς τε μιγέντων
ἐστι, φύσις τ' ἐπὶ τοῖς ὀνομάζεται ἀνθρώποισιν.

nature only as determined once for all by a 'First Cause,' or as directed by an immanent will. It is a vulgar error to suppose that invariable sequence excludes either a First Cause or an immanent will. Invariable sequence may be a fact of observation, but it explains nothing. Winter is not the 'cause' of summer, nor day of night. *Post hoc ergo propter hoc* is an anthropomorphism on the analogy of human purposive action. For an automatist it is absurd. Causation, used in its correct sense, is precisely what Bergson calls 'creative evolution,' and it does require *la durée*, as he says. But this constant operation of creative force may take place without any 'freedom' on the part of that which exhibits its effects. A watch is no more free when we push the hands about than when we leave it to keep its own time. Nor does Bergson even succeed in proving that a psychical series, in 'real Time,' is irreversible. He only makes it discontinuous, whether we read it backwards or forwards, for whenever a 'new' element is admitted, there is a breach of complete continuity. Lastly, he does not prove that it is unpredictable, but only that it is unpredictable by the laws which govern inorganic matter. What he calls creative evolution may be the orderly development of psychical or spiritual law, which a superior being could predict as the astronomer predicts an eclipse. In this case, the argument for free will falls to the ground, if we take free will to mean a real 'contingency in the heart of things,' to use a phrase of Dr. James Ward. Bergson rejects teleology, and therefore finalistic determinism; but he cannot get rid of either. If, with the Neoplatonists, we hold that 'Divine necessity coincides with Divine will,' we shall infer that we win freedom in proportion as we enter into the life of God, and make His will our will. Our freedom will then be our emancipation from our fancied subjection to the law of sin and death.

It seems more than probable that there is no radical difference between the laws which determine the sequence of events in the organic and in the inorganic worlds ;[1] but that as we rise to the higher forms of being the laws become more and more complex and therefore apparently irregular in their working. Human character is the most complex of all, and the most obviously ungeometrical. But only a superhuman intelligence could say whether there is any real indetermination in these manifestations. We have rejected the notion that one event is the cause of another. The cause of any event is the will of a spiritual being, of a mind which has willed it to happen in a certain series. That will is certainly not less free if it acts uniformly, linking events together as stages in a pre-determined action. Whether that will is human or superhuman is another question. For Plotinus, the will is that of the World-Soul, and individual Souls are free in proportion as they understand and obey the laws which the World-Soul has ordained alike for them and their environment. The World-Soul itself is the instrument of Spirit energising through it as the supreme will.

The 'idealistic reaction against Science' (the title of Aliotta's book) has made great play with the irregularities of concrete Nature, which only approximates ' on the average ' to the ' diagrams ' of science. It is argued that Nature ' really is ' irregular and unaccountable, the ' laws of Nature ' being only convenient methodological assumptions, indispensable for the special work of science. Plotinus would say that the laws are certainly the work of Soul, but that Nature is so too. Whatever may be the explanation of apparent disorders in Nature, no Platonist can observe with glee that the world does not seem to him to be a perfect cosmos. He may need a caution against ' mathematicising Nature '; but not against attempting to find universal law in the natural world. The synthesising labour to which he is always impelled is no mere

---

[1] What we call mechanism is itself psychical. Nothing is given without psychical activity. To ignore this is one of Bergson's chief errors.

'symbolism':[1] it is the pathway to reality.   It is thus that in the psychical world he discovers the truth of teleology, and in the spiritual world the eternal fountains of Truth, Beauty, and Goodness.   It may be suggested that the real object of that branch of science which deals with inorganic nature, is to discover the *inner meaning of what seems to us unconscious activity*.   This is a very different thing from drawing diagrams.

Time for Plotinus is *the form of willed change*.   Every distinct idea Yonder becomes a finite purpose Here. Every attribute of God's essence becomes an activity of His existence.   The time-process is not the necessary form of the self-evolution of God ; it is the product of His free but necessary creative activity.   But it is not necessary to suppose that in inorganic nature God has wound up the clock and left it to itself, while in living beings new interventions take place.   Rather, the same power which slumbers in the stone and dreams in the flower, awakes in the human soul.   The assumption that regularity is a sign of undirected movement is one of the strangest and most obstinate of human prejudices.   It is only a false idea of causation that makes us think that orderly evolution is not real change.   It is the same prejudice that makes men say that ' God does nothing ' because they cannot distinguish any particular event as an ' act of God.'[2]

Variation and heredity are both facts, both names for unknown laws.   Why should one be more ' spiritual ' than the other ;   and why should we confound freedom

---

[1] Aliotta (p. 438) seems to me very sound on this point.   ' If we examine any principle, law, or physical concept whatever, we shall find that experience is not simply copied or abbreviated, but is rather completed, perfected, and idealised.   In the scientific concept the phenomena given in perception attain to a higher degree of coherence and intelligibility than in the practical world, and hence to a higher degree of truth.'   The scientific concept is not a symbol ; for the symbol is always worth less than the thing symbolised, whereas the scientific concept is of greater value than the series of facts which acted as the starting-point of its formation.

[2] An act of God has been defined by a judge as an event of which no rational explanation can be found !

with the unpredictable ? We have no wish to reduce
even inorganic evolution to the terms of pure mathematics. In fact, no natural process does exhibit this
exactness. Nature always ' wobbles ' a little, as any
table of vital or meteorological statistics shows. But
irregularity is not a sign of higher or freer life. On the
contrary, the precision of the mathematical sciences
seemed to Plato and many of his school the very type
of the spiritual order. But there is a profound truth in
the saying of Proclus that only the highest and lowest
things are simple, while all between is complex. Mathematical truth may perhaps be compared to an empty
outline of the rich glory of the spiritual world. It is an
abstract and colourless presentation of supratemporal
reality. With the concrete individual there enters not
only ' a splitting up ' (as Plotinus says) of spiritual truth,
but some apparent dislocation of law—of mechanical
law in the physical world, of psychical law in the soul-
world. This dislocation seems relatively slight in the
material world, just because that world has so little
life ; it is more marked in the region of Soul, because it
is in this region that life is most fully revealed as a
struggle. But we do not know what a mechanical
psychical life would be ; we have no scales to weigh the
imponderable.

Time, for Plotinus, is not merely the ' measure of the
impermanence of the imperfect ' ;[1] it is the measure of
a definite finite activity directed to some end beyond
itself.[2] This remarkable statement proves that Plotinus
regards Time as a teleological category. What is real in
Time is the potentiality of qualitative change. ' Movement by itself does not need Time.' There is movement
in the spiritual world, but no qualitative change. Continuous regular motion is a form of stability. Time is
needed when the superior principle desires to make something ' according to the pattern showed in the mount.'

[1] Dr. Schiller.
[2] οὐκ αὐτὴ τελειοῦται, ἀλλὰ τὸ πρᾶγμα οὗ ἐστοχάζετο. 6. 1. 16.

Because this act of creation is willed, and willed as a process, there must be an interval between the inception and conclusion of the process. This interval is Time.

Past and Future

In what sense are the distinctions of past and future real ? Plotinus says that temporal differences Here are images of differences in order or arrangement (τάξει) Yonder. What is unreal in past and future is not the relation which under the form of Time appears as anteriority and posteriority, but the envisagement of temporal events from an imaginary point, ' the present,' within the process. Anterior and posterior events are, in their positions and not out of them, constituent parts of the individual fact to which they belong. Past and present are illusory ideas Real things do not come into being, nor pass out of being ; it is we who are moving through Time, as the traveller in an express train sees trees and hedges hurrying past his field of vision. But is this a legitimate comparison ? It runs counter to a deep-seated instinct, that Time and Space are not like each other. We readily grant that the ' not here ' is as real as the ' here ' ; but it is difficult for us to think of the past and future as being no less real than the present. Consider this curious difference. We none of us want to be ubiquitous ; but we do wish to be immortal. What is the ground of this difference ? One reason may be that we can move voluntarily in Space, but not in Time. The movement of Time carries us all with it, like the movement of the earth round the sun. There is also a mysterious and deeply important difference between the two tracts that lie behind and before the moment which we call the present. We are blind on one side. The apparent contingency and uncertainty of all that lies ahead of us seems to be the source of our ideas of cause, purpose, and freedom. If the future lay open before us, it is difficult to see how we could have these

ideas, which could never arise from a contemplation of
coexistence. Unless, then, our ideas of cause, purpose,
and freedom are illusory, futurity must indicate something more than a blind spot in our mental vision. This
ignorance must be a necessary condition of soul-life.
We must however be careful not to exaggerate the
difference between our knowledge of the past and our
ignorance of the future. Very much of the past is as
completely lost to us as the future ; and the whole would
be lost but for the mysterious faculty of memory. What
memory does for us with regard to the past, knowledge
of natural law does for us with regard to the future.[1]
We do know many things that have not yet happened.
But if we are to take Plotinus as our guide, we must
remember that the Soul is the creator of the phenomenal
world and the time-process, and that this creation is a
continuous act, being the activity which constitutes the
out-going life of the Soul. From this, the specifically
human point of view, there is a real generic difference
between the ' not yet ' and the ' no longer,' and we
cannot regard them as homogeneous parts of a landscape
which we traverse as passive spectators. The will, of
which Time is the form, has a wholly different relation
to the future from that which it has to the past. In
looking back, the will confesses its impotence ; in looking
forward it finds its scope and *raison d'être*. It is because
psychical reality is will, not memory, that we regard the
past as ' done with.' Memory indeed proves that our
consciousness of a moving present, perpetually passing
out of existence, is an illusion. It is a partial knowledge,
limited by the needs of our activity. Like all else, it
indicates that the Soul has ' come down ' on a temporary
adventure. But this attitude of the will is not something to be merely left behind when we climb from Soul
to Spirit. In the life of Spirit, Time is transcended ; but
the Eternity in which Spirit moves and has its being is
not an arrested and fixed present moment, truncated

---

[1] I do not mean that there is any parallel between them.

of its living relations to past and future ; it is a fuller and richer life in which all meanings are completely expressed, all relations acknowledged. The Soul must take its Time-experience up with it to the threshold of Eternity ; it will leave nothing behind as it crosses the threshold. The life of the Soul in its higher aspect is a contemplation of Spirit. That is to say, all real psychical ends belong to the spiritual world. Ends are striven for in Time, but there can be no ends in Time, which swallows its own children.

From the point of view of practical religion it makes a great difference whether we regard the phenomenal world as a mere polarisation of a timeless and changeless reality, or whether we hold that its being is radically teleological. The former doctrine deprives Time of all existence and all value. Philosophers of this school care nothing for history. The general tendency of Indian thought has been in this direction, in strong contrast with the Iranian and Hebrew religions, in which the revelation of God is sought from history, with which accordingly the sacred books of the Jewish people are largely occupied. It makes a great difference whether we make it our aim to understand reality or to help in making it. The religious genius, it is true, soon learns both that the truths of life can only be learned by practising them, and that on the other hand ' good works ' without ' faith ' are dead. But the caricatures of the two doctrines are very different. On one side we have the pushing, hustling European or American man of business, immersed in irrational activities which make him no wiser and the world no better ; and on the other the vacuous Indian contemplative, whose existence is a living death, steeped in dull torpor. Christianity has combined, without fully reconciling, the two views about Time. But in the countries of the West it has lost much of its idealistic element, through the vulgar conception of heaven as a fairy-land existence in Time and Place. To this error, and not to any essential part of Christian doctrine, is to

be attributed the spurious 'otherworldliness' which
disparages or denies the values of the world in which
we live.   To a similar error is also due the secularist
apocalyptic which seeks encouragement and inspiration
by 'making heavy drafts upon the future,'[1] a method
fatal to real insight and just appreciation of values.
The final satisfaction of human hopes within the temporal
series is for ever impossible.

The Platonic tradition leaned to the Indian view of
existence rather than to the Hebraic.   Plato was consciously leading a reaction against the disintegrating
tendencies of his age.   His thought was decidedly more
Oriental than that of Plotinus, who had Aristotle and the
Stoics to keep him a good European.   The view of Time
as the form of the Will is certainly to be found in the
Enneads, though it is less insisted on than a modern
reader would desire.   Metaphysically, Plotinus' doctrine
of Time anticipates some of the best thought of our own
age, and is still highly instructive.

Cosmology

We must not expect to find in Plotinus any contribu-
tions to natural science.   He does not even choose well
among the discoveries, some of them very brilliant, which
earlier philosophers had made about the constitution
of the universe.   Only here and there we find valuable
suggestions, as when he says[2] that though the substance
of the stars is in perpetual flux, this does not impair their
immortality, because all the flux goes on *within* the
universe, and the sum-total of the material is never
either augmented or diminished.[3]   I have already said

---

[1] Bosanquet, *The Value and Destiny of the Individual*, p. 291.
[2] 2. 1. 3.
[3] The newest astronomy teaches that Matter, in the sense of
ponderable stuff, is gradually wasting away into radiation.   But
I cannot believe that 'annihilation'—the word used by Professor
Eddington—is the right word for the end of this process.   I agree
with those who refuse to be troubled by the dismal predictions based
on the Second Law of Thermo-dynamics.   Even if the universe is
running down like a clock, we may assume that whatever power
wound up the clock once will be able to do so again.   Whittaker
thinks that the acceptance of the opposite view would be fatal to
Neoplatonism.

that modern physics seems to be approximating to the
Plotinian doctrine of Matter.   And the Greek theory of
recurring cycles[1] is, as I shall show presently, much more
in accordance with what we know about the history of
the heavenly bodies than the utterly unscientific notion
of an automatic ' law of progress,' that strange will-o'-the-
wisp of nineteenth-century thought.   Other lucky hits
might perhaps be found ; but on the whole the chapters
which deal with cosmology are among the least valuable
in the Enneads.

Plotinus assumes that the sublime reconciliation of
change and permanence, which is found in the spiritual
world, must have its reflexion in the phenomenal world.
No better symbol of this rest-in-motion could be found
than a body revolving round a fixed centre, and at the
same time rotating round its own axis.   The perfection
of the spiritual world is symbolised in the lower order
by a closed system of movements which repeats itself in
successive æons.   The underlying unity of all phenomena
binds the whole of nature together in a subtle web of
occult sympathies.   The recognition of these sympathies
gives a certain justification to the lore of astrology and
natural magic, which Plotinus cannot decisively repudiate,
though he dislikes and distrusts it.   When Neoplatonism
tried to become a popular religion, as it did in the fourth
century, a flood of superstition entered by this door,
which Plotinus would fain have kept closed, though not
locked.

Fate of the World

Plotinus believed that the universe is eternal, in the
sense that it had no temporal beginning and will have
no temporal ending.[2]   He cannot allow that the Ideas

---

[1] This was an Orphic doctrine.   The wheel of birth is governed by
the circling of the heavens.   The Soul, caught in the circle, passes
through various forms, now man, now beast, now plant.   The cycle
consists of ten thousand solar years ; at the end of each cycle the
Soul may escape from its captivity, and a new world-order begins.
This theory is a conflation of the old belief in reincarnation with the
Babylonian astronomy, which taught that after long intervals the
stars all come back to their original positions.

[2] 5. 8. 12.

at one time existed apart from Matter and then entered into it. Plutarch indeed tried to defend such a theory from the *Timaeus*, but in so doing he deserted the orthodox Platonic tradition. Longinus, who had a controversy with Plotinus, did not hold this theory. He only argued that the Divine Mind contemplates the Ideas as existing objectively over against itself. Plotinus, as we shall see, makes Spirit and the Spiritual World (Mind and the Ideas) inseparable and interdependent.

The doctrine of the eternity of the universe is compatible with the view that every individual in it perishes, the type alone persisting and renewing itself in successive individuals. Plotinus however asserts positively that there are Ideas of individuals; and since the phenomenal world derives whatever reality it has from the Ideas, this is conclusive. Individuality is a fact in the real world, and therefore indestructible. 'Nothing that really is can ever perish' (οὐδὲν ἀπολεῖται τῶν ὄντων).

The world-order evolves regularly till the end of an astronomical cycle, and then the whole process is repeated, perhaps exactly. When all the seminal Logoi have produced individuals, according to the plan of the Universal Soul, a new world-order will begin.[1] Thus the history of the Universe consists of an infinite number of vast but finite schemes, which have, each of them, a beginning, middle, and end. This view is in every way far superior to the loose theories of perpetual progress which are so popular in modern Europe and America. An infinite purpose is a contradiction in terms. Such a purpose could never have been formed, and could never be accomplished.[2] There may be a single purpose— hardly 'an increasing purpose,' as Tennyson puts it in a well-known line—in the present world-order taken as a whole; but only on condition of our admitting that the present world-order had a beginning and will have an end. Physical science of course is well aware of the fate in store for this planet. The achievements of humanity will one day be wiped off the slate. They will

[1] 5. 7. 3. [2] Cf. 1. 5. 2.

be as completely obliterated as a child's sand-castles by the next high-tide ; they will vanish and ' leave not a wrack behind.' So our modern apocalyptists, who, rejecting belief in a spiritual world, project their ideals into an unending terrestrial future, suffer shipwreck both in philosophy and science.   The ancient doctrine of alternate integration and dissociation is alone tenable ; and man must find consolation for the inevitable fate of his species either nowhere or in a heaven where all values are preserved eternally.

The belief in recurring cycles belongs to Asia as well as to Europe. ' In India there was the mythical dream of vast chronological cycles, each divisible into four epochs, until a new *mahá-yuga* or great cycle begins.'[1] The old Persian religion encouraged the hope that evil would not last for ever, but never connected this optimism with any doctrine of gradual progress.   In Hesiod there is no mention of cycles : he traces a gradual decline through the ages of gold, silver, brass, and iron, only intercalating the *heroic* age (the legends of which were too strong for his theory) between the last two.   The evolution of man out of lower forms was taught by Empedocles ; his advance from bestial savagery by Æschylus in the *Prometheus Vinctus*, and by Euripides.[2]   The doctrine of cycles is part of Orphism, and of Stoicism. ' The Stoics,' says Nemesius, ' taught that at fixed periods of time a burning and destruction of all things takes place, and the world returns to the same shape that it had before ; and that the restoration happens not once, but often, the same things being restored an infinite number of times.'[3]   Lucretius, in some of the finest lines of his poem, predicts the final destruction of the present world-order :—

Quorum naturam triplicem, tria corpora, Memmi,
Tres species tam dissimiles, tria talia texta,

[1] Flint, *Philosophy of History*, Vol. 1, p. 89 ; P. Leroux, *De l'Humanité*, Vol. 2, chap. 8.
[2] Euripides, *Supplices*, 201–218.
[3] Nemesius, *De Nat. Hom.* 38.

Una dies dabit exitio, multosque per annos
Sustentata ruet moles et machina mundi.' [1]

Virgil thinks that the Golden Age was ended that man
might work out his own salvation.[2] Pliny leans to the
superstition of the nineteenth century. 'We must
firmly trust that the ages go on continuously improving.'[3]

It is perhaps not easy to reconcile the theory of recurring cycles, every phase of which is a necessary part
of the universal order, like the alternate opening and
shutting of valves in the human body, with the doctrine
that the Soul has sinned in coming down into the world
of change. I shall argue in the next chapter that this
latter doctrine has an insecure place in the system of
Plotinus, and was never accepted by him whole-heartedly.
Historically, the two doctrines had separate origins, the
former belonging to what Mr. Cornford calls the Dionysiac
tradition, the latter to the Orphic. They were first
brought together by Parmenides. Aristotle confines the
cyclic mutation to the history of the earth and mankind,
thus falling back behind Plato, and still more behind
Heracleitus and Empedocles.[4]

Categories of the World of Appearance

The enquiry into the categories, initiated by the
Pythagoreans, was first prosecuted in detail by Aristotle.[5]
It also held an important place in the writings of the
Stoical school. In Plotinus we find a good deal of space
given to the subject. The first three books of the Sixth
Ennead, and the sixth of the Second, are devoted to it ;
and several discussions in other parts of his work are
based upon these classifications. Zeller, differing from
Steinhart, thinks that the doctrine of categories has
but little influence upon the philosophy of Plotinus, in

[1] Lucretius, 5. 92–95 ; and cf. Ovid, *Met.* 1. 89–150 ; 256–258.
[2] Virgil, G. 4. 121–146. [3] Pliny, N.H. 7. 31.
[4] Gomperz, *Greek Philosophers*, Vol. 4, p. 125.
[5] Modern philosophers have treated the Aristotelian categories
with very scant respect. Kant thinks that Aristotle jotted down his
ten γένη just as they occurred to him ; Hegel that he threw them
together anyhow ; Mill that they resemble a division of animals into
men, quadrupeds, horses, asses, and ponies.

spite of the large space allotted to it in the Enneads.
My own impression is that Plotinus is hampered, as in
some other cases, by the Platonic tradition, which obliged
him to accept, not the Aristotelian list, but the five
categories of the intelligible world which are laid down
in the *Sophist* of Plato—ὄν, στάσις, κίνησις ταὐτότης and
ἑτερότης. The category of ' Being ' is, as I shall hope to
show, unsatisfactory. It needs to be resolved into
Thought and its Object, in order to bring it into line
with the two pairs of inseparable opposites or correlatives
which follow as the other categories of the spiritual world.
Plotinus in reality sees this quite clearly, and sometimes
gives us six categories of the spiritual ; but the Platonic
classification introduces some confusion into the categories of the World of Sense, which we have now to
consider. He is concerned to prove that the categories
of the spiritual world are not applicable to the world of
phenomena, but that at the same time the two run
parallel to each other, so that the names of the spiritual
categories may be used, in an incorrect sense, of the
phenomenal world. In the spiritual world, Thought and
its Object, Stability and Movement, Identity and
Difference, are not mutually exclusive : they are united
in the harmony of eternal life. In the world of appearance
this unity is broken up by a want of complete correspondence between Thought and its Object, caused by
the fact that neither Thought nor its Object is purely real
and true. The following extract [1] will make it clear in
what manner, and with what hesitation, Plotinus lays
down his categories of the phenomenal world.

' Let us first speak of what is called Reality (or Being)
here below. We must recognise that the corporeal
nature can only be called Reality in an incorrect sense,
or perhaps it should not be called Reality at all, since
it is in perpetual flux ; the word Generation would be
more appropriate. . . . We may also distinguish in
bodies, on the one side Matter, on the other the Form
impressed upon Matter, and make a category of each of

[1] 6. 3. 2.

these taken separately, or we may unite them in the same
category, calling it, incorrectly, Reality, or generation.'
(Thus he proposes to make of Matter and Form one
category in the phenomenal world, just as Thought and
its Object are combined in the intelligible or spiritual
category of Real Being.) 'But what can there be in
common between Matter and Form ? And how can
Matter be a category, and what would this category contain ? What distinctions are there within it ? And in
what category shall we place the composite of Matter
and Form ? Matter and Form are the constituent elements of corporeal Being ; but neither of them is Body ;
can we place them in the same category as the composite,
Body ? But though we must abandon the attempt to
identify the categories of the phenomenal with those of
the spiritual world, we may admit analogous divisions.
Instead of spiritual Being, we have here below, Matter ;
instead of spiritual Movement, we have Form, which
gives to Matter life and perfection ; instead of spiritual
Stability, the Inertia of Matter ; instead of Identity,
Resemblance ; instead of Difference, Unlikeness.
Matter, however, neither receives nor possesses Form
as its life or proper activity ; on the contrary, Form
introduces itself into Matter from outside. Further,
while in the spiritual world Form is essentially activity
and movement, in the sensible world Movement is something strange and accidental. Far from being Movement, the Form impressed upon Matter communicates
to it rather Stability and immobility ; for the Form
determines Matter, which is naturally undetermined.
In the spiritual world, Identity and Difference apply to
one and the same Real Being, at once identical and
different. But here a Being is different only adven-
titiously. As for Stability, how can we attribute it to
Matter, which is constantly taking different forms from
outside ? We must therefore abandon this division.
What classification then shall we adopt ? We have first
Matter, then Form, then the Composite of these two,

I.—O

and finally the things which belong to these three and are affirmed of them, whether as attributes or as accidents ; and among accidents, some are contained in things, others contain them ; some are activities of them, others passive states, others again consequences.' He goes on to say that the class of ' accidents ' includes Time and Place, Quality and Quantity. Then he decides to include Form, Matter, and the Composite in one category, that of ' Reality incorrectly so called ' (ὁμώνυμος οὐσία), and to add, as further categories, Relation, Quality, Quantity, Time, Place, Movement.

We need not follow further an argument which is one of the most obscure and least attractive parts of the Enneads. What is most necessary to remember is that while in the eternal world Thought and its Object, Stability and Movement, Identity and Difference, are taken up into a higher unity, in the world of our ordinary experience there are unsolved contradictions, which proceed from the fact that the Soul cannot create anything better than an imperfect copy of spiritual reality.

Relations of the ' Two Worlds '

Plotinus speaks so often of ' Here ' and ' Yonder,' as if they were two countries, that we can hardly avoid accepting the ordinary language which has so often led critics of the Neoplatonists to accuse them of teaching a rather crude dualism. But strictly there is only one real world—the spiritual world or κόσμος νοητός. The world of sense has not only a lower value ; it has a lower degree of reality. The difficulty for a modern philosopher is to decide whether Plotinus meant us to regard the world of sense as merely our imperfect view of the world of Spirit, or whether it is, from the point of view of perfect knowledge, an actually existing second world. In order to answer this question, we must remember that there is only one sharp line intersecting the field of experience —that which divides things which have οὐσία, Real

Being, from those which have it not. The kingdom
of οὐσία includes Soul, but nothing lower than Soul.
Accordingly, the phenomenal world, which is created by
Soul, is not in itself real. Nevertheless, it is a necessary
product of Soul, and without it none of the Divine
principles would be knowable for what they are. Plotinus
is very emphatic about this. Without the phenomenal
world, the spiritual world would not be ἐνεργείᾳ ;[1] it
would have been hidden.[2] If the Soul's potency or
potentiality (δύναμις) were unmanifested, the Soul
would be non-existent (οὐκ οὖσα), not being really exis-
tent (ὄντως οὖσα).[3] Still more strongly, in a passage of
supreme importance for the right understanding of
Plotinus, we read : ' It is necessary that each principle
should give of itself to another ; the Good would not
be Good, nor Spirit Spirit, nor Soul Soul, if nothing
lived dependent on the first life.'[4] It is the nature of
each principle in the hierarchy to create something
which, though necessarily inferior to its creator, yet reflects faithfully, so far as is possible in an imperfect
medium, not its creator, but the principle next above its
creator, the ideal towards which the gaze of its creator,
even in the moment of creating, is turned. Thus all
grades of life are bound in ' a golden chain about the feet
of God.' But of what nature is the necessity which
impels each principle to create ? To suppose that
spiritual existences, the Divine Ideas, have to bathe in
the flowing river of Time before they can take their place
in the world of perfect and eternal Being, would be to
misunderstand Plotinus. The higher does not need the
lower ; God does not need the world ; though without
it His character would have been ' hidden.' The necessity
lies in the inner nature of all which derives its being from
the One who is also the Good. Proclus[5] says that God

---

[1] 6. 7. 9.   [2] 4. 8. 6.   [3] 4. 8. 5.
[4] ἀνάγκη ἕκαστον τὸ αὑτοῦ διδόναι καὶ ἄλλῳ, ἢ τὸ ἀγαθὸν οὐκ ἀγαθὸν
ἔσται, ἢ ὁ νοῦς οὐ νοῦς, ἢ ἡ ψυχὴ μὴ τοῦτο, εἰ μή τι μετὰ τὸ πρώτως ζῶν
ζῴη καὶ δευτέρως ἕως ἐστι τὸ πρώτως. 2. 9. 3.
[5] Proclus, in Timaeum, 112.

created the world by his goodness, his will, and his providence, a trinity in unity (ἐνοειδὴς τριάς) of motives. These correspond to the three attributes which he ascribes to Spirit—Being, Power, Activity. The Soul descends into the phenomenal world 'because it desires to imitate the providence of the gods.' Another statement, which is found in Plato, is that it is always *love* which is the motive in creation. But this love is not love for the creature which is to be created, but the love which the creative principle feels for what is above itself. This longing reproduces, as it were, an image of its object. Plotinus is also fond of two metaphors to represent the relation between the higher and the lower worlds. He speaks of the higher principle 'as it were overflowing'; and he speaks of a luminary pouring forth its light. He prefers the latter image because, in accordance with the science of his day, he believed that the sun loses nothing of its own heat and light by shining upon the world, and he wishes to insist that the higher principle loses nothing of its own substance or power by creating. The activity of the higher principle in creating is always an activity outside itself. Now there are philosophers who deny that such activity is possible, even in the spiritual and psychical spheres. Nothing, they say, can be done without a reaction on the agent. If they are right, the whole philosophy of Plotinus falls to the ground. For his system depends entirely on the assumption that Spirit can act upon Soul, and Soul upon Matter, without losing anything in the process. The relations between higher and lower are one-sided. The lower needs the higher; the higher is complete without the lower. The higher possesses certain qualities which necessarily impel it to creative activity, and it is therefore impossible that it should live without creating. But the world is the manifestation of God's character, not a constituent of His existence. The Divine power is

'ipsa suis pollens opibus, nihil indiga nostri.'

To deny this is surely to destroy not only Platonism, but all theism. The analogy of mechanical laws, which preclude any possibility of one-sided activity, need no longer frighten us. Spiritual life is not subject to these laws.

The world of sense, then, is created by Soul after the pattern shown her by Spirit. But it is no coherent, consistent world, with which we are dealing in this lecture. It is a construction of superficial experience, a rough-and-ready synthesis based on very imperfect data. The world of sense must not be confused with the world described by natural science. This latter is an attempt to interpret the universe as a self-consistent harmonious system or law. Its categories are quantitative only,[1] and a rigorous application of its principles would reduce the world to pure mathematics. The quantities with which it deals are hypothetical, since the individual concrete never absolutely conforms to type. In practice, of course, the scientist cannot refrain from assigning values, though in doing so he is transgressing the limits which he laid down for himself. But the world of common experience is not the world of natural science. It is a blurred and confused picture of the spiritual world, distorted in innumerable ways by defects in the organ of perception, and split up by the very conditions of Soul-life into Here and There, Past and Future. But for all this, it is a glorious vision of the eternal realities. There is nothing 'Yonder' which cannot be found 'Here.'[2] And all things Here that have $εἴδη$—that is to say, that represent some thought in the Divine mind, have a secure abiding-place Yonder. It is only things 'contrary to nature' that have no place in the eternal world.[3] These have a place in reality only when they are completely transformed into parts of a larger scheme.

Consequently, Plotinus has no sympathy with the

---

[1] It may be objected that (e.g.) chemical affinities imply non-quantitative relations. But I do not think that this objection is valid.
[2] 5. 9. 13.   [3] 5. 9. 10.

half-Christian Gnostics who disparage this beautiful
world and hand it over to the evil principle.   In reply
to the suggestion that the world was created through
a lapse of the Universal Soul, he says : ' We affirm that
the Soul created the world, not because it looked downward, but because it did not look downward.   In order
to look downward, the Soul must have forgotten the
spiritual world ; but if it has forgotten it, how can
it create the world ?   Where could it find its pattern,
except from what it saw yonder ?   But if it remembers
the spiritual world while creating, it does not look
downwards at all. . . . We must not allow that the
world is ill made, because it contains much that is disagreeable.   That would be to claim too great a perfection
for the sensible world and to confound it with the spiritual
world of which it is only the image.   But could there be
a more beautiful image ?   Could there be a better fire
than ours, after the fire yonder ?   Could one conceive a
better earth than this, after the earth yonder ?   Could
there be a more perfect sphere, better ordered in its
movements, after the revolution of the spiritual world ?
After the sun that is yonder, what sun could we have
other than the one that we see ? ' [1]   In the same book
he says indignantly, ' Do not suppose that a man becomes
good by despising the gods, the world, and all the beauties
that are in it.   They [the Gnostics] have no right to profess respect for the gods of the world above.   When we
love a person, we love all that belongs to him ; we extend
to the children the affection which we feel for the father.
Now every Soul is a daughter of the Father in heaven.
How can this world, with the gods which it contains, be
separated from the spiritual world ?   Those who despise
what is so nearly akin to the spiritual world, prove that
they know nothing of the spiritual world, except in
name.' [2]   In another place he says[3] that this world is
worthy of its Author, complete, beautiful, and harmonious.   Those who find fault with it make the mistake of

[1] 2. 9. 4.   [2] 2. 9. 16.   [3] 3. 2. 3.

considering it piecemeal. There are no doubt minor defects in it ; but ' we do not take Thersites as the type of the human race.' For anyone who has seen anything of the beauty of the spiritual world, this world is full of echoes of that beauty, full of order, harmony, and grace. And the more we can train ourselves to take large and comprehensive views of this world, disregarding petty details, the more we shall be convinced of its divine origin. What is most real in this world is that which reflects the purpose, meaning, and plan which called it into being. By fixing our attention on this, we are taking the only path by which anything in heaven or earth can be understood, that is to say, by viewing it in its relation to what is next above it. So the broken lights of the Divine which irradiate this world of ours will flow together ; and in rising above the flux of changing phenomena we shall leave nothing behind. Sun, stars, and all that is good and beautiful ' here below ' exist also ' yonder.'[1] All things on earth were in heaven ; ' for whence else could they have come ? '[2] ' Spirit is the first lawgiver, or rather the law of all being.'[3]

We must be content to acquiesce in the multiplicity, change, and strife which are conditions of existence in such a world as that which we inhabit. We recognise these conditions as imperfect, just because we are not debarred from knowledge of the perfect. Thus the flaws which we justly observe in the world of Time and Space are themselves evidence that the Soul has her home in another and a higher sphere.

[1] Cf. a remarkable modern parallel in *A Modern Mystic's Way*, p. 17. ' She told me of "going into the Blue." It is a place, she said, as real as earth, but it seems to be made of some different and finer stuff. There are trees and flowers and grass and men and women, all like the people and things of earth, yet seeming of earthly life transfigured,' etc. The whole passage closely resembles what Plotinus says of life in the spiritual world.

[2] 3. 2. 4.   [3] 5. 9. 5.

LECTURES IX–XI

THE SOUL (ψυχή)

THE idea of 'Soul,' or 'Life,'[1] may have had its
source in primitive religion—'animism.' 'Nature,'
for the Ionians, was 'a material continuum charged
with vital force.'[2] They did not at first distinguish
mechanical motion from vital activity. Aristotle's[3]
comment on the doctrines of Soul in early philosophy
is worth quoting. 'Those who have concentrated their
attention on the fact that what is animate is in motion
have regarded Soul as that which is most capable of
movement: those who have directed their observations
to the fact that the Soul knows and perceives things
existing, identify Soul with the elementary principles of
all existence, whether they recognise a plurality of these
or only one. Thus Empedocles makes Soul to be compounded of all the elements, and at the same time considers each of these to be a Soul. His words are as
follows :—

> Earth we perceive by earth, and man knoweth water by water,
> Air the divine by air, by fire sees fire the destroyer,
> Love he beholds by love, by discord horrible discord.[4]

So Plato in the *Timaeus* constructs Soul out of the
elements. Like is known by like, he maintains, and the

---

[1] I have resisted a temptation to render ψυχή throughout by
'Life'; we must keep this word for ζωή. But 'Soul' is laden with
alien associations, and the reader of Plotinus must bear in mind that
'Life' would often represent the idea of ψυχή better. In Stoicism also
soul is the principle of *action*, while the body is the passive part of man.

[2] Cornford.   [3] Aristotle, *de Anima*, I. 2.

[4] The Greek is quoted on p. 138.

objects of knowledge are composed of the elements of
existence . . . While, however, thinkers agree in reducing the Soul to elements or principles, they differ as
regards the name and number of the principles ; some
make them corporeal, others incorporeal ; some reduce
them to one, others regard them as more in number. . . .
Democritus regarded the Soul as identical with Mind
(νοῦς), which belongs to the class of primary and indivisible bodies, and possesses the faculty of movement.
. . . Anaxagoras sometimes seems to distinguish Soul
and Mind, but he really identifies them, except that he
makes Mind the principle of all things. . . . Heracleitus
also identifies the Soul with his principle in describing it
as the " fiery process " out of which he derives other
existing things, his ground being that it is that which
is least corporeal and in constant movement. . . . Thus
with the exception of the earth all the elements have
gained a vote.'

The Orphics were the first to teach that the Soul of
man is 'fallen ' ; it is in prison until the end of the
cosmic year of ten thousand solar years. Till then, it is
'an exile from God and a wanderer.' It retains its
individuality (this is distinctive of Orphism) through all
its transmigrations. The Pythagoreans held to this
doctrine of a multitude of immortal souls, thus breaking
up the older doctrine that 'Soul' generically is the
active power or manifestation of one spiritual Being.
One of the main problems of the later Greek philosophy
was to preserve the truth of human personality, thus,
rather late, recognised, without sacrificing the right to
believe in Divine immanence and in the ultimate
unity of all the creatures in God. The doctrine which
insisted on the individuality and personal responsibility
of the human Soul contained a theodicy ; for, as Empedocles and Pindar before him taught, the Soul is in
prison because it sinned—stained itself with blood, or
'followed strife,' or committed perjury—in an earlier
state of existence. If love and strife are the contending

principles which constitute the life of the immortal Soul, sin must be the following of strife, and its punishment the rupture of the bond of love which unites souls with each other and with God. The eating of flesh, forbidden by the Orphics, was a kind of sacrament of strife, an acceptance of the sad law that creatures must live by killing one another. The flesh itself, in which we live our outer lives, is an ' alien garment,' the sign that we are divided from one another. When ' loving-kindness burns like a fire,'[1] we are on the way to conquer strife by love, and the Soul may look for an end to its wandering in the wilderness. Thoughts like these help to reconcile panentheism (Divine immanence) with belief in the distinct soul-life of human individuals.

Plotinus thus inherited a double tradition about the nature of Soul. Some of his predecessors had almost identified it with Mind or Spirit; that is to say, they made Soul the power of God in the world, a spiritual energy like that ascribed to ' Wisdom ' in late Jewish literature.[2] Others had thought not of Soul but of Souls, and had elaborated a semi-mythical doctrine of the fall of the Soul from its heavenly home, and of its return thither. Philosophy was attempting to combine two very different theories, just as Christianity tried to find room for the very different religious ideas of Judaism and Hellenism. From the point of view of the rigorous logician and metaphysician, this kind of syncretism can hardly escape the charge of halting between two opinions ; but the attempt to do justice to two legitimate views of the world, and to bring them together, is a worthy task for a philosopher. In matters of religion especially, it is better to leave some ragged edges than to purchase consistency by onesidedness.

The Soul is in the centre, not at the summit, of Plotinus' philosophy. It stands midway between the phenomenal

---

[1] φιλοφροσύνη δὲ δεδήει, Empedocles, *Frag.* 130.

[2] I do not, of course, mean that the early philosophers, named by Aristotle in the passage just quoted, held this view.

world, of which it is the principle, and the world of Spirit, which is its principle. But the Soul is not only an intermediary between appearance and reality. It is the point where all converging and diverging lines meet ; ' it binds extremes together,'[1] and it is in vital correspondence with every region to which these lines lead. Within the Soul all metaphysical principles are represented. It touches every grade in the hierarchies of value and of existence, from the super-essential Absolute to the infra-essential Matter. It has its own centre, a life proper to itself ; but it can expand infinitely in every direction without ceasing to be itself.[2] The Soul is a microcosm ; as Aristotle says, ' the Soul is the real world.'[3] There is a sense in which each of us *is* the spiritual world[4] ; and we also share the being of the universal Soul. The Soul is the last Logos of the spiritual world, and the first of the phenomenal world, and is thus in vital connexion with both.[5] To maintain this connexion by constant movement is part of its nature.[6]

No limit has been set to its possible expansion. When the Soul raises itself to the realm of Spirit, ' it will see God and itself and the All ; it will not at first see itself as the All, but being unable to find a stopping-place, to fix its own limits and determine where it ceases to be itself, it will give up the attempt to distinguish itself from the universal Being, and will arrive at the All without change of place, abiding there, where the All has its home.'[7]

In modern idealism the Soul or self-conscious self tends to be the fixed centre, round which all revolves. In Plotinus it is the wanderer of the metaphysical world.

[1] 4. 4. 23. συνάπτει τὰ ἄκρα ἀλλήλοις.
[2] The Soul is ἐν μέσῳ, 4. 6. 3 ; μέσην τάξιν ἐν τοῖς οὖσιν ἐπισχοῦσαν 4. 8. 7 ; ὥσπερ κέντρον, 5. 1. 11 ; ἀρχὴν καὶ μέσα καὶ ἔσχατα ἔχει, 1. 8. 14.
[3] Aristotle, *De Anima*, 3. 8. 1. τὰ ὄντα πως ἡ ψυχή ἐστιν.
[4] ἐσμὲν ἕκαστος κόσμος νοητός, 3. 4. 3 ; νοοῦμεν ἐκεῖνα ὄντες ἐκεῖνοι, 6. 5. 7 ; ἔχει ἕκαστος αὐτὸν (νοῦν) ὅλον ἐν ψυχῇ τῇ πρώτῃ, 1. 1. 8.
[5] So for Clement the Soul is ἄλογον, σαρκικὸν, σωματικὸν πνεῦμα (πνεῦμα = the Neoplatonic νοῦς).
[6] 4. 7. 7.
[7] 6. 5. 7.

The life which we know in our external experience is not
the Soul's life. The Soul is in truth a stranger among the
things of sense. It realises itself by turning towards its
principle, and away from its own creations, which none
the less are good and necessary. But the world of sense
is, as it were, only the shadow of Soul cast by the sun of
Spirit ; and the more the Soul lives in the light of Spirit,
' turned towards ' that which is above itself, the more
creative it becomes, though its work is done with its
back turned.

Soul is the offspring of Spirit,[1] which, having perfect
life, must necessarily procreate and not be barren. It is
an energy thrown off by Spirit.[2] As an image of Spirit,
it resembles its principle closely. But while on one side
it is closely attached to Spirit, of which it is the effluence,[3]
on the other it touches the phenomenal world. Soul is
still a part of the Divine world, though the lowest part.[4]
' It is not Matter and Form, but Form only, and power,
and energy second to that of Spirit.'[5] Soul is eternal
and timeless. It may be compared to a moving circle
round the One, while Spirit is an unmoving circle.[6] Soul
is ' indivisible even when it is divided ; for it is all in all
and all in every part.'[7] Individual souls are Logoi of
Spirits,[8] more evolved (ἐξειλιγμέναι), that is to say, less
fully unified, than Spirits. It is only bodies, not souls,
that are in space, and subject to the mutual exclusiveness and incompenetrability of spatial existence. Soul is
distinguished from Spirit not by being localised, but,
among other things, by the presence of unfulfilled *desire*
in Soul, Spirit being free from all desires. Soul, as an
activity proceeding from Spirit, is in labour to create
after the pattern which it saw in Spirit, and from this
desire ' the whole world that we know arose and took its
shapes.'[9] Soul is separated from Spirit as word from
thought, as activity from power, as manifestation from
essence. It is of the nature of Soul to look both up and

---

[1] 5. 1. 7.　　　　[2] 5. 2. 1.　　　　[3] φῶς καὶ ἴχνος, 5. 1. 7.
[4] μέχρι τούτων τὰ θεῖα, 5. 1. 7.　　　[5] 4. 4. 16.　　　　[6] 4. 4. 16.
[7] 4. 2. 1.　　　　[8] 4. 3. 5. ; 5. 1. 6.　　　[9] 4. 7. 13 ; 3. 2. 2.

THE SOUL 205

down,[1] and so to be the intermediary between Spirit
and the world that we know. The Soul has its proper
place in this intermediate sphere.[2]

The Universal Soul

The Third Person in the Neoplatonic Trinity is not
the aggregate of individual Souls, the 'world of spirits'
which some modern philosophers have made the centre
of their systems, but 'the Soul of the All.' To this World-
Soul Plotinus assigns attributes which bring it very near
to the nature of Spirit.[3] The World-Soul is exalted above
Time and Space; it remains itself at rest while it vivifies
the world and gives it all the being that it has. The
World-Soul is not in the world; rather the World is in it,
embraced by it and moulded by it.

The individual Soul can understand itself only by contemplating the universal Soul. The passage in which
Plotinus urges us to this holy quest is one of the finest
in the Enneads. Part of it is familiar to thousands who
have never read Plotinus, because it has been closely
imitated by St. Augustine in a famous chapter of his
Confessions. ' The Soul ought first to examine its own
nature to know whether it has the faculty of contemplating spiritual things, and whether it has indeed an
eye wherewith to see them, and if it ought to embark
on the quest. If the spiritual world is foreign to it, what
is the use of trying? But if there is a kinship between
us and it, we both can and ought to find it. First then
let every Soul consider that it is the universal Soul which
created all things, breathing into them the breath of life [4]

---

[1] 4. 8. 8.   [2] 4. 8. 3.

[3] Plotinus thus distinguishes them (4. 8. 3) : ' Besides its spiritual
character, Soul has another character, in which its proper nature consists. By looking up to that which is above itself, it sees the spiritual
world; by recalling its gaze to itself, it maintains its own life; by
looking down at that which is below itself, it adorns, administers, and
governs it.' Soul is like the moon, Spirit like the sun; the moon shines
with borrowed light (5. 6. 4).

[4] ἐμπνεύσασα αὐτοῖς ζωήν. It is an interesting question whether
this is a conscious allusion to Genesis 2. 7. In 4. 3. 17 he has the phrase
φῶς ἐκ φωτός, which has a Christian sound. But the resemblances
may be accidental.

—into all living things which are on earth, in the air, and in the sea, and the Divine stars in heaven, the sun, and the great firmament itself. The Soul sets them in their order and directs their motions, keeping itself apart from the things which it orders and moves and causes to live. The Soul must be more honourable than they, since they are born and perish as the Soul grants them life and leaves them ; but the Soul lives for ever and never ceases to be itself. But how is life imparted, in the whole and in individuals ? The Great Soul must be contemplated by another Soul, itself no small thing, but one that makes itself worthy to contemplate the Great Soul by ridding itself, through quiet recollection, of deceit and of all that bewitches vulgar souls. For it let all be quiet ; not only the body which encompasses it, and the tumult of the senses ; but let all its environment be at peace. Let the earth be quiet and the sea and air, and the heaven itself waiting.[1] Let it observe how the Soul flows in from all sides into the resting world, pours itself into it, penetrates it and illumines it. Even as the bright beams of the sun enlighten a dark cloud and give it a golden border, so the Soul when it enters into the body of the heaven gives it life and immortality and awakens it from sleep. So the world, guided in an eternal movement by the Soul which directs it with intelligence, becomes a living and blessed being ; and the heaven, after the Soul has made it her habitation, becomes a thing of worth, after being, before the advent of the Soul, a dead body, mere earth and water, or rather darkness of Matter and

---

[1] I formerly thought that Kirchhoff's ἀκύμων (a word used by Plotinus in 1. 6. 5) was probably right for the MS. ἀμείνων. But I have now no doubt that Professor Sleeman's ἀναμένων (Professor Dodds had already suggested ἅμα μένων) is right. Cf. 6. 8. 9. ἀναμένειν δεῖ τὰ ἄλλα τί ποτε ὁ βασιλεὺς φανείη. Augustine closely imitates this passage in *Confessions* ix. 10. Dicebamus ergo : Si cui sileat tumultus carnis, sileant phantasiae terrae et aquarum et aëris, sileant poli, et ipsa sibi anima sileat, et transeat se non se cogitando ; sileant somnia et imaginariae revelationes, omnis lingua et omne signum, et quidquid transeundo fit, si cui sileat omnino ; quoniam si quis audiat dicunt haec omnia : non ipsi nos fecimus, sed fecit nos qui manet in aeternum.

above or 'before' it, the other with what is below or
'after' it. The practice is irritating to the logician, who
rightly insists that the intercalation of intermediate
terms bridges no gaps ; but as a picture of life it is true.
The higher Soul, having in itself the eternal light of life,
imparts it to all living beings as they are able to receive it.
Life alone begets life ;[1] even the One 'cannot be alone.'[2]
So the Soul must 'unroll' ($\dot{\epsilon}\xi\epsilon\lambda\dot{\iota}\tau\tau\epsilon\iota\nu$) its powers by
creating down to the utmost verge to which it can pene-
trate.

The connexion between Soul and Body is mediated by
Pneuma, a word which has far less importance and
dignity in Plotinus than in Christian theology. The
curious passage[3] in which, following Plato's *Timaeus*, he
speaks of the 'spherical motion' of Pneuma, does not
help us at all to understand the part which he wishes to
assign to it in the scale of existence. Porphyry and
Proclus say that Pneuma is the vehicle of the Soul ; the
former says that when the Soul is separated from the
Body it does not quit the Pneuma, which it has received
from the celestial spheres.[4] The idea seems to be that
the disembodied Soul remains invested with an ethereal
form, a sort of gaseous body. We find this ghost of
materialism even in Christian writers. Dante, following
no doubt some scholastic authority, clearly held it :[5]

> ' Tosto che luogo lì la circonscrive,
>> La virtù formativa raggia intorno,
>> Così e quanto nelle membra vive.
> E come l'aer, quand' è ben piorno,
>> Per l'altrui raggio che in sè si riflette,
>> Di diversi color si mostra adorno ;
> Così l'aer vicin quivi si mette
>> In quella forma, che in lui suggella
>> Virtualmente l' alma che ristette ;
> E simigliante poi alla fiamella
>> Che segue il fuoco là 'vunque si muta,
>> Segue allo spirto sua forma novella.'

---

[1] 3. 8. 5.   [2] δεῖ μὴ μόνον ἐν εἶναι, 4. 8. 6.
[3] 2. 2. 2.   [4] Porphyry, 'Ἀφορμαί, § 32.
[5] *Purgatorio*, xxv. 88–99.

The Pneuma is corporeal, though its substance is of extreme tenuity. It is an invisible, intangible body, the first incorporation of the Soul. Plotinus adds that there are very many ἄψυχα πνεύματα.[1] Such a conception seems to have no philosophical value, and Plotinus makes very little use of it. It would have been better if he had discarded it altogether.

And yet it is impossible to leave this important word, which fills so large a place in Christian Platonism, without some further comment. Reitzenstein says that the Pauline uses of Pneuma are all to be found in the Hermetic literature and magical papyri. 'The Spirit,' or 'the divine Spirit,' is contrasted with 'Body' and with 'Flesh.' Sometimes Pneuma and Soul seem to be identical. But in other passages Pneuma and Soul are contrasted, the latter being the principle of natural human life, the former of Divine inspiration or indwelling. He thinks that the Gnostic classification of men as 'sarkic, psychic, and pneumatic' is not borrowed from St. Paul, but from the mystery-religions. But in the mystery-documents the 'pneumatic' seems to be always a man in a state of ecstasy, whereas it was one of the great achievements of St. Paul's theology to ethicise the conception of Pneuma which he found in the Old Testament, and to teach that the Holy Spirit is an abiding possession of the true Christian. This makes Pneuma much more like the Plotinian Nous ; and it is important to observe that the two words are sometimes interchangeable, both in the papyri and occasionally in St. Paul.[2] In Origen the identification of Pneuma with the Neoplatonic Nous is almost complete. Pneuma is sinless ; it is the master and judge of the Soul.[3]

The activity of the Soul is truly creative ; all life comes

---

[1] 4. 7. 4.
[2] References and quotations in Kennedy, *St. Paul and the Mystery Religions*, p. 149. For St. Paul see Rom. 11. 34 ; 1 Cor. 2. 16. But generally in St. Paul νοῦς=λογικὴ ψυχή. The Pauline terminology is complicated by his occasional use of καρδία for the inner life generally.
[3] Origen, *in Rom.* 2. 9.

from life.[1] Below its influence we can find nothing but
the absolute indeterminateness of Matter. The extent
to which the contents of the world are animated by Soul
varies infinitely, so that nature presents us with a living
chain of being,[2] an unbroken series of ascending or
descending values. The whole constitutes a harmony,[3]
in which each inferior grade is ' in ' the next above.[4]
Each existence is thus vitally connected with all others.
This conception, which asserts the right of the lower
existences to be what and where they are, is difficult to
reconcile with the Platonic doctrine of a ' fall of the
Soul.' It is, however, Plotinus' own view, whenever he
is not hampered by loyalty to the tradition. His critics
have not emphasised nearly enough the unbroken connexion of higher and lower, which in this philosophy is
much closer than that which connects individual objects
on the same plane with each other. These latter are
connected indirectly, though the connexion of each with
a common principle ; the bond of unity between the
higher and lower products of Soul is the aspiration, the
activity, the life (ἔφεσις, ἐνέργεια, ζωή), which is the
reality of the world of becoming.

Faculties of the Soul

Sensation (αἴσθησις)

The Neoplatonic theory of knowledge is best discussed
in connexion with the faculties of the Soul, as enumerated
by Plotinus. Beginning at the bottom, only omitting the
feeblest manifestations of Soul, in vegetable life, we shall
first consider Sensation.

The ' Soul in Matter ' (ἡ ἔνυλος ψυχή)[5] has as its proper

---

[1] ζωὴ ἐκ ζωῆς, 3. 8. 5.   [2] τάξιν ἐφεξῆς, 2. 9. 13.
[3] συμφωνία, 4. 3. 12 ; τὸ πᾶν ἓν καὶ μία ἁρμονία, 2. 3. 5 ; σύνταξις
μία, σύμπνοια μία, 2. 3. 7.   [4] 5. 5. 9.
[5] 2. 3. 17. This soul includes ἡ φυτικὴ ἐνέργεια, τὸ θρεπτικὸν, τὸ
αὐξητικὸν, τὸ γεννητικὸν ; also the power of feeling pleasure and pain ;
this power is called ἡ ἕξω αἴσθησις or ἕξις παθητική. Further, it includes
ἡ φαντασία, τὸ ὀρεκτικὸν, τὸ ἐπιθυμητικὸν, and τὸ θυμοειδές.

character Sensation, which resides in the part which is 'common' to Soul and Body. Plotinus insists that we must not regard Sensation as a passive impression made by external objects on the perceiving faculty. It is an activity (an ἐνέργεια, not a πάθος) ;[1] 'a kind of force' (ἰσχύς τις).[2] It is not the eye which sees, but the active power of the Soul (4. 6. 3). 'External sensation,' he says, impresses forms (τύποι) on the 'animal nature' (τὸ ζῷον), and these forms which are spiritual things (νοητά) can be perceived by the Soul.[3] Sensation is a reception of Form, for the nature of Form must be an activity, which creates by being present.[4] The difference between sensations and spiritual perceptions (νοήσεις) is one of degree ; sensations are dim spiritual perceptions, spiritual perceptions are clear sensations.[5] This doctrine of sensation or sense-perception as an activity of the Soul is found also in Wordsworth. Sir Walter Raleigh says :[6] ' In the Lines written above Tintern Abbey, and often elsewhere, Wordsworth makes division of ' all the mighty world of eye and ear ' into ' what they half-create, and what perceive.' The shaping energy of the mind is never dormant. Perception itself is largely the work of imagination ; it is a transaction between the outer powers that operate on the mind through the senses and the inner powers of the mind itself, which impose their own powers on the things submitted to it. Berkeley's doctrine is very similar.[7] ' Sense supplies images to memory. These become subjects for fancy to work upon. Reason considers and judges of the imaginations. And these acts of reason become new objects to the understanding. Each lower faculty is a step that leads to one above it. And the uppermost naturally leads to the Deity. There runs a chain through the whole system of

---

[1] 3. 6. 1, αἰσθήσεις οὐ πάθη ἀλλ' ἐνέργειαι περὶ τὰ παθήματα. Aristotle De Anima, 2. 5, had asserted the contrary ; but with qualifications. See Wallace, Aristotle's Psychology, p. lviii.
[2] 4. 6. 3.   [3] 1. 1. 7.   [4] 1. 1. 2.   [5] 6. 7. 7.
[6] Wordsworth, p. 158.
[7] I do not mean that Berkeley makes sense an activity.

beings. In this chain one link drags another.'[1] We may add that every sensation implies an intellectual reference, including a distinction between the actual fact and the preceding moment.

The actual process of sensation is explained by the doctrine of sympathies, a very important part of this philosophy. All the activities of the Soul are 'movements,' including that activity which gives life to a body. This vital force possesses a sort of consciousness which embraces all the parts of the being which it vivifies.[2] From this unity, and consciousness of unity, proceeds a 'faint sympathy,'[3] which pervades, in various degrees, the whole world, proving that it is itself a living individual. This sympathy extends to the organs of the body and to the sensible objects which come in contact with them. The fact of sensation is thus evidence of the living unity of nature.

The powers of the sensitive Soul are localised in certain parts of the body. Sight, hearing, taste, and smell have each their own organs. Only the sense of touch is present wherever there are nerves.[4] But the real organ of sensation is the seminal Logos, just as Soul is the organ of discursive reason.[5]

The knowledge which sensation gives is only 'belief' (πίστις),[6] since the Soul in sensation has not in itself the things which it perceives.[7] The object perceived by the senses is only an image of the spiritual reality ; sensation is a kind of dream of the Soul.[8] Or we may say that sensation is the messenger of the King, Spirit.[9]

---

[1] Berkeley, *Siris*, § 303.
[2] ἡ συναίσθησις τὸ τῆς ψυχῆς εἴδωλον μετὰ τοῦ σώματος ἔχει, I. I. II.
[3] ἀμυδρὰ συμπάθεια, 4. 5. 2.
[4] 4. 3. 23.
[5] 6. 7. 5. 7.
[6] In Proclus (*Theol. Plat.* I. I) πίστις has quite a new dignity. See note on p. 89.
[7] 5. 5. I.
[8] τὸ τῆς αἰσθήσεως ψυχῆς ἐστιν εὐδούσης, 3. 6. 6.
[9] αἴσθησις ἡμῖν ἄγγελος, βασιλεὺς δὲ ἐκεῖνος (=νοῦς), 5. 3. 3.

Modern psychologists have raised the question whether there is actually a sensational level of experience, as distinguished from the perceptual. Plotinus, if I understand him rightly, would deny that a purely sensational experience can exist. It is a limit, like ' Matter ' ; a limit to which the lower kinds of experience approximate in various degrees. But consciousness, it is probable, always implies perception. In all consciousness there is a synthesis of sense-material, an interpretation and combination of elements ; and this, as Plotinus rightly says, is an activity of the Soul. Whenever we recognise an object as a definite thing, we begin to apply the categories of identity and difference, of the universal and the particular. Practically, we also always recognise change. And since it is only the permanent that changes, the recognition of change involves that of permanence. Thus, if it is difficult to draw any line between sensation and perception, it is equally difficult to say where perception passes into thought.

Plato discredited sense-perception on the ground that it pictures reality as in a state of growth and decay, which cannot be true, since real being cannot pass into not-being. Modern philosophy, leaving these dialectical puzzles, has studied the physiology of sensation, and has maintained the old distinction between primary and secondary qualities. Sugar, it is said, is not ' really ' sweet ; it only tastes sweet ; and there is no resemblance between the sensation and the object which evokes it. Waves of ether are not at all like light. On the other hand, bodies are ' really ' extended and movable and solid. But it is very doubtful whether this distinction can be maintained.[1] Our ideas of primary qualities are derived from sensation ; and the space-picture is not taken in from the external world, but produced in much the same manner as our perceptions of secondary qualities. According to Lotze, we have no more ground for regarding extension

[1] There is an excellent discussion of this in Professor Pringle-Pattison's *Idea of God*, p. 120, sq.

as an absolute property of things than taste or colour. If this is so, the conclusion will certainly be drawn that we have no ground for believing in the objective existence of Body at all. But Plotinus does not anticipate Berkeley. Reality for him is not mental, though there can be no reality without mind. If we reduce the phenomenal world to a mere thought of the Soul, we shall have to make the spiritual world a mere thought of Spirit, and this is by no means what Plotinus intended. The illusory but not wholly imaginary οὐσία of the objects of sense-perception is an imperfect picture of the real οὐσία which is known by Spirit.

Pleasure and Pain

Pleasure and Pain belong neither to the Body nor to the Soul, but to 'the compound,' that is to say, to the Soul present to the Body, or the Body present to the Soul. The higher or reasonable Soul, in which our personality resides, does not *feel* these sensations, though it is aware of them.[1] The higher part of the Soul wears the Body, with its pleasures and pains, like a garment;[2] they belong to it, but it is detached from them. Pleasure and pain are only possible because the union of 'the compound' is unstable ; we feel pain when we recognise that 'the Body is deprived of the image of the Soul'; we feel pleasure when harmony is restored between them.

Plotinus is right in saying—for this is his meaning—that pleasure and pain are not pure sensations, since they are states of consciousness ; and, on the other hand, that they are not affections (πάθη) of the Soul. What is characteristic of pleasure and pain is that they 'tell us nothing beyond themselves, have no meaning, and suggest no object or idea.'[3] And when they are over, they are as if they had never been. We do not feel better for

---

[1] ἡμῖν δὲ ἡ τούτου ἀλγηδὼν καὶ ἡ τοιαύτη ἡδονὴ εἰς γνῶσιν ἀπαθῆ ἔρχεται, 4. 4. 18.   [2] 4. 4. 18.
[3] Bosanquet, *The Value and Destiny of the Individual*, p. 37.

having had a good dinner last week, nor worse for having
had a bad toothache the week before. (We are speaking
only of physical pleasure and pain : psychical and spiritual
experiences, whether happy or miserable, have often a
vitality as strong as our own lives.) This isolation and
ephemeral character of pleasure and pain stamp them
as being very slightly connected with the real or spiritual
world. They are associated exclusively with finite *foci*,
and cannot pass beyond them. The Soul can therefore
to a large extent conquer them by living upon its own
highest level. It will then continue to be conscious of
them, but not as states of itself.

Memory (μνήμη—ἀνάμνησις)

Memory and Imagination (φαντασία), which in Plotinus
are closely connected,[1] belong to the Discursive Reason
(διάνοια). Memory has no place in the Spiritual World,
which is above time. For Memory is always of something
which was but is no longer ;[2] the object present to pure
Spirit is eternal and unchanging. The chief difference
between Memory and Imagination is that the phantasm
carries with it little connotation of truth or falsehood with
reference to any external object, and implies no relation
to any time in past experience at which it was originally
presented.[3] Memory, on the other hand, implies at once
an object to which it corresponds, and it is attended by
a consciousness of some time in the past at which the remembered event actually happened. Consequently, as
Aristotle saw, it is only those living beings which possess
a sense of time that are capable of Memory. Aristotle,
however, distinguishes between Memory proper (μνήμη),
which is the passive faculty of retention, ' the permanent
possession of a sensuous picture as a copy which represents the object of which it is the picture,'[4] and Recollec·

---

[1] τοῦ φανταστικοῦ ἡ μνήμη, 4. 3. 31.   [2] 4. 4. 6.
[3] Wallace, *Aristotle's Psychology*, xciii.
[4] *De Anima*, 451 a, 15.

cion (ἀνάμνησις), the power of active search or recall. Modern psychologists in the same way distinguish between spontaneous and voluntary Memory.[1] Even Plotinus, who clearly holds that there can be no Memory without an activity of the Soul,[2] speaks of μνήμη as a πάθημα τῆς ψυχῆς.[3] Recollection demands a higher kind of volitional and rational activity, and is confined to man, while Memory is found also in the lower animals. In ' Recollection,' which gives actuality to the notions which the Soul possessed only potentially, ' time is not present.' Plotinus transforms Plato's ' Recollection ' into a doctrine of innate ideas potentially present. Memory is always of something which the Soul has experienced, not of something innate. Recollection, on the other hand, is of things which belong to the Soul, but which are not always active in it. The term ' Memory ' is incorrectly applied to the spiritual energising of the Soul in accordance with its innate principles.[4] Time belongs to memory, not to recollection. The higher Soul, which constitutes our personality, has Memory, though Spirit has it not ; the lower Soul has a Memory of its own. In a sense, Memory constitutes the empirical *ego*.[5] After death these two Souls are separated, though each retains a dim consciousness of what belongs to the other.[6] Both preserve a Memory of friends, country, etc. ; but the inferior Soul mixes them with passive emotions, while the superior remembers only the higher experiences.[7] The superior Soul is by choice forgetful of all that is foreign to its true nature. At the same time, it *recovers* ideas which belong to earlier and nobler states of existence, which it has forgotten here below. Lastly, Memory is of images only ; spiritual perception (νόησις) is first transformed into an image reflected in the mirror of imagination ; and Memory is that which grasps this

---

[1] Maher, *Psychology*, p. 179. [2] 3. 6. 2.
[3] 4. 3. 26, a criticism of the Stoical theory of impressions.
[4] 4. 3. 25. [5] 4. 4. 3, οὗ μνημονεύει ἐκεῖνό ἐστι καὶ γίγνεται.
[6] 4. 3. 27. [7] τὰ ἀστεῖα τῶν παθῶν, 4. 3. 32.

image.[1] We do not 'remember' νοητά, because we contemplate them as permanent activities of our highest self. The Soul when contemplating spiritual things does not 'remember' even itself; self-consciousness, which on the psychic plane always involves Memory, is not the highest state of the Soul.[2] There is such a thing as unconscious Memory.[3]

In spite of his doctrine that there is no Memory Yonder, Plotinus would not have combated the following statement of Paulsen.[4] 'The fact that we retain the past in memory gives us an idea of the permanent relation between the individual Soul and the universal Spirit.' It might also be maintained that what we remember is always the significance—the noëtic correspondences—of a past event, though we may often misinterpret that significance.

Imagination (φαντασία)

In Plato φαντασία, or τὸ φανταστικόν, 'the image-making faculty,' holds the lowest rank among the intellectual faculties of the Soul. It is the mental representation of an object actually absent, the memory of a sensible object. It is the waking dream of the Soul. Plato indulges in a characteristic fancy when he makes the liver the seat of the Imagination. The power proceeding from Nous sends upon this organ thoughts (διανοήματα), which, reflected on its bright surface, are transformed into images. The Imagination is the faculty of representing thoughts under the form of images.[5]

In Aristotle φαντασία is defined as 'the movement which results upon an actual sensation,' i.e. the continued presence of an impression after the object which first excited it has been removed from actual experience. So

---

[1] 4. 3. 30.   [2] 4. 4. 2; 4. 4. 4.; 3. 9. 3.; 5. 3. 4.
[3] 4. 4. 4.   J. W. Gregory (*Making of the Earth*) says 'crystals have a longer memory than any organic life.' This theory of unconscious memory is of considerable importance in recent thought. Professor James Ward, among others, has dealt with it.
[4] *Introduction to Philosophy*, p. 243.
[5] Plato, *Timaeus*, 71.

Hobbes defines fancies as 'motions within us, reliques of those made in the sense.'[1] Imagination is closely associated with sensation ; the faculty which receives sensations is identical with that which forms pictures ; but they are manifested in different ways. And there are obvious differences between the two : sense requires an object to excite it into activity, imagination does not ; sense is always ready to act, imagination is capricious ; sensation belongs to every animal, imagination only to those which are more highly organised. The reports of sense are, so far as they go, true ; those of imagination are often false, and sometimes have no relation to any external fact. We can exercise imagination when our eyes are shut. Imagination differs from opinion ($\delta\acute{o}\xi a$), in that opinion is always attended by belief ($\pi\acute{\iota}\sigma\tau\iota s$), which implies an act of thought and reason. Nor can we regard imagination as a combination of opinion and sensation. Our opinion does not always coincide with our conception of our sensations. Our eyes tell us that the sun is an inch or two across ; but our opinion is that it is larger than the earth.

The faculty of forming pictures is so independent of the judgment that illusions frequently occur. 'Movements of the senses themselves,' without any objective excitation, produce the same pictures as those which arise when the object of sensation is itself in movement. During sleep especially, the restraints put by the understanding on the image-making faculty are inhibited ; and the phenomenon of dreaming is the result.

This theory of imagination appears at first sight to be pure materialism. The impressions of sense are conceived as strictly analogous to the impressions of a seal upon wax. But for Aristotle the impressions of sense are not themselves material ;[2] they are generalised conceptions ; and so the pictures of the imagination tend to pass into ideas.

---

[1] Wallace, *Aristotle's Psychology*, p. lxxxvii.
[2] They are $a\iota\sigma\theta\acute{\eta}\mu a\tau a$ $\check{a}\nu\epsilon\upsilon$ $\check{\upsilon}\lambda\eta s$.

The Stoics conceived the human mind as a material
substance, which at birth is like a sheet of clean paper.
Impressions (φαντασίαι) are made upon it through the
senses. Some of these impressions are true ; others are
false. False impressions may be subjective delusions ;
or they may be the result of carelessness, or of excite-
ment. True impressions conform to and resemble the
objects ; and they have a distinctive power of gripping
the mind and being gripped by it. We recognise a true
impression by its irresistible clearness ; it is (literally,
for the Stoic materialist) stamped, with every outline
distinct, on the surface of the Soul.[1] These impressions
are turned into concepts by the free assent of the mind,
on the basis of man's common experience. Men differ,
not about the natural concepts themselves, but in the
application of them : e.g. the Jews and Romans agree
in preferring holiness to all things, but differ as to whether
it is impious to eat swine's flesh.[2] The crude materialism
of this theory of mental impressions is easy to criticise ;
but we have seen that even Aristotle used somewhat
similar language. In fact it was not till a late stage of
Greek philosophy that materialism was recognised as
such, and rejected. The doctrine of irresistible impressions (καταληπτικὴ φαντασία) as a criterion of certainty,
is not valueless. The Stoics insist that it is only the
healthy mind that can trust its clear convictions ; also
that the standard is not private and subjective, but the
consensus of sane, calm, careful, and unprejudiced persons. Assent to sense-impressions is a voluntary act ;
and the will that accepts or rejects them is a moral and
rational will, already convinced that the world is an
ordered system, which makes for righteousness.

Plotinus deals with imagination in the First and Fourth
Enneads. In the First Ennead[3] he defines imagination

---

[1] So Descartes (*Discours sur la Méthode*, Part 4) says, ' I judged
that I could take for my general rule that the things which we conceive very clearly are all true.'

[2] Epictetus, *Diss.* I. 22.   [3] I. 8. 15.

as 'the impact from outside on the irrational soul.' This, however is only the 'sensible imagination'; there is also an 'intellectual imagination.' He returns to the subject in the Fourth Ennead,[1] where he says that the higher imagination is attached to the rational, the lower to the irrational soul.

Imagination, opinion (δόξα), and reasoning (διάνοια) have their places in an ascending scale between sensation and νόησις. Perception, as an act of knowledge, seizes the forms (εἴδη) of sensible objects. At the summit of this faculty, when the percept (αἴσθημα) becomes a purely mental representation, the faculty takes the name of imagination (τὸ φανταστικόν) in presence of the object, of memory in its absence. Imagination transforms into images both the forms of sensible objects, and our thoughts about them. Imagination is midway between sensation and reasoning; in its higher state it passes into opinion (δόξα).

Here, as elsewhere, we are troubled by difficulties of nomenclature. Φαντασία is not exactly 'imagination,' being nearer to the German Vorstellung; and the representation of material objects apart from their presence, which Plotinus calls φάντασμα, modern philosophy incorrectly calls an idea.[2] The differences between the idea or phantasm and the percept, presentation, or impression, are well summed up by Mr. Maher.[3] The idea is almost invariably very faint in intensity as compared with the impression. The representation is transitory, the perceived object is permanent. The image is normally subject to our control; the sensation, so long as the sense is exposed to the action of the object, is independent of us. Most important of all is the reference to objective reality which accompanies the act of sense-perception, but is absent from that of the imagination.

[1] 4. 3. 30, 31 ; and cf. 4. 4. 13.
[2] An idea should mean, according to the invariable usage of the ancients, a universal representation of Noûs.
[3] Psychology, p. 163.

Imagination plays a more important part in mental
life and progress than is often supposed. ' The imagination is the prophetic forerunner of all great scientific
discoveries.'[1] Even in the most abstract of sciences,
such as mathematics, it has its indispensable place. In
religion it has had, and still has, an immense influence.
' Mythology is an observation of things encumbered
with all that they can suggest to a dramatic fancy. It
is neither conscious poetry nor valid science, but the
common root and raw material of both. . . . It belongs
to a level of thought, when men pored on the world with
intense indiscriminate interest, accepting and recording
the mind's vegetation no less than that observable in
things, and mixing the two developments together in
one wayward drama.'[2] At all levels of culture, it fills
innumerable gaps in experience, and builds bridges over
many a *salto mortale*.

Wordsworth[3] has a magnificent passage in praise of
spiritual imagination, the νοερὰ φαντασία of Plotinus.

> ' This spiritual love acts not nor can exist
>   Without imagination, which in truth
>   Is but another name for absolute power
>   And clearest insight, amplitude of mind,
>   And reason in her most exalted mood.'

This exalts imagination to a higher position than
Plotinus could have conceded to his φαντασία. Imagination, for Wordsworth, is Spirit creating, after its own
image, ideas which are the lode-star or guiding light of
the soul, up to the very end of its Godward course. Even
' intellectual love,' the νοῦς ἐρῶν which conducts Plotinus
above the world of Spirit to the vision of the One, is for
Wordsworth inseparable from imagination. It is this

[1] Baldwin, *Senses and Intellect*, p. 236.
[2] Santayana, *Reason in Religion*, p. 49.
[3] *Prelude*, xiv. 188. Reference must also be made to the eloquent
pages in Ruskin's *Modern Painters*, which treat of imagination asso-
ciative, penetrative, and contemplative, and its difference from fancy.
Imagination, for Ruskin as for Wordsworth, is a mystical faculty
which sees into the heart of things.

faculty which gives us faith in God and immortality, by
presenting to us clear images of eternal truths. The
difference between this teaching and that of Plotinus is
not so great as appears, because the Greek philosopher
acknowledges the fact and value of these spiritual images,
though he would ascribe them to a higher faculty than
imagination. And Wordsworth himself knew that in
the mystical trance imagination is quiescent. But the
doctrine that ' intellectual love ' is in indissoluble union
with imagination, and creates images which are the
reflection of ' reason in her most exalted mood,' is highly
important. It is the key to the understanding of religious
symbols generally, which have a high truth as creations
of imagination and love acting together, but which have
a fatal tendency either to petrify or to evaporate, losing
in the process both their truth and their value. When
they petrify, they become flat historical recitals, imposed
tyrannically upon the mind and conscience as tests of
institutional loyalty. When they evaporate, they become
poetical fancies, emotional luxuries which form the
content of a spurious and superficial mysticism. Wordsworth indicates this latter danger in his useful distinction
between imagination and fancy, the latter a wayward
and sportive faculty, which invents types and sympathies
instead of finding them. Fancy, as Ruskin says, is never
quite serious ; and the religion which gives it the rein is
seldom quite serious either.

Principal J. C. Shairp[1] analyses poetic imagination as
follows. To our ordinary conceptions of things it adds
force, clearness, and distinctness. It seems to be a power
intermediate between intellect and emotion. In its
highest form, it would seem to be based upon moral
intensity. The emotional and the intellectual in it act
and react on each other. In its highest form it is that
intense intuition which goes straight to the core of an
object, and lays hold of the essential life of a scene.
It is that by which Shakespeare read the inmost

[1] Shairp, *Aspects of Poetry*, pp. 6–8.

heart of man, Wordsworth of nature. It is also the combining and harmonising power, and it is the power which clothes intellectual and spiritual conceptions in appropriate forms. As Shakespeare says, it 'bodies forth the forms of things unknown.' But it can also spiritualise what is visible and corporeal, filling it with a higher meaning. It is not, as has sometimes been supposed, a deceiving faculty ; rather it is pre-eminently a truthful and truth-seeing faculty, perceiving aspects of truth which can find no entrance by any other inlet. It is accompanied by a delight in the object or truth beheld, a thrill which is one of the most exquisite moods that man ever experiences.

Opinion (δόξα)

This, in Plotinus, is simply the superior form of imagination. It consists of unsystematised isolated beliefs about things.

Reason[1] (διάνοια)

In the discursive reason the proper function of the Soul is achieved.[2] The most instructive passage is in 5. 3. 3. 'Sensation has seen a man and furnished the image (τύπον) of him to reason. And what does reason say ? It may say nothing yet, but takes knowledge of him and there stops. But if reason reflects with itself 'who is this ? ' and having met him before, calls in the help of memory, it says, 'It is Socrates.' If it develops the form of Socrates, it divides what imagination gave it. If it adds that Socrates is good, it speaks still of things known by the senses, but what it affirms—' goodness '— it takes from itself, because it has with it the standard of the good (κανόνα τοῦ ἀγαθοῦ). But how can it have the good in itself ? Because it has the form of the good

---

[1] Perhaps ' understanding' would have been the best English word for διάνοια.

[2] Plato three times in the *Republic* uses διάνοια for νόησις. There is no sharp division in Plotinus, for νοήσεων ἐνέργεια ἡ διάνοια ἡ ἀληθής, I. I. 9.

(ἀγαθοειδής) and is strengthened for the perception of goodness by the Spirit which shines upon it ; for this pure power of Soul receives the prints of Spirit which is just above it. But why should we call all that is superior to sensation Soul rather than Spirit ? It is because the power of the Soul consists in reasoning, and all these operations belong to the reasoning faculty. But why do we not attribute self-knowledge to Soul, and so make an end ? Because we have assigned to reason the busy examination of external things, while Spirit, we say, examines only itself and what it has in itself. If anyone says, ' Why should not reason, by another faculty of the Soul, examine what belongs to itself ? ' the answer is that then we should have pure Spirit, and not reason. ' But what hinders that pure Spirit should be in the Soul ? ' ' Nothing hinders.' ' But does it belong to Soul ? ' No, it is rather ' our Spirit,' something other than the reasoning faculty, something that has soared up, something that is still ours, though we do not count it among the parts of the Soul. It is ours and not ours. We use it and we use it not, though reason we use always. It is ours when we use it, and not ours when we use it not. What do we mean by using it ? Is it not that we become it, and speak as if we were it—or rather as if we were made like it (κατ' ἐκεῖνον) ? For we are not Spirit ; we are made it by our highest reasoning faculty which receives Spirit. For we perceive by our perceptive faculty ; and it is we who perceive. Do we then reason in the same manner ? It is we who reason, and who think the spiritual thoughts that are in the mind (νοοῦμεν τὰ ἐν τῇ διανοίᾳ νοήματα). This is ourselves ; while the products of spiritual activity are above us, and the products of sense-perception below us. This is the proper sphere of the Soul, between sense-perception and Spirit. We all agree that sense-perception belongs to us, because we always have it. We are not sure whether Spirit is ours, because we do not use it always, and because it is detached from us—detached in so far as it does not bend down to

us, but we rather have to look up to it. Sense-perception
is our messenger, Spirit is our king.'

In such a passage the difficulty of finding English
words for some of the most important technical terms in
the philosophy is acute. But my hearers will have understood by this time that νοῦς and its derivatives always
refer to the inner life of Spirit in the world of eternal
reality, while διάνοια and its verb refer to the discursive
reason, the ordinary processes of thought. Sensation
and sense-perception operate on a lower level than
διάνοια, which is the proper activity of Soul.

In another place[1] he asks how we can account for the
blunders of opinion and discursive reason. Spirit, it is
admitted, is impeccable; is the Soul impeccable too?
He answers, as usual, that Soul or personality is not a
fixed entity. The 'true man, the pure man,' possesses
spiritual virtues, which belong to the detached or separated (χωριστὴ or χωριζομένη) Soul. The Soul may win
detachment even on earth. But 'we are double'; and
the lower Soul is entangled in the illusions of bodily
existence. The most intimate and characteristic activities of the Soul (ἴδια τῆς ψυχῆς) are those which 'do not
need the body for their exercise.'

The Soul and Consciousness

Self-consciousness belongs to the reasoning faculty.
The Soul 'turns to itself and knows itself and the things
that belong to it.' Consciousness is not primitive; it
accrues (γίγνεται). The psychic principle of life is reflected as in a mirror, in which 'we see ourselves as
another.'[2] The Soul knows itself truly only when it
knows itself as Spirit. But the highest activity of
the Soul is not self-conscious[3] in the ordinary sense,
though in another sense we may say that Spirit alone is
self-conscious. What we commonly mean by self-
consciousness is awareness of ourself as an object different

[1] 1. 1. 9.   [2] 1. 4. 10.   [3] 5. 3. 14; 5. 8. 11.

from the perceiving subject. But this is a sign that we
have not yet reached our goal, which is that the seer and
the seen shall be as one. Consciousness is aroused most
sharply by what is alien and hostile, just as when the
body is in health it is not conscious of its organs; 'we do
not feel ourselves nor what belongs to us.' 'We cannot
get outside ourselves.' Plotinus observes also that we
do things best when we are not thinking of ourselves as
doing them.[1] Thus what we usually call self-consciousness
is for Plotinus consciousness of externality. When we
'lose our Soul and find it' in Spirit, we are what we contemplate, and can no longer objectify it as something
other than the perceiving mind. So R. L. Nettleship
says, 'I am getting more and more convinced that being
conscious of something is just *not* the idea or consciousness
of what we say it is, but of something else. It means that
we are *not* ourselves fully.' This seems to me perfectly
sound. Consciousness of self is in truth consciousness of
a contrasted not-self, with which notwithstanding we
claim kinship. Strictly speaking, there is no such thing
as self-consciousness. 'We cannot too strongly insist,'
says Professor Taylor, 'that if by self-consciousness we
mean a cognitive state which is its own object, there is
no such thing, and it is a psychological impossibility that
there should be any such thing as self-consciousness.
No cognitive state ever has itself for its own object.
Every cognitive state has for its object something other
than itself.'[2] What we call self-consciousness is an

---

[1] So Raphael is said to have observed to Leonardo da Vinci: 'I
have noticed that when one paints one should think of nothing; everything then comes better.' In some arts the automatism of the expert
performer is obvious. The thoughts of the professional bowler at the
moment of delivering the ball cannot be of a very complex nature.
Sir James Paget 'remembered once hearing Mdlle Janotha play a
presto by Mendelssohn, and he counted the notes and the time occupied.
She played 5,595 notes in four minutes three seconds.' In art, men
begin to theorise only when inspiration has died down. This is plain
from architecture, sculpture, and painting. And in morals, two of the
chief Christian graces, humility and purity, are entirely spoilt when
we begin to think about them.

[2] A. E. Taylor, *Elements of Metaphysics*, p. 79.

experience which has its place in mental growth; it is useful for certain purposes; but it is not an ultimate state of the human Spirit. In our best and most effective moments, when we really ' enter into ' our work, we leave it behind. But there is an experience of living—a ' waking state,' as Plotinus calls it, which becomes ours when we are identified with the object of our knowledge. This is the experience of pure Spirit, especially when it ' turns towards the One.' When we reach this state, we often doubt whether the experience is real, because the senses ' protest that they have seen nothing.' Of course they have not, because we are then concerned with the supersensible. Hence there is a kind of unconsciousness in the highest experiences of the Soul, though we can no more doubt them than our own existence.[1] Plotinus also shows that in the spiritual world it is nonsense to separate thought and the consciousness of thought.[2]

Plotinus distinguishes two forms of consciousness: (1) συναίσθησις, which is sometimes called αἴσθησις and παρακολούθησις—the knowledge which a being has of the unity of its parts;[3] (2) ἀντίληψις—the consciousness of the opposition of subject and object in self-consciousness. It is the prerogative of Spirit to know itself as itself;[4] Soul knows itself ' as another's.'[5] The Soul, in knowing itself, knows ' that there is something better than itself.'[6] Discursive thought, the characteristic activity of the Soul, contains within itself neither the material nor the formal nor the final conditions of its own thinking. It reasons about data supplied by sense, in order to gain knowledge. Its powers are directed to transcending the conditions of their own activities. It is not the presence of the subject-object relation which for Plotinus is the sign of inherent limitations in discursive thought; but the conscious *opposition* of the self and the not-self. When the level of spiritual perception

---

[1] 5. 8. 11.   [2] 2. 9. 1.
[3] It knows τὰ ἔνδον γιγνόμενα, 5. 3. 2.
[4] 5. 3. 4.   [5] 5. 3. 6.   [6] 5. 3. 4.

is gained, the externality of the object has wholly
disappeared, though the duality which is the condition of thought remains. Discursive thought is the
polarised 'copy' of νόησις, which is at once creative and
immanent activity. Discursive thought, as opposed to
creative or purposive thought, 'of itself moves nothing,'
as Aristotle says ; but διάνοια is in fact never separated
from νόησις at one end, and creativeness (ποίησις) at
the other. Plotinus intentionally makes νοῦς and
διάνοια overlap. He speaks of 'reasoning Spirit, Spirit
in differentiation and motion.'[1] Soul, on the other hand,
is 'the Matter of Spirit, being of spiritual form.'[2] Soul
is itself within the world of Spirit and must of necessity
be unified[3] with it. Soul is οὐσία ; there is no line between
it and Spirit. The realm of Soul is the 'world of life' ;[4]
it is in this world that individuals live and move ; Spirit
is 'above us.'[5] That part of the Soul which remains when
we have separated from it the body and its passions is
'the image of Spirit.'[6] And yet Plotinus reminds us that
even 'the Soul here below,' which is not the Soul in its
full potency, possesses true Being, and hence the wisdom,
justice, and knowledge which it possesses are not mere
shadows—they too are real. Indeed, if we include in
'the sensible world' the Soul and all that belongs to it,
there is nothing Yonder that is not also Here.[7] But the
world of Soul, as we know it, is only real when it is taken
as a whole. It is split up among individual *foci* of consciousness, and in time. The soul-world, as we know it in
experience, is a world of claims and counter-claims, in
which *things* are known as *instruments* for the striving
individual. This experience does not express the highest
truth about the contents of this world. The pity of it is
that language, which was made for the fireside and the

---

[1] νοῦς λογιζόμενος, νοῦς ἐν διαστάσει καὶ κινήσει, νοῦς μεθεκτός.
[2] νοῦ ὕλη νοοειδὴς οὖσα, 5. 1. 3.
[3] ἡ ψυχὴ ἐν τῷ νοητῷ οὖσα . . . εἰς ἕνωσ ν ἐλθεῖν τῷ νῷ ἀνάγκη 4. 4. 2.
[4] κόσμος ζωτικὸς is identified by Proclus with ψυχή. Plotinus, too,
calls ψυχὴ ὁ τῆς ζωῆς κόσμος, 6. 4. 12. [5] 1. 1. 8.
[6] 5. 3. 9. Bouillet well comp res a passage from the *Fons Vitæ* of
Ibn Gebirol. [7] 5. 9. 13.

market-place, helps to stamp this view of life on our minds, since it cannot easily express any other. Wordsworth, and other poets and prophets too, have lamented this incurable imperfection in human speech. But the world of souls, and of soul-making, is after all the world in which we have to live. There are ' other heights in other worlds, God willing,' and these are not wholly out of sight ; but the world in which we profess ourselves to be only strangers and sojourners is, for the time being, our home.

What has been said will make it plain that consciousness, for Greek thought, is continuous with the infraconscious on one side and with the supra-conscious on the other. The Greeks were less interested in the gradual emergence of consciousness out of the unconscious than with the gradual emergence of order and purpose out of inertia and meaninglessness. Soul-life is the immediate experience of an organic individual, from the moment when he begins to be an organic individual. This experience is conscious and self-conscious in various degrees. Its ideal perfection is such an all-embracing experience as will break down all barriers between the individual Soul and the Universal Soul. ' The Soul is potentially all things.' ' We are a spiritual world.'

This refusal to ascribe a primary importance to human consciousness, which we have found in Plotinus, is characteristic of almost all philosophy which is in sympathy with mysticism, and can claim much outside support. Campanella follows the Neoplatonists in holding that there is a dim knowledge in plants and even in minerals. Leibnitz uses similar language ; each of his monads, though impenetrable, was supposed to be a kind of microcosm, sleeping, dreaming, or awake. He insists that there are unconscious perceptions in man. Ferrier[1] says, ' What do we mean by the word consciousness, and upon what ground do we refuse to attribute consciousness to the animal creation ? In the first place, we mean

[1] Quoted by Rickaby, First Principles, p. 344.

by consciousness the notion of self which in man
generally, but by no means invariably, accompanies his
sensations, passions, emotions, play of reason, or states
of mind whatsoever. Man might easily have been
endowed with reason without at the same time becoming
aware of his endowment, or blending it with the notion
of himself.' So Bain says, ' Consciousness is inseparable
from feeling, but not, as it appears to me, from action
and thought.' Lewes holds that ' we often think as
unconsciously as we breathe,' and Maudsley that consciousness is ' an incidental accompaniment of mind.'[1]

An elaborate attempt has lately been made, by Arthur
Drews, to connect the philosophy of Plotinus with that
of Hartmann, author of *The Philosophy of the Unconscious.*
This attempt seems to me to have failed completely, for
the simple reason that Hartmann's system is vitiated by
fundamental inconsistencies which are certainly not to
be found in Plotinus. Hartmann tries to combine the
pantheism and pessimism which he learned from Schopenhauer with an evolutionary optimism which his own
character prompted him to accept. But the pessimism of
Schopenhauer was the direct consequence of disillusioned
egoism and hedonism. No one is likely to despair of the
world who has not tried to exploit it for anti-social aims.
This kind of pessimism is almost as foreign to Neoplatonism as to Christianity. And how is it possible to
reconcile it with the optimistic teleology which finds the
principle of the world in an ' over-conscious clear-seeing
intelligence,' which is transcendent as well as immanent,
and the beneficent designs of which are opposed only by
the ' blind irrational will ' of conscious creatures ? Hartmann's attempts to bring together the discrepant sides of
his theory seem to me only to demonstrate their incom-
patibility. At the same time, there are many of his utterances which agree with and illustrate Plotinus very
well ; as when he says ' To know oneself as of divine
nature does away with all divergence between self-will

[1] Rickaby, l.c.

I.—R

and the universal will, and with all alienation between man and God ; to regard the life of one's spirit as a spark of the divine flame engenders a resolution to lead a truly divine life ; . . . we acquire the will and power to think, feel, and act as if God were in us, and to transfigure each finite task in the divine light.' Such utterances belong not to the disciple of Schopenhauer, but to a moralist who wished to substitute for traditional Christianity a spiritual religion which should include the discoveries of modern science and especially the doctrine of evolution.

Bergson has been studying and lecturing upon Plotinus, and there are indications that the great Neoplatonist has had some influence upon his thought. In his Huxley Lecture (1911) he identifies mind with consciousness, and almost identifies consciousness with memory. ' A consciousness that retained nothing of the past would be a consciousness that died and was re-born every instant— it would be no longer consciousness. Such is just the condition of matter ; or at least it is just the way we represent matter when we wish to oppose it to consciousness. Leibnitz defined matter—that is to say, what is not consciousness—by calling it momentary mind, an instantaneous consciousness. And in fact an instantaneous consciousness is just what we call unconsciousness. All consciousness then is memory ; all consciousness is a preservation and accumulation of the past in the present.' But, he adds, consciousness is not only memory of the past ; it is also anticipation of the future ; it is a hyphen between past and future. How far, he proceeds to ask, is consciousness traceable in nature ? It seems to us to be dependent on the possession of a brain. But just as low organisms are able to digest without a stomach, so when the nervous substance is merged in the rest of living matter, consciousness may be diffused in an attenuated form, and may exist feebly wherever there is life. But the truth seems to be that while consciousness—which means the capacity of *choice* —is in principle present in all living matter, many organisms, such as parasites and nearly all vegetables, do not use it, so that it has become or remains dormant and atrophied. As action becomes automatic, consciousness is withdrawn from it. 'Two careers are open to a simple mass of protoplasmic jelly.' It may follow the path towards movement and action, which requires an increasing exercise of consciousness ; or it may prefer the humdrum existence of a placid vegetable soul. Life is something that encroaches upon inert matter, over which necessity sits enthroned. Life means indetermination—freedom. There is 'a slight elasticity in matter,' which gives liberty its chance. The dynamic is an 'explosive,' a portion of solar energy absorbed in food. Thus consciousness 'takes possession of matter,' and directs energy in a chosen way. So we have on one side an immense machine, subject to necessity, and on the other free consciousness. Behind this activity of consciousness there is a climbing impulse, driving organic beings ' to run greater and greater risks in order to arrive at greater efficiency.' But consciousness, which enters matter with the objects just stated, is sometimes ensnared by it. Liberty is dogged by automatism, and, except in man, is stifled by it. Matter, however, is necessary ; it plays at once the rôle of obstacle and of stimulus, and without it no effort would be put forth.

The view thus briefly sketched has some obvious affinities to the philosophy of Plotinus. But it is at bottom irreconcilable with it. It is based on the assumption—which underlies all Bergson's philosophy—that caprice and eccentricity are the marks of freedom and spiritual activity. The spontaneity of life is supposed to show itself in motiveless diversity, while regularity—all that can be predicted—is a proof of thraldom to blind necessity and mechanism. It is no wonder that superstitious supernaturalism holds out both hands to this philosophy. But such a view is abhorrent to Platonism, since it hands over nature, not indeed to a malignant power, but to purposeless machinery, and the formative

and directive agency which interferes with the regularity
of its working is not the Universal Soul, which for Plotinus
is responsible for the whole visible universe, including
those parts of it which seem to us devoid of life, but a
plurality of finite spirits, who act upon the world from
outside, as it were, and triumph in proportion as they
can introduce the unpredictable into the predetermined.
All this is contrary to the genius of Greek philosophy,
and especially of Platonism. For Plotinus, the purpose-
fulness and relevance of the world here below, across
which no hard lines are drawn, are the image of the
complete harmony which prevails in the eternal world. We
are not driven to assign some phenomena to mechanism
and others to miracle ; Soul, and behind Soul Spirit,
are at work everywhere. It follows that the presence
of purpose in the world does not depend upon the inter-
ference of finite consciousness with mechanical movements. The great dramas of organic evolution and of
human history are in no sense the life-story of any individual ; the actors for the most part are quite unconscious of the larger aspects of their lives. But these
larger purposes certainly exist, and they are prior to
and independent of the consciousness of the actors.[1]
The *foci* which we call ourselves exist as limiting *foci*
only for soul-consciousness ; Spirit enjoys an enriched
form of consciousness not tethered to any *foci*, in which
the contrast between externality and internality is
transcended. This is like what Bucke calls cosmic consciousness. But Plotinus is not fond of the word consciousness in relation to Spirit. ' Does the Soul Yonder
remember itself ? ' he asks.[2] ' It is not probable. He
who contemplates the spiritual world does not recall
who he is, or reflect whether he is Soul or Spirit. Giving
himself entirely to the contemplation of the spiritual
world, he does not return upon himself in thought ; he
possesses himself, but he applies himself to the spiritual

[1] Bosanquet, *The Principle of Individuality and Value*, p. 195.
[2] 4. 4. 2.

and becomes the spiritual, towards which he plays the part of Matter.' Self-consciousness, in a word, is another name for inattention.[1]

The suggestion may be hazarded that the chief function of consciousness, which is only one of Nature's many instruments, is the formation of new habits. It seems clear that it belongs to beings who are in course of change and development, and to times when they are not acting from habit. It appertains to psychic life as we know it, and in the eternal world it must be raised to a higher form, widely different from our present experience.[2] 'Spirit *is* what it possesses,' says Plotinus.[3]

The Soul and the Ego

The abstract ego is a different conception from that of the Soul. It seems to imply three assumptions, all of which are disputable. The first is that there is a sharp line separating subject and object, corresponding to the uncompromising antithesis of ego and non-ego. The second is that the subject, thus sundered from the object, remains identical through time. The third is that this indiscerptible entity is in some mysterious way both myself and my property. Just as Lucretius says that men fear death because they unconsciously duplicate themselves, and stand by, in imagination, at their own cremation, so we are seriously concerned to know whether that precious part of our possessions, our 'personality,' will survive death. Plotinus will have nothing to say to the first of these assumptions. Not only do subject and object freely flow into each other on the psychic

[1] Schopenhauer says that we are never conscious of ourselves in ourselves, independently of the objects of knowledge and will. Pure introspection is looking at a void. Hence, he argues, the individual must be only phenomenon.

[2] Royce, *The World and the Individual*, Vol. 2, p. 260–265, has the interesting thought that self-consciousness (=consciousness of self) depends on a series of 'contrast-effects' which arise from our social life. 'Never do I observe myself as a single and unambiguous fact of consciousness.' [3] 4. 4. 4.

level, but on the spiritual level there are no barriers at
all. To the second he would answer that the empirical
self is by no means identical throughout, and that the
spiritual ' idea,' the ' Spirit in Soul,' which we are to
strive to realise, is only ' ours ' potentially. To the
third he would reply that no doubt individuality is a
fact (δεῖ ἕκαστον ἕκαστον εἶναι), but that the question
whether it is *my* self that has its distinct place ' yonder '
is simply meaningless.[1]

We have to admit that in Plotinus there are traces of
a real conflict between the Orphic doctrine of individual
immortality, and the Heracleitean doctrine that there
is only one life, which animates every creature during
its transit from birth to death. The doctrine of rebirth,
which rests on the idea of Souls as *substantiae*, does not
agree well with the idea of the World-Soul. A statement
which throws much light on Plotinus' view of personality
is in the form of an answer to the question, how the
higher part of the Soul can possess sensation.[2] The
answer is that the objects of sensation exist in the spiritual
world, and are there apprehended by a faculty analogous
to what we call sensation. The Soul here below combines
and systematises the *data* of sensation, and thereby
assimilates them to the harmony which exists in the
spiritual world. ' If the bodies which are here below

---

[1] Eckhart says, ' It is not *my* soul which is transformed after the
likeness of God.' In Plato the relation between Soul and Souls is
almost undiscussed.

[2] 6.7.6. This important section is unfortunately corrupt. In the
second line the Medicean manuscript reads ἢ τὸ αἰσθητικὸν τῶν ἐκεῖ
ἀναισθήτων, with dots under the first two letters of the last word,
indicating that the true reading is αἰσθητῶν. Ficinus translates
' quæ illic dicuntur sensibilia.' Kirchhoff reads ἀναισθήτων, which
Müller translates. I am convinced that αἰσθητῶν is right, and that
Volkmann need not have despaired of the passage. Plotinus answers
the question, how the higher soul can possess αἴσθησις, by saying
that ' it perceives those things which are objects of perception in the
spiritual world, and as objects of perception exist in the spiritual
world.' He insists that πάντα ἐνταῦθα ὅσα κἀκεῖ. The objects which
the senses perceive and identify here below, are discerned in their
true nature ' yonder.' In the sixteenth line of this section (Volkmann's
edition), I should read οὐ γινόμενος ἐκεῖνοι (for ἐκείνοις), ἀλλὰ παρακείμενος
ἐκείνοις.

existed also yonder, the higher Soul would perceive and
apprehend them. The man of the spiritual world
(ὁ ἄνθρωπος ὁ ἐκεῖ), the Soul adapted to life there, can
apprehend these things ; whence also the lower man,
the copy of the spiritual man, has powers (λόγους) which
are copies of spiritual powers ; and the man in the
Spirit (ὁ ἐν νῷ ἄνθρωπος) is a copy of the man who is
above all men. This highest man illuminates the second
man, and the second the third. The lowest man in a sense
possesses the others, not that he becomes what they are
but that he is in contact with them. One of us is active
in accordance with the third and lowest man ; another
receives also something from the second, another from
the first.[1] Each man's self is determined by the principle
of his activity (ἔστιν ἕκαστος καθ' ὃν ἐνεργεῖ) ; though
each individual possesses all the three ranks, and possesses
them not.' The meaning of this cryptic passage is that
there are three planes on which a man may live, and that
his rank in the scale of existence depends on the choice
which he makes. He may live a purely external life,
obeying his natural instincts and not reflecting. Or he
may live in accordance with his discursive reason, the life
of an intelligent but unspiritual man. Or lastly, he may
live on what is really a superhuman plane—' that of the
gods and godlike men,' the life of Spirit. The Soul, as
a microcosm, has within it the potentiality of all three
lives ; but it chooses which of its faculties it shall develop,
and which shall remain latent. If we have to choose one
kind of activity as characteristically *human*, and say that
our personality as individuals resides in that sphere of
activity, we must select the second grade, that of the
discursive intellect ;[2] because the merely sensuous life

---

[1] Plotinus says ' the third,' i.e. in the ascending scale, although
in the preceding sentence ' the third ' means the lowest of the ' three
men.'

[2] See 4.8.8 ; 2.1.5 ; 5.3.3. For the Soul, when living its own life,
Sensation is its servant, Spirit is its king. This is the doctrine of the
Christian mystics. Cf. (e.g.) *The Cloud of Unknowing*, Chap. 8. ' In
the lower part of active life a man is without himself and beneath
himself. In the higher part of active life and the lower part of con-

is infra-human, and since in the life of the Spirit we are really raised above the conditions and limitations of earthly existence, no man, while in the body, can live permanently on this level. But we cannot remind ourselves too often that Plotinus allows us no fixed fulcrum of self-consciousness as the centre of our world and our activities. *We* are potentially all things ;[1] our personality is what we are able to realise of the infinite wealth which our divine-human nature contains hidden in its depths. This being so, we must not lay much stress on the tripartite division of soul-life which we have just been considering. It represents three stages in the ladder of existence and value, but these shade off into each other. Elsewhere he tells us that ' every man is double ' ;[2] and that even the universal Soul has its higher and lower sphere of activity. Every living thing has a vital connexion with what is above and with what is below itself, and the choice between the better and the worse is continually offered. But neither the ' double ' nor the ' threefold ' man must be interpreted as a hard and strict classification. ' A man must be *one*,' as he says himself ; and ' the Soul cannot be divided quantitatively.' Even here below Soul is ' undivided ' (ἀμέριστος) as well as ' divided,' and ' sees with that part by which it keeps the nature of the whole.'[3]

The whole trend of Neoplatonism is towards those philosophies which teach that the ego or self is not *given* to start with. Our nature, our personality, is in process of being communicated to us. The individual is a microcosm striving after unity and universality. We do not yet know ourselves ; the Soul feels itself to be an exile and a wanderer from God (φυγὰς θεόθεν καὶ ἀλήτης). It is impelled by home-sickness to struggle up

templative life a man is within himself and even with himself. But in the higher part of contemplative life a man is above himself and under his God.'

[1] So Keyserling says : ' Das Ich eine Kraft ist, die als solche keine Grenzen kennt.'

[2] διττὸς ἕκαστος, 2. 3. 9.   [3] 4. 1. 1.

towards the world of Spirit, in the travail-pangs (ὠδῖνες) through which the new birth is effected. The great saying of Christ about losing one's soul in order to find it unto life eternal would have been quite acceptable to Plotinus, who would indeed have understood it better than most modern Christians. For the repudiation of the 'me' and 'mine' which follow from it has seldom been accepted without qualification by Christian moralists. It occupies the centre of the teaching of the *Theologia Germanica* and other mystical books; but outside this school it is rare to hear Divine justice (for example) treated from this point of view. Individualistic justice belongs to the world of claims and counter-claims which the Soul must learn to leave behind. Neither God nor Nature allows such claims, and the good man does not make them for himself. It is just here that the modern exaggeration of human individuality with its rights and claims is proving a disintegrating influence in social and national life. The ethics of militarism are as much superior to those of industrial democracy on this side as they are inferior to them in other respects.

Does this view of the self lead logically to Nirvana? If we hold that every enhancement and expansion of the personal life make it less personal, by spreading their experience over what was before external, and bringing the outside world into ourselves, would not the theoretical consummation of this process be complete absorption in the Absolute? And if finite selfhood is an illusion, how are we to explain the persistence of the illusion, which indeed seems to most of us a very solid fact indeed? And further, is it true that we are only divided from each other by differences in our interests? If two hearts could really 'beat as one,' would they lose their individuality, and perhaps therewith the possibility of love —since we do not love ourselves? These are difficult questions, which involve the whole problem of personality, divine as well as human. Lotze held that 'we have little ground for speaking of the personality of finite beings : personality is an ideal, which like all ideals is proper only to the infinite in its unconditioned nature, but to us is, like every other good thing, only vouch-safed under conditions and therefore imperfectly.' On the other hand, it may be urged that personality is no ideal, but only the name for our delimitation of individual existence. ' Personality only exists because we are not pure spirits, but have a visible and sensible basis to our existence, in passions, limbs, and material conditions.'[1] Personality can only belong to one who is not everything, but stands in relations to others outside himself. Such conditions cannot apply to the Deity. This contradiction illustrates very strongly the fact that personality, like morality, always strives to subvert the conditions of its own existence. It aspires to be all-embracing, and is potentially all-embracing ; but if it could realise this aspiration, it would cease to be individual. For a person only exists as such in relation to other persons ; and yet we are not fully personal (as Lotze argues) while there are other persons over against ourselves.[2] Plotinus says that the Soul does attain complete personality in the spiritual world, where individual *foci* are not abolished, but are each the centre of an infinite circle. And having attained this perfection, the glorified Soul does not rest in its fruition, but in complete self-forgetfulness looks up with yearning eyes to the Absolute One, in whom there are no more persons. And while thus looking, it creates unceasingly in the world of Soul.

The analogy between personality and morality is not accidental. Personality is above all things a quality which expresses the moral nature of man.[3] Or we might say that it expresses the social nature of man. We

---

[1] Wallace, *Lectures and Essays*, p. 278.

[2] This subject is further discussed in Vol 2, p. 229, where it is argued that Plotinus avoids the contradiction which Bradley finds in ' finite centres.'

[3] Leibnitz's definition is : ' Persona est cuius aliqua voluntas est seu cuius datur cogitatio, affectus, voluptas, dolor.' This is perhaps to identify personality too closely with consciousness.

recognise ourselves as persons very largely by contrast
with the other persons whom we meet in friendship or
rivalry. Thus thought first increases the illusions of
separate individuality, and at last transcends them.[1]
We begin to know ourselves by realising the stubborn
externality of the not-self, and then by degrees these
barriers are broken down, and we find a larger self in the
extension of our knowledge and sympathy. But the
truest way to regard personality is as the expression and
vehicle of a unitary purpose. The self is a teleological
category. Here I may refer to Royce,[2] who has stated
this view most excellently. For us the self has indeed
no independent being; but it is a life, and not merely
a valid law. It gains its very individuality through its
relation to God; but in God it still dwells as an individual; for it is a unique expression of the Divine
purpose. And since the self is precisely, in its wholeness,
the conscious and intentional fulfilment of this Divine
purpose, in its own unique way, the individual will of
the self is not wholly determined by a power that fashions
it as clay is fashioned and that is called God's will;
but, on the contrary, what the self in its wholeness wills is
just in so far God's will, and is identical with one of the
many expressions implied by a single Divine purpose, so
that the self is in its innermost individuality not an
independent but still a free will, which in so far owns no
external master, despite its unity with the whole life of
God, and despite its dependence in countless ways upon
nature and upon its fellows, for everything except the
individuality and uniqueness of its life. This uniqueness, he goes on to explain, is 'unique precisely in so
far as it is related to the whole.' Royce also insists
that 'in our present form of human consciousness the
true self of any individual man is not a datum, but an
ideal.'

[1] This point is argued admirably by Carveth Read, *Natural and
Social Morals*, p. xvii. sq.; and cf. Royce, quoted on p. 245.
[2] Royce, *The World and the Individual*, Vol. 2, p. 286.

Finally, we may say that the particularism of our experience is the cross which we have to bear, and that in
the overcoming of it is the sole realisation of human
happiness.   Almost all unhappiness is rooted in a feeling
of isolation.

The Soul and Will, or Purpose

Plotinus has been criticised for having no intelligible
theory of causation.   He recognises, in fact, that the
mode of action of the higher upon the lower is mysterious ;
it is not essential that we should understand it.   He
concentrates his attention upon what does concern us—
the return-journey of the Soul to God.   The Soul lives in
the consciousness of purpose ; ' it only knows itself in
so far as it knows that it depends on a higher power ' ;[1]
it ' turns towards ' the idea which it lives to realise.   The
World-Soul must live in the consciousness of the all-
embracing purpose, or rather purposes, of the universe.
Individual Souls while on earth have to aim not so much
at what has been called ' cosmic consciousness,' as at a
full understanding of the finite and particular purpose for
which we are living our present lives.   Since this purpose
exists in relations, it involves very wide ramifications.
The centre must be our prescribed station ; to the circumference there is no necessary limit, since our life is
continuous with that of the Universal Soul.   Time is the
form of the Will, and belongs to the activities of Soul, not
Spirit.   It is true that Plotinus once or twice seems to
identify Will with νόησις ; but it is only as an activity
of Spirit that Will belongs to the eternal world.   The
idea of Will necessarily carries with it the notion of a
hierarchy of value and existence, for while thought
energises in pari materia, Will necessarily gives form to
what is, for it, in the position of Matter   Soul has its
own inner activities, in which its happiness consists ;[2]

---

[1] 5. 3. 6.

[2] 1. 5. 10, ἡ ἐνέργεια τῆς ψυχῆς ἐν τῷ φρονῆσαι καὶ ἐν ἑαυτῇ ὧδὶ ἐνεργῆσαι.
καὶ τοῦτο τὸ εὐδαιμόνως.

but as Will its activity is inspired from above, and the sphere of its activity is below itself.[1]

In Eckhart, always a good interpreter of Plotinus, the Will is above *Verstand*, but below the higher *Vernunft*, which is the ground of the Soul.

The objection may be raised : if Soul belongs essentially to the eternal world, though near its lower limit, how can it live in unfulfilled purpose ? Hegel, in the third book of his *Logic*, says that ' in teleological activity the end is the beginning, the consequence is the ground, the effect is the cause, a case of becoming is a case of what has become.' He adds that our belief that ends are not yet accomplished is an illusion, though on this illusion depend all our activities and all our interest in life. Hegel has been ridiculed for this theory of teleology ; but the sentence quoted is by no means absurd if we take it as an attempt to describe the consciousness of *achieved ends*, or of purposes viewed, *sub specie aeternitatis*, as inseparable from their fulfilment.[2] The higher Soul, according to Plotinus, must view ' the World as Will ' much in this manner. But the temporal succession, in which purposes are worked out, is certainly not mere ' illusion.' To call it so would be to banish Time and Will from the nature of things. The activity of Will or Purpose is precisely that which links the world of ordinary experience to spiritual reality ; it is the most real thing in our world. The Will effects nothing in the world of Spirit, which is the source from which the Will itself flows ; in the world of Soul it is the proper life and activity in which the Soul expresses itself.

---

[1] I. 4. 9, ἐσμὲν ἡ τοῦ νοοῦντος ἐνέργεια.

[2] Plotinus too insists that τέλος ἅπασιν ἀρχή, 3. 8. 7.

The Descent of the Soul

We have seen that Plotinus conceives the universe as a living chain of being, an unbroken series of ascending or descending values and existences. The whole constitutes a ' harmony ' ;[1] each inferior grade is ' in ' the next above ;[2] each existence is vitally connected with all others. But those grades which are inferior in value are also imperfectly real, so long as we look at them in disconnexion. They are characterised by impermanence and inner discord, until we set them in their true relations to the whole. Then we perceive them to be integral parts of the eternal systole and diastole in which the life of the universe consists, a life in which there is nothing arbitrary or irregular, seeing that all is ordered by the necessity that eternal principles should act in accordance with their own nature. The perfect and unchangeable life of the Divine Spirit overflows in an incessant stream of creative activity, which spends itself only when it has reached the lowest confines of being, so that every possible manifestation of Divine energy, every hue of the Divine radiance, every variety in degree as well as in kind, is realised somewhere and somehow. And by the side of this outward flow of creative energy there is another current which carries all the creatures back toward the source of their being. It is this centripetal movement that directs the active life of all creatures endowed with Soul. They were created and sent into the world that they might be moulded a little nearer to the Divine image by yearning for the home which they have left. This aspiration, which slumbers even in unconscious beings, is the mainspring of the moral, intellectual, and æsthetic life of mankind.

This is the world-view of Plotinus. It provides an

[1] 4. 3. 12, $\beta\iota\omega\nu$ $\dot{\omega}\rho\iota\sigma\mu\acute{\epsilon}\nu\omega\nu$ $\epsilon\dot{\iota}s$ $\sigma\upsilon\mu\phi\omega\nu\acute{\iota}a\nu$; 2. 3. 5, $\tau\dot{o}$ $\pi\hat{a}\nu$ $\dot{\epsilon}\nu$ $\kappa a\grave{\iota}$ $\mu\acute{\iota}a$ $\dot{a}\rho\mu o\nu\acute{\iota}a$. Other expressions used are $\sigma\acute{\upsilon}\nu\tau a\xi\iota s$ $\mu\acute{\iota}a$, $\sigma\acute{\upsilon}\mu\pi\nu o\iota a$ $\mu\acute{\iota}a$.
[2] 5. 5. 9. ' Harmony ' in Greek does not mean concordant notes played simultaneously.

explanation of the Soul's position in the sphere of time
and place. The Soul, itself a Divine principle, would be
false to the nature which it shares with the other Divine
principles, if it did not create a world which it could strive
to fashion after the likeness of its own Creator, Spirit.
'See that thou make all things according to the pattern
showed thee in the mount,' is the sum of the 'marching
orders' issued by God to all His creatures. There is no
necessary fall, or humiliation, or pride, or forgetfulness,
in a Soul which has its temporary habitation among the
tents of Kedar. Its descent into the world was not its
own choice, but the ordinance of God. Whether the Soul
has one life to live on earth, or more than one, its earthly
course, both in its external activities and in its inward
growth, is a task committed to it by God, and a part of
the Divine scheme in which it is privileged to co-operate.

But Plotinus is not able to rest content with this as
an adequate and satisfactory theory of temporal existence. The Soul while on earth is, after all, living in the
midst of its enemies, and it is often its own worst enemy.
Those instruments which, according to the theory stated
above, it has itself created in order to 'mould them nearer
to the heart's desire,' appear in experience to be clogs
and weights which prevent it from using its wings ; and
too often the Soul, or the lower part of it which is in
immediate contact with the world of sense, loves to have
it so. When we view the condition of the majority of
incarnate Souls, we cannot help asking ourselves, Would
it not have been better for them to have remained Yonder
in the world of spirits ?[1] Can it have been God's will that
they should smirch their wings and wallow in mud here
below ? Must we not assume that it was pride, or
curiosity, or wilfulness, that led to such a fall ? So his
master Plato seems to have thought ; and is not such a
theory, which asserts 'original sin, the corruption of
man's heart,' less superficial, in spite of all its difficulties,
than the facile optimism which takes no account of evil,
making the Soul, as well as Spirit, impeccable, and 'the

[1] Cf. Calderon, 'Pues el debito mayor del hombre es haber nacido.'

chain of our sins ' only an inert resistance to a kind of magnetic attraction ? Plotinus, who always seems to be thinking aloud, never conceals his real perplexities. In this case he throws out suggestions which do not pretend to be consistent with each other, and leaves it to his readers to choose between them.

The fullest discussion is in the eighth book of the Fourth Ennead. Plotinus says that often, when he has ' awaked up out of the body,' and has been conscious of the blessedness of union with God and of the untrammelled activity of the Spirit which has freed itself from the life of sense, he has returned to earth again with a sense of wonder how the Soul, which even here is capable of such experiences, comes to find itself imprisoned within a material body. Heracleitus tells us that the pendulum of life swings necessarily between contraries ; that ' the way up and the way down are the same ' ; and that change is good in itself, bringing relief from *ennui*. This is guesswork, says Plotinus ; and too obscure to carry conviction to others. Empedocles speaks of the ' law ' which obliges erring souls to come down to earth, the region of ' raging discord ' ; but neither he nor Pythagoras makes his meaning clear. ' Poets are not obliged to speak plainly.' It remains to interrogate ' the divine Plato.' But Plato does not always use the same language about the descent of the Soul. He is emphatic in disparagement of the world of appearance ; he speaks of it as the cave, the prison, the tomb of the Soul ; he says that the Soul suffers a moulting of its wing-feathers ($\pi\tau\epsilon\rho o\rho\rho\acute{\upsilon}\eta\sigma\iota\varsigma$) by contact with Matter. And yet, if we turn to the *Timaeus*, we find this world praised as ' a blessed god ' ; and we are told that the Creator sent Soul into the world to make it the abode of intelligence ($\check{\epsilon}\nu\nu o\upsilon\nu$), as it ought to be, and with a view to its perfection. Both the Universal Soul and our individual Souls were ' sent by God,' with this intent ; for it is necessary that everything in the world of Spirit should be represented also in the world of sense. It is not, then, a fault

in the Soul, that it should give to the body the power of
Being ; ' we may care for that which is below us, without
ceasing to abide in the highest and best.' In this comment upon Plato, Plotinus allows us to see clearly that his
master's disparagement of the material world is not quite
to his taste. It is in the *Timaeus*, and not in the *Phaedrus*,
that he finds the doctrine which satisfies him.

The Universal Soul, he proceeds, governs the world in
a royal way, by simple commands ; individual Souls by
direct productive action (αὐτουργῷ τινι ποιήσει). This
particular superintendence brings into activity the latent
powers of Soul. It is indeed the proper nature of the
Soul to set in order, rule, and govern ; it has its duties to
that which is beneath itself, and cannot remain always
in contemplation of the world of Spirit. The Soul of the
World suffers no contamination ; for it does not enter
into bodies, nor belong to bodies ; they are rather in it.
It is free, therefore, from the two dangers which Soul
incurs by contact with body—that of being hindered in
its spiritual life, and that of being occupied by thoughts
of pleasure and pain. Individual Souls, as if desiring a
more independent life than the blessed community of
the spiritual world, separate themselves partially from
this close intercommunion, and animate particular
bodies. They live an ' amphibious ' life (οἷον ἀμφίβιοι),
passing from the spiritual to the sensuous and back
again. Plato says, speaking mythically, that ' God '
planted them there ; but the whole movement is in
accordance with nature and necessity. There is then,
Plotinus thinks, no contradiction between the two theories
of the descent of the Soul which are countenanced by
Plato. It is permissible to say that God sent the Souls
down to earth, for ' the operation of the highest principle,
even though there are many stages between, can be traced
down to the end of the process.' And yet the Soul commits two faults, one, and the greater, in ' coming down,'
the other in entering into bodies. It does so by choice
(ῥοπῇ αὐτεξουσίῳ), and because it desires to bring order

into what is below. If it returns quickly, it suffers no hurt. It has gained knowledge of good and evil, and this knowledge is a good thing;[1] it has put forth its latent powers, which would have been unperceived and useless if it had not become incarnate. Indeed, if the Soul's powers were unmanifested, it would not be fully real (οὐκ οὖσα, μηδέποτε ὄντως οὖσα). In Chapter 6 (4. 8. 6) he traces in detail how the One could not be alone, for then nothing would exist; and how Spirit also and Soul must communicate their gifts, down to the lowest degree possible. The Soul (Ch. 7) learns its true good by the experience of contraries; though stronger Souls can understand evil without experience of it.[2]

In another place we read that the Soul descends into the body prepared for it, when the time comes, as if summoned by a herald.[3] In the Second Ennead,[4] where he is maintaining, against the Gnostics, that the Creator of this world is good, he puts the alternatives, either that the Souls are 'compelled to come down by the Universal Soul,' or that they come down willingly. In any case, he adds, the universe is so constituted that it is possible for us, while we live here, to gain wisdom, and to live the life of the Spirit while still in the flesh. In the seventh book of the Fourth Ennead he states what is perhaps his own inmost thought upon the matter when he says that the Soul has a longing to go forth and set in order 'according to what she has seen in the spiritual world' (καθ' ἃ ἐν νῷ εἶδεν); the Soul is with child by Spirit and must give birth to her offspring; this is why she creates in the world of sense.[5] And in the third book[6] of the same Ennead he clearly asserts that the ascents and descents of Souls are necessary and integral parts of the universal harmony.

In spite of the beauty of several passages in which

---

[1] 1. 8. 15.
[2] Porphyry suggests that God sends Souls down, that they may see evil and so be liberated from any desire for it. Augustine, *De Civ. Dei*, 9. 30.
[3] 4. 3. 13.   [4] 2. 9. 8.   [5] 4. 7. 13.   [6] 4. 3. 12.

Plotinus speaks of the sojourn of the Soul in the lower world, there is a want of firmness and consistency in this part of his philosophy. We cannot blame him for recognising that man is in a ' fallen ' state here ; but he hesitates in answering the question whether (had it been possible) it would have been better for the Soul to have remained in the Spiritual World. He tells us indeed that the descent of the Soul into Matter is strictly parallel to the νοερὰ διέξοδος of Spirit down to Soul and back ; [1] and to this latter process no shadow of blame can be attached   And he also admits that if the Soul had not claimed the measure of independence which involved its ' descent,' its powers would have been undeveloped, and the riches contained in Spirit would have remained for ever hidden. But the numerous passages in Plato, in which contact with Matter is assumed to be a defilement to the spiritual principle, have an attraction for him apart from the weight of authority which they carry. It is just here that the miserable state of society in the third century warps his thought by impelling him, as many Christian saints have been impelled, to sigh with the Psalmist, ' O that I had wings as a dove, for then would I flee away and be at rest.' There were then no obvious and practicable tasks of social reform to call the philosopher from his lecture-room, the saint from his prayers. Plotinus could not even console himself with the delusive hope of an approaching end of the world. The apocalyptic dream, which has been the strangest legacy of the later Judaism to Christianity, never consoled or troubled the mind of Pagan philosophers. They must have felt that *tempora pessima sunt,* but they could not say *hora novissima.* Deliverance, for them, was not hoped for in the future, but half-seen beyond the veil in the present. It was a different kind of *Weltflucht* from that of monastic Christianity ; both alike rest on truth mixed with illusion, on faith and courage which are still not faithful and courageous enough. The Christian doctrine of the

[1] 4. 8. 7.

Incarnation, which Augustine sought for and could not find in the Platonists,[1] puts the keystone in the arch. It is not derogatory to the Divine principle, nor injurious to it, to mingle in the affairs of a sinful and suffering world. On the contrary, the Divine is never more itself than when it 'empties itself' in self-sacrificing love.[2] Nor is it necessary to the nature of pure Spirit that it should operate always without effort, and as it were with its back turned. Perfect in itself, it is nevertheless impelled by its very perfection to put forth all its strength against evils which, we must suppose, are allowed to exist for this very purpose. God reveals Himself as a suffering Redeemer ; and on a lower plane the Soul does not 'shed its wings' but rather grows them in struggling with the impediments of an evil world. This truth was imperfectly grasped by Plotinus. But we must not misunderstand him by taking literally his metaphors of 'abiding in her own place,' and 'coming down.' No movement in space is even thought of. Spirit and Soul are everywhere and nowhere ; we are in heaven whenever 'we in heart and mind thither ascend' ; we are 'immersed in Matter' whenever we forget God. The fault of the Soul, whether it be due to pride ($\tau\acute{o}\lambda\mu\alpha$), curiosity, sensuality, or mere 'forgetfulness of its Father,'[3] does not, for Plotinus, consist in exercising the creative activities which are an integral part of the world-order, but in treating as ends those constituents of the temporal order which were intended to be instruments. The Soul is 'deceived' and 'bewitched' by the charm of sensuous things, which bear an illusory resemblance to the world of Spirit.[4] It beholds itself in the mirror of Matter,[5] and, like Narcissus, falls in love with the image, and plunges

---

[1] Augustine, *Confessions*, 7, 9 and 21.

[2] The well-known controversy in Christian theology as to whether the Incarnation was part of the eternal counsels of God, or was made necessary only by the fall of man ('*O felix culpa!*') seems to me a close parallel to this perplexity of the Neoplatonists.

[3] 5. 1. 1. Cf. Eckhart, 'If the soul could have known God, as the angels know Him, it would never have come into the body.'

[4] 4. 6. 3.   [5] 4. 3. 12.

in after it. The whole duty and happiness of a spiritual
being is to remember that 'its source must be also its
end.' It is a stranger and pilgrim upon earth ; its affections must be set on its heavenly home. But as its
'descent' implies no local or material absence from the
heaven which surrounds and penetrates us always and
everywhere, so its ' flight ' homewards implies no local
or material severance of the ties which bind us to the
scene of our probation. The detachment is spiritual ;
and spiritual detachment is not only consistent with
a beautiful and beneficent external life ; it is the very
condition of such a life. ' Things here ' are not all
shadows ; even the Soul in its essential nature (αὐτοψυχή)
is ' here, though perhaps not as we know it here.'[1] ' There
is nothing Yonder that is not also Here,' if among things
Here we include the Soul and what belongs to it. But
when we shut out the light of heaven from ' things Here,'
all is dark, evil, and deceitful.

' Does the Soul all descend ? '

Does the individual Soul ' come down ' entire into the
lower world, or does part of it remain above ? This
question, with its unfortunate though inevitable spatial
imagery, raises a problem which we must try to understand. It will come home to us more easily if we try to
dispense with the spatial metaphor, and ask instead,
Can the Soul itself sin ? Is the empirical Ego, which
thinks and acts and suffers, sinning, repenting, and
struggling, the true self, or a projection from it ? Can the
real Soul remain pure and uncontaminated, though to
outward appearance the character has not been free from
faults ? Is there, as the medieval mystics taught, a
' spark ' at the core of the Soul, which never consents to
evil, a Divine nucleus in the heart of the personality,
which can take no stain ? Plotinus teaches that there
is ; and it is exceedingly interesting to find that most of

[1] 5. 9. 13.

his successors in the Neoplatonic school, in spite of their
extreme reverence for their master, here refuse to follow
him. The first to revolt against the doctrine was Iamblichus, who perhaps deserves more credit for originality
than has commonly been allowed to him. There is no
'pure Soul,' he says, which remains sinless while the
'composite nature' goes astray. For 'if the will sins, how
can the Soul be sinless?'¹ Proclus, Simplicius, and
Priscian all follow Iamblichus, while Theodorus and
Damascius remain true to the doctrine of Plotinus. Proclus is quite emancipated from the Platonic doctrine of
πτερορρύησις. He makes the creation of the world, with
all its imperfections, an essential movement of Spirit.
'All Spirit,' he says, 'in the act of spiritual perception
(τῷ νοεῖν) posits what comes next in order to itself. Its
creativeness consists in its spiritual perception, and its
spiritual perception in creativeness.'² In the same way
the Soul, in the act of exercising its proper function,
which is the realisation of spiritual ideas under the form
of rational and moral ends, produces the sensible world
to be the sphere of its activity. It is impossible for Souls
to remain always in the spiritual world; all Souls must
trace the circle again and again. Clearly there is no question of sin here in the Soul's incarnation; its wanderings
and returns are the pulsation of unending life. Proclus
indeed gives a very clear answer to the question why the
Soul comes down. 'It is because it desires to imitate
the providence of the gods.'³ What nobler enterprise
could the Soul set itself, than to hand on to other created
beings the gifts which God has given to itself?

Plotinus tries to father his doctrine on Plato.⁴ It is not
difficult to understand why he shrank from the idea that
the Soul says good-bye to its heavenly home when it
enters the body. The whole physical organism is for him

---

¹ Proclus, *in Tim.* 341, εἰ δὲ ἡ προαίρεσις ἁμαρτάνει, πῶς ἀναμάρτητος ἡ
ψυχή;
² Proclus, *Inst. Theol.* 174, πᾶς νοῦς ᾗ ᾧ νοεῖν ὑφίστησι τὰ μετ' αὐτὸν, καὶ
ἡ ποίησις ἐν τῷ νοεῖν, καὶ ἡ νόησις ἐν τῷ ποιεῖν.
³ Proclus, *in Tim.* 338. ⁴ 5. 1. 10.

something 'separable' (χωριστόν), no part of the real
man. The Soul must maintain its connexion and com-
munications with the spiritual world; and if the law
holds that like can only be known by like, how can a Soul
which has entirely 'come down' into a body live as a
spirit among spirits, or have any knowledge of the
spiritual world? Plotinus, as a mystic, treasures the
belief that the Soul can always find God and heaven
within itself. Lastly, he would have agreed with Dr.
Bosanquet,[1] that ' no activity is *ours* in which we do not
remain at home as well as go abroad.' Behind the
activities of the Soul in the world, there must be the life
of the Soul itself, to which its activities are referred, and
this life is spiritual.

There is, as has been already suggested, a possible
reconciliation of the two views. The Soul is a spiritual
being, with its home in heaven—the heaven that is within
us, even while it is in the body.[2] But it has brought down
this heaven with it into the time-process in which it
energises. There is no contamination whatever in these
activities, so long as the Soul remembers that it has been
sent into its present life as God's fellow-worker, 'to imitate the Divine providence,' as Proclus says. The more
deeply it penetrates into the darkest recesses of the nature
which has fallen furthest from God, the more faithfully
it is fulfilling the Divine will, and vindicating its Divine
origin. Its inmost life and being are safe, because the
Soul is the child of God; but it is not allowed to remain
always on the mount of vision; there are devils to be cast
out in the plain below. The return-journey is rough
and arduous, because the task given to great souls is
great and heroic. Temporary failure is of no importance;
God has all time to work in, and the Soul has all eternity

---

[1] *Principle of Individuality and Value*, 1. 66.
[2] This is not far from the doctrine of Plotinus, 6. 4. 12, τὰ δὲ τῆς
ψυχῆς δεῖ λαμβάνειν ὡς οὐκ ὄντος αὐτῆς τοῦ μὲν ἐν σώματι τοῦ δὲ ἐφ' ἑαυτοῦ, ἀλλὰ
ὅλου ἐν αὐτῷ καὶ ἐν πολλοῖς αὖ φαντα ζομένου. He goes on to say that the
presence of the Soul ' here ' is only an appearance—ἔστιν ἐν ἑαυτῷ
καίτοι δοκοῦν ἐνταῦθα ἐλθεῖν.

in which to enjoy that rest which is another word for unbroken activity in accordance with the law of its being.

From another point of view we may be disposed to agree with Plotinus. There are many persons who from some physical defect, such as malformation of the brain, are condemned to lead a *vie manquée* here below. In their case the Soul does not seem to have ' come down ' entire. In all of us there are some hindrances to a perfect life, hindrances which cannot be overcome. It is a legitimate hope that in another life the Soul may be able to act more freely.

INDEX

DATE DUE

	WITHDRAWN		
	UML LIBRARIES		
GAYLORD			PRINTED IN U.S.A.